Michèle is a stand-up comedian, freelance writer, and social commentator. Originally trained as a journalist in 1979 and with a degree from Victoria University in English Literature and Drama, Michèle won 'NZ Female Comedian of the Decade' in 2010, and has been writing a weekly column on social issues for *The Press* since 2008. Michèle has been on New Zealand TV screens since 1987 and still turns up when they let her. She talks a lot — sometimes on radio, sometimes in pubs — and works the comedy circuit in places like San Francisco, Las Vegas, Vancouver, Brisbane, Adelaide, Auckland and Mangawhai. She likes to say she has a 'portfolio career', which includes corporate work as an MC and entertainer. Michèle has one child — her daughter, Holly, born in 1993 — and didn't have any more because Holly was so spectacular, any subsequent children would have been a disappointment. Michèle lives on Auckland's North Shore with her favourite husband. This is her first actual book.

Michèle A'Court

STUFF I FORGOT to TELL MY DAUGHTER

HarperCollins*Publishers*

HarperCollins*Publishers*

First published in 2015
by HarperCollins*Publishers* (New Zealand) Limited
Unit D1, 63 Apollo Drive, Rosedale, Auckland 0632, New Zealand
harpercollins.co.nz

HarperCollins*Publishers*
Unit D1, 63 Apollo Drive, Rosedale, Auckland 0632, New Zealand
Level 13, 201 Elizabeth Street, Sydney NSW 2000
A 53, Sector 57, Noida, UP, India
1 London Bridge Street, London, SE1 9GF, United Kingdom
2 Bloor Street East, 20th floor, Toronto, Ontario M4W 1A8, Canada
195 Broadway, New York, NY 10007, USA

A catalogue record for this book is available from the National Library
of New Zealand.

Cover and internal design by areadesign.co.nz
Front cover photograph by Jane Ussher
Back cover photograph by Stephen A'Court
Typeset in Bembo Std by Kirby Jones
Printed and bound in Australia by Griffin Press
The papers used by HarperCollins in the manufacture of this book are
a natural, recyclable product made from wood grown in sustainable
plantation forests. The fibre source and manufacturing processes
meet recognised international environmental standards, and carry
certification.

CONTENTS

For Holly, of course.
And for Ariana-Rose.

PROLOGUE

In early 2012 my daughter, Holly, got a job and went flatting. She didn't move to Syria or anything — just another suburb in our city about 15 minutes' drive away.

Holly and I have always adored each other. For a while, when she was little, it was just the two of us, and we've remained a pretty tight unit ever since. But by the time she reached 18, I think we were both sick of hearing me say 'What time do you call this?', and neither of us believed me any more when I pulled out the previously infallible 'Because I said so'. Plus, there are things an 18-year-old wants to experiment with that a mother doesn't need to witness first-hand — purple eyeshadow, navel studs and lace hot-pants among them.

Keen to 'get on with my life' as she put it, she left Unitech, found a job and moved in with a bunch of her friends. Remarkably, I didn't suffer the 'empty-nest syndrome' angst that apparently smacks other parents in the head when their only child leaves home. Like I say, it felt like time, and I was excited to see her make her own way in the world and hear her stories ('My boss is an idiot!', 'My flatmates are dicks!') when we met for lunch a couple of times a week.

I finally got her room as clean and tidy as I'd been asking her to make it for several years, and was delighted to discover that it really is possible to properly get rid of the smell of sock and armpit. It is one of life's great truths that the perfect kid's room — the one that looks delicious and inviting, ready for a photo-shoot, just like a bought one — is the kid's room that doesn't actually have a kid living in it.

And suddenly liberated from 24/7 motherhood, with a lot less cooking, cleaning, washing and taxi-driving to do — and fewer questions to answer — I was able to enjoy a proper thought process for the first time in 18 years. Mostly, I spent the initial couple of months wandering around the house thinking 'Oh, my God, did I tell her everything she needs to know? Did I explain how to store ginger? Can she do hospital corners? Did we ever talk about feminism?'

Because of my job as a comedian and a writer, I get invited to speak at school and university graduations, where I tell other people's kids all kinds of wise and important things about work and life and relationships. I'd go and do that, and then I'd come home and tell my daughter to hold her fork properly. So I started making a list. A list of all the things I had forgotten to tell my daughter. Because often we're so busy telling our kids to sit up straight and do their homework that we forget to talk to them about the Big Things — social activism, finding your tribe, the power of youth. And okay, yes, also the Small Things, like not touching your eye when you've just sprinkled something with cayenne pepper.

That list of stuff I forgot to tell my daughter became a one-hour comedy show at the NZ International Comedy Festival in 2013. Wisdom wrapped up in jokes. People came, and it resonated with them. Often mothers brought their daughters, and sometimes fathers brought their sons. Afterwards, parents would thank me for saying out loud the things they had either forgotten to say, or couldn't find the words for. Standing beside them, the kids would look relieved that someone other than their actual mums had introduced them to the concept of middle-aged people having sex.

And people suggested more things that we all might have forgotten to tell our daughters. The list kept getting longer. Until it turned into this book. If you are a mother, my hope is that this book says some of the things you haven't found words for, or reminds you of things you forgot to say. I like to think it will inspire conversations between the two of you.

If you are a daughter, and your mum has left this on your bedside table, I like to think of you reading it and then getting back to her to ask supplementary questions. Try to wrap your head around the idea that your mother once felt a lot like you do now. (See Chapter 4, 'Middle Age'.) Mothers are much smarter than we assume they are when we are young and sometimes ticked off with the world.

Or if you found the book all by yourself: good work, well done. I am hoping that, once you've finished reading it, you will give your mother a hug and tell her she is freaking awesome.

Mothers adore those random acts of love — though they can also throw them a bit and make them nervous. Which daughters quite like. So that's a win-win.

And if you are a father or son: welcome! I am thrilled to have you here. Sometimes when I have written 'she' or 'her', you will need to substitute that in your head with 'he' and 'him' so you feel included. Don't worry: ladies have to do that all the time when they read books or listen to songs or hear daft old buggers talk. It's a bit tiring, but you get used to it.

CHAPTER 1

WHY WE FORGET TO TELL OUR KIDS STUFF

So yes, back in 2012 my daughter went flatting for the first time. I think we can all imagine what that looked like. Staying up late, sleeping in, eating what you like when you like, riotous parties, wild sex … I had no idea what she was doing, but I was *loving* it.

There is a reason for this sudden rush of energy. Once the kids are gone, you realise that the properly exhausting thing about parenting is that you have to know everything, all the time. They ask endless questions, kids, and you need to be able to answer all those questions, because, if you can't, you lose your authority and they won't eat their broccoli.

I remember when Holly was about three years old and she asked, 'Mummy, why is the sky blue?'

'Well, sweetheart,' I said, 'light is made up of all the colours in the rainbow from red right through the colour spectrum to

THEY ASK ENDLESS QUESTIONS, KIDS, AND YOU NEED TO BE ABLE TO ANSWER ALL THOSE QUESTIONS, BECAUSE, IF YOU CAN'T, YOU LOSE YOUR AUTHORITY AND THEY WON'T EAT THEIR BROCCOLI.

blue. The red light-waves are short, so they pass through the gaseous particles in the atmosphere. But the blue light-waves are long, so they bounce off the gaseous particles — or "refract" — and bend back towards the Earth, where our eyes pick them up. So really, the sky is made up of all the colours of the rainbow, but we can only see the blue. Eat your broccoli.'

Obviously, you've all had that same conversation with your kids at some point, so I'm not telling you anything you don't already know. But as they get older, they start asking you questions that you don't know the answer to, so obviously you have to start making stuff up or, as I say, you lose your authority and they won't eat their broccoli.

When she was 11, Holly asked me: 'Mummy, how does the internet work?' I took a deep breath and gave it a jolly good go. 'Okay, sweetheart, so when you ask the computer questions, those questions go through the computer and out the fibre-optic cables into the sky. Where the fairies catch them. And the fairies feed those questions to, um, unicorns, and the unicorns eat the questions and think about them for a bit — or "digest" them — and then they poo them out as answers. But, honey, if you spend too much time on the computer, then the fairies feed the unicorns too many questions and that upsets their tummies and they fart. And that's what thunder is. Eat your broccoli.' I have yet to meet an IT specialist who can prove to me that that's not true.

Once the kids are out of the house, you don't have to answer these questions any more. Having relinquished responsibility for their broccoli intake, you are free to stop faking omnipotence. It is tremendously liberating, this not-having-to-know-stuff.

Not long after she moved out, Holly was over for a visit and she said, 'Mum, what are the Kardashians for?'

'I don't know, darling,' I replied cheerfully. 'Really, nobody's got the answer to that. It's one of life's mysteries. Make Mummy a cocktail.'

IT IS TREMENDOUSLY LIBERATING, THIS NOT-HAVING-TO-KNOW-STUFF.

My point is: we should never underestimate how much children eat your brain. They are a constant distraction throughout their growing-up years with this barrage of questions, and their need to be kept safe and fed, and to be dropped off at hip-hop class and picked up from basketball. Their brain-eating powers are undeniably at their peak in that first year of life. If you think back to the year your baby was born, I'm guessing you can remember little or nothing of the socio-political goings-on of the period.

I've often thought that, if you asked a breastfeeding mother the kind of questions they ask someone who is suspected of having a brain injury (Who is the prime minister? Is it Wednesday?), she'd be made to immediately lie down in a hospital bed for 24-hour observation. The prospect of which — horizontal in clean sheets with the possibility someone might bring you a cup of tea — is inordinately appealing to a new mum.

The year Holly was born — 1993 — is a total blank space in my understanding of world history. Born six weeks premature and weighing two kilograms, Holly spent her first week in intensive care, fed through a tube down her nose. Rather than waiting for her to let me know when she was hungry, I needed to wake her every few hours to feed, so there was a complex roster of feed/burp/engage/sleep tasks to be followed. I used a colour-coding system and Post-its. I had also moved to a new city shortly before she was born, so I was without a support system of family or friends who might nip around with a casserole and let me know when I smelt whiffy. Not playing for sympathy here — I don't even like casserole — just providing context for the all-consuming dizziness of my first taste of parenthood.

My major contact with the outside world was Plunket, bless them: New Zealand's extraordinary mother-baby service. I can vividly recall one particular wintertime visit to the local Plunket rooms. I dressed my tiny baby in Michelin Man layers — cotton singlet, wool singlet knitted by her grandma, stretch-and-grow, wool booties (also grandma), special wool hat (yes), which grandma had knitted prem-size to fit a small orange, and a baby puffer-jacket. Having stuffed Holly into her portable car seat (I had to loosen the straps), I opened the front door to head to the car and was shocked by just how cold it was outside. At which point I looked down and realised I was wearing a nightie and a pair of socks. We were late for the appointment. They were very understanding.

So in amongst all that hoo-ha I failed to stay on top of current events. I missed the Waco tragedy in Texas and the World Trade Centre bombing in New York — two significant examples of domestic and international terrorism of the time. Even now, whenever these events are referenced in relation to more recent terrorist activities, my brain goes mother-fuzzy and I'm overwhelmed by an urge to go check on the baby. Not a terrible instinct, but not particularly useful when you don't have an actual baby any more, and it does get in the way of fruitful dinner-party conversations with my more geo-politically savvy friends.

I was completely unaware, too, of the genocide taking place in Rwanda, and what the Hutu majority did to the Tutsi. Mind you, the United Nations was similarly unaware of the deaths of up to half a million people, and that was actually their job. Perhaps they were breastfeeding, too. It is hard to comprehend any other explanation.

A decade later, I rented *Hotel Rwanda* from the video store, assuming it might be a character drama set in an exotic locale — a sort of African *Gosford Park*. I was traumatised. I lay awake all night, sobbing 'How did I not know?!', fairly certain it was my inattention that had ruined Don Cheadle's life. For weeks afterwards I would burst into tears and, when people asked, explain, 'I'm still very upset about Rwanda.'

I recall no movies at all from 1993. I didn't even see that year's number-one film, *Jurassic Park*, and still haven't seen it. It feels too late now for me to develop any expertise in dinosaur cloning. Apparently there is a character in *Jurassic Park* named Robert Muldoon who is a game warden. I find it impossible to suspend disbelief sufficiently to accept that Robert Muldoon could be anything other than a New Zealand prime minister. And if *he* was ever going to appear in a movie, it could only make sense if he turned up as an evil hobbit in the DVD extras for *Lord of the Rings*.

And I totally missed out on the phenomenon that is Grunge. Nirvana? Pearl Jam? Stone Temple Pilots? Nope, nothing. Fortunately, I have spent the past 15 years living with a man who has floppy hair and wears check shirts, so I feel like I've caught up nicely, thanks for asking. Twenty years after they were hot, I'm putting Pearl Jam on while I do the housework. Big crush on Eddie Vedder, me. I like to pretend it's still 1993 and I'm a bit cool. Neither of those things is true.

I MIGHT HAVE PASSED FOR GRUNGE. THOUGH MORE COBAIN THAN COURTNEY. SIMILARLY BLEARY, BUT DEFINITELY MORE CHIPPER.

Ironically, when I look back at the photos of Holly's first year — she dressed immaculately, me with unwashed hair and a crumpled button-through plaid shirt for easy breastfeeding access — I might have passed for Grunge. Though more Cobain than Courtney. Similarly bleary, but definitely more chipper.

The only news story that captured my attention in 1993 was the one about Lorena Bobbitt. Lorena was the American woman who got out of bed one night, went to the kitchen for a glass of water and came back with a kitchen knife and cut off her husband's penis. Then she went for a drive and threw the penis out the car window. The story had a happy ending. The police found her husband's penis on the side of the road and he had it stitched back on. At least, they said it was his penis. Might have been anything really — all kinds of stuff ends up on the side of the road. Could have been a bit of fried chicken; we'll never really know. But that's the only news story that filtered through the baby-haze in 1993. It's funny what you notice.

Before we go any further, I need to say that I didn't forget to tell my daughter *everything*. I did tell her heaps of stuff. For starters, I have fond memories and photographic evidence of the day I taught her to spit water like a dolphin spraying from its blowhole. It wasn't so much about the spitting. Really, what I was teaching her was how to pronounce 'hospital' properly. Like a lot of new people, Holly had initial difficulties sounding some letters correctly and putting them in the right places. In an effort to tidy up 'hostible', we worked on putting the 'spit' — literally — into 'hoss-spit-al'. While in the bath, obviously, with a cup of clean water at hand. We'd say 'hoss', then say 'spit' with a mouthful of water, followed by 'al'. Slowly at first; then sped up until it sounded like a word. It was tremendously successful. You're welcome.

A big focus on verbal communication, then. And books, music and dance — all the major food groups. We also put a fair amount of focus on learning the kinds of things that would make her a welcome guest in other people's houses. An only child needs to socialise, and mamas who work at night need an occasional lie-in. So 'please' and 'thank you', obviously. And table manners. Holly knew early on to start with the cutlery on the outside and move inwards; that it was her bread roll on the left and her glass on the right. If Holly had been invited to dinner at Government House when she was four (she wasn't), she would have been ready.

We talked about love and death and appropriate language and spelling and maths — lots of Big and Little Things. But not all of them. I knew I had forgotten to tell Holly about some stuff because of the Bread Defrosting Incident. Visiting our house from her flat one day while we had a power cut, Holly said she was hungry.

'Make a sandwich,' I said.

'There isn't any bread,' she said.

'It's in the freezer,' I said. (It's always in the freezer.)

She gave me one of those looks that only a teenage girl can give her mother — the one that says, unmistakably, 'Mummy, you are a complete fucktard.' What she actually said was, 'Oh, Mummy! How can I defrost bread without electricity?'

Let's start there.

CHAPTER 2

HOW TO DEFROST BREAD WITHOUT ELECTRICITY

Wait.

That's pretty much it. Bread out of the freezer, put it on a plate and ... wait.

For people raised on microwaves and instant gratification, however, 'waiting' lacks the kind of technical complexity they're used to. Waiting for bread to defrost is the culinary equivalent of checking the letterbox every day for a week for a birthday card from Gran with a postal note inside, which you then have to take to the post office to have turned into a dollar. What? Why? How much? No! No one's got the time for that sort of carry-on any more.

If we are going to wait for things, it will be high-tech waiting, right? Here, then, are a couple of other options for defrosting bread without electricity.

The bread house

Take two pieces of frozen bread and lean them against each other as though they were the pointy roof on an invisible house. Once the bread has defrosted sufficiently, the two slices will automatically (like magic) collapse, at which point you will know they are ready for sandwiching. If it helps, you can say 'Ding!' at or near the moment of collapse.

My first microwave

Alternatively, try placing one slice of frozen bread on a plate. Gently rotate the plate clockwise while making a combined humming/buzzing sound with your lips. For an ultra-high-tech version of this, take a light source in your spare hand (a torch or, more likely, the torch app on your mobile) and shine it on the bread. Scientific studies suggest the rotational movement and light application will not result in the bread defrosting at a faster rate than, say, for example, waiting. But you may find the complexity of it all reassuring.

Seriously: just wait.

CHAPTER 3

HOW TO STORE GINGER ... AND OTHER 'MUST-KNOWS' IN THE KITCHEN AND THE LAUNDRY

Let's stay in the kitchen for a moment, then nip briefly into the laundry. Not that I am, I can assure you, any kind of domestic goddess.

In the kitchen

After several years of solo-parenting, cooking (by which I largely mean 'reheating') was about producing sufficient food on a regular enough basis to stop my daughter and me starving to death. The concept of 'cooking as relaxing diversion' remains alien to me. I reckon there is something fundamentally wrong with the preparation-to-consumption ratio. An hour to create,

10 minutes to consume, another hour to wash, dry, put away and scratch rogue bits of onion off the skirting boards? The maths is all wrong.

But I've been lucky and a bit clever, too. The lucky bit is that my husband, Jeremy, is an enthusiastic cook who finds marinating, sautéing and whipping up sauces a meditative experience. I buy him fancy cookbooks. He puts on a food show. Everybody wins.

The clever bit is that I pretended quite convincingly during the first years of our living together that I couldn't cook. Burnt some stuff. Left other things sloppy in the middle. Failed to demonstrate any kind of enthusiasm, or reveal that my great-aunt had taught me to make really good short pastry. Over time, our household fell organically into a comfortable rhythm whereby he does the lion's share of the cooking while I eat and clean.

Faffing about in the kitchen where things are dangerously hot and sharp was never a mother–daughter bonding ritual. Hence the panic after Holly went flatting: had I taught her any kitchen stuff? I knew that, thanks to her grandmother, she had a copy of the *Edmonds Cookery Book*, and I'd seen her watching the Food Channel on the tele while sitting on the couch hoovering instant noodles — but did she know how to keep her ginger fresh?

So here are some things I forgot to tell my daughter that are unlikely to be covered by the great chefs, or the ones on the TV.

Ginger
Buy some ginger root at the vegetable shop. It looks like a fairytale stepmother's hand, but tastes heaps nicer in stir-fries

and soups and hot drinks. If you put fresh ginger in a zip-lock bag it will keep in the vege-crisper* for a few weeks, or in the freezer for several months. If you go the freezer option, remember you don't have to defrost it (or 'wait') to use it — just slice it or grate it while it is still frozen and throw it into whatever you're making.

Alternatively, you can peel the ginger and preserve it in a jar of vodka. After about six weeks, feel free to toss the ginger and drink the vodka.

Chillies

We like things spicy at our place, so a bit of chilli is one of our go-to flavours. The dried flakes and chilli pastes are handy, and easier to judge in terms of the kind of heat and flavour they will provide, but whole chillies are beautiful, and I like the Russian-rouletted-ness of the experience: one day, a couple of chillies will give a dish a bit of excitement; another day, they'll blow the top of your head off.

They're not expensive, but as you only use a few at a time and you don't want to waste the rest, again, put them in a zip-lock bag and whack them in the vege-crisper for a short time, or the freezer for a long time.

One thing to note: after handling chillies, make sure you wash your hands before you touch your eyes. Or change your tampon. Same goes for cayenne pepper. I still shudder when I recall being a student in a cold, damp Wellington flat decades ago, and trying to warm up on a winter's day by grilling cheese-on-toast with a sprinkle of cayenne pepper for added spicy

---

* The drawer in the fridge where most people keep their beer.

PEEL THE GINGER
AND PRESERVE IT
IN A JAR OF VODKA.
FEEL FREE TO TOSS
THE GINGER AND
DRINK THE VODKA.

heat … And then going to the loo while it grilled. Yep. In some cultures, women aren't allowed in the kitchen when they've got their period. I'm not sure that this has everything to do with the specific dangers of touching your lady-parts after handling spices, but it could explain some of it. I recommend yoghurt as an effective antidote. Though not for your eye.

Signature dishes

As much as I am not a fan of preparing 21 meals a week, I'm happy to do it now and again. A girl's got to eat. If you're like me, then, it is useful to have a Signature Dish — one main meal, one dessert — that you can whip up with cheerful confidence. Both of mine are ones you can make the day before, which means I'm not stuck in the kitchen alone while everyone else is having a riotously good time in the living room, drinking all the ginger vodka.

Chilli con Carne

It's not pretty, but it's really good. Mostly I make it as comfort food for us, but if we have guests, I encourage them to think of it as 'rustic' and bang on a bit about the joy of peasant food. It is also one of those dishes that you can do really well without everyone suddenly assuming you have a special talent for cooking in general, and therefore expecting you to host dinner parties all the time. It can be, if you want, your One Hit Wonder — your gastronomic equivalent of 'Who Let the Dogs Out' or 'Achy Breaky Heart' or Pachelbel's 'Canon in D'.

I've been loose in my descriptions of quantities here — they really don't matter down to the gram. I get anxious when I read

'85g tin' of whatever and my supermarket only stocks the 80g kind. When I say 'a tin', I mean the thing you imagine when someone says 'a tin can'. Not the tiny ones, or the huge ones, the size of tin that makes those other ones appear relatively tiny or huge. This isn't baking a cake where half-a-teaspoon too much baking soda ruins your life. This is Chilli. I suspect the people who invented it were sunburnt and drunk. They weren't measuring grams.

YOU WILL NEED

2 onions, chopped

1 tablespoon of olive oil

2 sticks of celery, chopped

1 capsicum (also known as a bell pepper) — red or green (Cut off the
top, take out the core, rinse off the seeds and chop it up.)

1kg mince (Either the expensive lean stuff, or the cheap stuff.
Who cares? You hardly ever cook — their long-term
cardiovascular health is not your concern.)

Worcestershire sauce

soy sauce

brown sugar

salt and pepper, to season

2 tins of diced or crushed tomatoes

2 tins of chilli beans

chilli — flakes, paste or fresh

2 zucchinis (also known as courgettes)

1 tablespoon of flour

METHOD

Chop the onions. If you (like me) cry like a fool when you chop onions, try keeping them in the freezer and then cut them while they're still frozen. It works, though they do go a bit mushy as you cook them. Which might matter if you were making a stir-fry of onions with lightly sautéed truffles, but it doesn't matter here. Alternatively, get someone else to chop your onions. Or chop the onions while talking to someone and pretending to be really upset about something. This can be fun. You will be weeping desperately, but your voice will sound remarkably calm. It looks like maturity.

Bravely pull yourself together, then heat the oil in a large saucepan and throw in the onion. Once it is soft and transparent, throw in the celery and capsicum. In Louisiana's Cajun cuisine, these three ingredients are known as 'the Holy Trinity'. It is a great flavour base for almost anything. Also, telling people this makes you look a bit clever. As a person, not as a cook.

(Note: There are other cuisine Holy Trinities. The French insist on onion, celery and carrot, and call it *mirepoix*. In Spain, it's *sofrito* — garlic, onion and tomato. The Chinese go for garlic, ginger and chilli; in India, it's garlic, ginger and onion; in the UK, it's fat, salt and potatoes; and so forth, all around the world. Every culture's got a Holy Trinity. Don't go on about this too much, though. Knowing about just one of them will do, or you'll end up sounding like a wanker. Being able to recite long lists of things is not a great sell. I know a dude, for example, who can list all the capital cities in the world, and occasionally does. I really like him, but it is despite this, not because of it.

And yes, Chilli con Carne is really a Spanish dish, so you could go for the *sofrito* trinity, but I like Cajun flavours best right now. If anyone challenges you on your Holy Trinity choice, just say 'It's fusion,' and toss your hair a bit.)

Once your Holy Trinity starts to look hot and soft, crumble in all the mince. Stir it around until the meat is browned all through, with no pink bits left.

Then have fun with the Worcestershire sauce, soy sauce and brown sugar. Don't measure them — just wave them about with confidence — maybe a tablespoon-ish of each. Then a sprinkle of salt and a good grind of pepper. Make it look like you know what you're doing, even if no one is watching. You're watching. Put on a show. This is the fun part of cooking. Grab it where you can. And taste as you go. The flavours won't develop for a while, but it will start to smell quite promising.

Then add the tinned tomatoes and tinned beans and check the chilli-ness of it. The chilli beans might have done enough for you, but I like more. Start with one chilli or half a teaspoon of chilli flakes or a teaspoon of chilli paste. Add more if you want. Don't touch your eye.

Chuck in the chopped zucchini. Put the lid on, and simmer it for anything between 40 minutes and an hour; you can't cook this too long — it just gets better. Once you are happy with the flavour, take a clean jam jar and fill it a third of the way up with cold water, add 1 tablespoon of flour, shake it up, and pour it into the saucepan. That will thicken up the chilli and help all the flavours properly hold hands. Either serve it then, or take it off the heat, put the lid on, and leave it until the next day. When you reheat it, bring it to the boil, then let it simmer for 10 minutes, or as long as it takes you to whip up the ginger-vodka cocktails.

Serve it in bowls, with crusty bread or corn chips on the side. If you can be bothered, sprinkle each person's serving with Cheddar or Parmesan cheese. No pressure. You've done enough, really.

And a dessert ...

Cherry-sherry Trifle
This is my favourite — I love making it, I love eating it, and I love it that it rhymes. That's honestly why I put the cherries and sherry together ... and only discovered afterwards that they taste really good with each other. At some point, I may try rum and plums. The Cherry-sherry Trifle is famous in our family; we have it every Christmas. People know I love them if I make it for their birthdays.

Like the main course, this is one of those dishes where everything goes into one container, so it is all about flavours and getting the ingredients talking to each other rather than anything to do with presentation. I make my trifle in a big glass bowl, so you can see inside all the gooey layers of red and yellow.

YOU WILL NEED
plain sponges (the two-in-a-pack kind helpfully labelled 'trifle
sponge' in the bakery section of your supermarket)
1 jar of cherry jam
2 tins or jars of cherries with the stones taken out (they do
this for you before they stick them in the jar)

some sherry — probably half a cup (any old kind — sweet, dry,
    ruby, whatever you have lying about or can find cheaply
    in the fortified-wine section at the supermarket)
2 litres of custard
whipped cream

THE NIGHT BEFORE

Smear cherry jam over the two sponges with a knife, as though you
were putting it on toast. Then cut the sponges into rough cubes;
throw enough in the bowl to cover the bottom. Don't try to be neat
and tidy about this — it is messy to make, and you will get very sticky
fingers. Let yourself enjoy it. Scatter one-third of the cherries
over the sponge layer. Drizzle a bit of sherry over the sponge. You
can use the cherry juice instead, if you don't want any alcohol in
the dessert, or you can use a mixture of the juice and sherry. Use
enough liquid to make it a bit damp, but not too soggy. Pour a layer
of custard over this — just enough to cover it.

Then do another layer of jammy sponge plus cherries; another
drizzle of sherry and/or juice; and another layer of custard.

And then one more layer, finishing with the custard.

Cover the bowl with cling-wrap and keep it in the fridge
overnight. All the ingredients will enjoy each other's company and
fuse together, so that by the next morning it will be a delicious
custardy, fruity, boozy concoction.

ON THE DAY

Shortly before you serve it, whip the cream and smear a layer over
the top of the trifle. It is really hard to make whipped cream look
smooth, so I like to not even try. I take the tip of a clean knife and

tap it across the top in long lines, a bit like tiny footprints. If you want, you can grate some chocolate gently over the top. This is entirely unnecessary, but go for your life if you fancy it.

If there is any left over (unlikely), a Cherry-sherry Trifle lasts for a couple of days in the fridge and, in my opinion, gets even more delicious the longer all the ingredients meld together. It is a superb breakfast.

... and now nipping into the laundry

Okay, we're not in the kitchen any more. I always slip out of there as fast as I can. The laundry is one of my favourite places in the house. I recently had mine painted bright orange and I've hung pretty stuff on the walls. From the window over the tub I can see cabbage trees, and fairly often there is a tui or kereru or two. This is where I go to clean stuff, and make things new. It is a good thinking place — when I get stuck with writing or just want to do something with my hands rather than my head, I often end up here, hand-washing some knickers. I find that soothing.

Many years ago — 1984 — when I was living in another damp student flat, a friend of mine was dying of cancer. Loys had been like a second mother to me when I was growing up, and her daughter, Lesley, is still my dearest friend. Lesley's son, Jason, is my godson, and at this point he was a newborn baby. So, during the days, I would go over to visit, play with Jason, make cups of tea and generally try to be useful. It was a pretty sad time — you feel totally involved in one event and disconnected from the rest of the world, and a bit useless. While you are waiting for the worst thing to happen, it feels like nothing really happens for days and days.

Each day I would go home to my flat and clean things. I scrubbed benches and floors, and washed curtains. I did a lot of laundry, because it felt good to make things fresh and new, like you were taking them back to their beginning. When I ran out of clothes that were dirty, I started hand-washing things that were already clean — woollen jumpers and scarves, underwear, anything I could find. When I ran out of my own, I volunteered to do my flatmates' laundry.

I HAD BEEN MADLY CLEANING THE WORLD, TRYING TO TAKE IT BACK TO ITS BEGINNING.

This went on for a long time, even after Loys died. Eventually, I kind of 'woke up' and realised what I had been doing: madly cleaning the world, trying to take it back to its beginning.

I said to my flatmates, 'Seems I've been a bit mental with this cleaning thing.'

They said yes, they'd noticed.

I said, 'Why didn't you say something?'

They said they'd really enjoyed living in a very clean house.

So cleaning is my thing. And my laundry is a good place. I had an epiphany there once: one of those moments when you suddenly see an aspect of the world very clearly.

My daughter would have been two years old and had some kind of tummy bug. It was 3am and I was hunched over the stainless-steel tub, scraping vomit off her bedsheets. Holly had been washed and cooled and soothed and tucked down again, and I was hoping she might sleep for a couple of hours before we'd need to rinse and repeat.

I had my own hot-cold, hollow feeling — part anxiety, part exhaustion, and a tiny bit of anger about the unfairness of it all. I'd already had a Big Day and another one was going to start in a few hours, and there seemed sod-all chance for any sleep in between. This wasn't the first time I'd understood Life Wasn't Fair, but it was the first time I properly understood there was nothing you could do about it — no protest movement, no frank discussion with the boss, no appeal to someone in charge. This, it occurred to me (possibly a little late in the piece), was Motherhood.

THERE WE ALL WERE, SOMEWHERE ON THE PLANET, UNITED BY THIS PRE-DAWN VOMIT-SCRAPING THAT SAID: 'LOOK. WE ARE MOTHERS. THIS IS WHAT WE DO.'

Which was when it dawned on me that right at that moment, all over the world, there were other mothers scraping vomit off sheets in *their* laundries. This was a thing we all did that made us part of the same tribe. I remember wishing I could phone some of them for a chat. (This was pre-Facebook when you had no way of posting a status update with 'washing vomit off child's sheets' and receiving a 'like'.) I also understood in that moment that even the mothers who weren't currently alone in their laundry had been, and would be again. There we all were, somewhere on the planet, united by this pre-dawn vomit-scraping that said: 'Look. We are mothers. This is what we do.'

We don't celebrate that enough. I don't mean the vomit, obviously, but the shared experience of motherhood. Somewhere along our feminist road, in insisting (quite correctly) that being a housewife and mother wasn't our only destiny, we managed to stop giving serious regard to motherhood. Although I'm not sure it was ever properly valued, except in the way I've heard described as 'romantic paternalism' — the good little woman holding it all together so other people could get on with doing the important things. US Supreme Court judge William J. Brennan described it in 1973 as women placed 'not on a pedestal, but in a cage' and wives and mothers everywhere nodded in recognition. We've certainly never valued motherhood by paying money for it, which is usually the way we say what something is worth. Which is why, when asked 'What do you do?', our first instinct is to define ourselves by our paid work. More than that, we often hide the work we do as mothers from employers and colleagues. We don't often talk about the detail of it, because, honestly, scraping vomit off sheets doesn't serve our image as liberated, professional, successful people.

So any time you end up in the laundry at 3am scraping vomit off sheets, I'd encourage you to reach out and feel the sisterhood. In some parallel time and space, all the world's mothers are there with you. It is one of the many things I like about being a woman — that we are part of a tribe that can cross race, class and geographic boundaries because of our shared experiences.

25

The Blood Bucket

And while we're in the laundry talking about experiences women share ... Periods, obviously. We are, in my family, serious bleeders. Part of my rite of passage on reaching puberty was to hear graphic stories from my mother, grandmother, aunts and great-aunts about that cream wool coat or this coral evening dress or the freshly upholstered couch utterly ruined, ruined I tell you, by the curse of our monthly curse.

That was, in fact, a pretty thrilling moment in my life. Brought up on good manners to say the right thing at the right time, there was something deliciously liberating about hearing all these beautifully dressed, well-behaved women get properly earthy in my Great-aunt Ruth's kitchen about the messes they'd made. And endlessly comforting in the ensuing years, knowing that any time I left a wet, red patch on the back of a school uniform or a bicycle seat, I wasn't so much making a mess as fulfilling my womanly familial destiny. Every time I spent an afternoon with my school jumper tied around my waste to cover a stain, I was reminded of my Great-uncle Frank's habitual romantic gesture of always walking behind Ruth as they left a movie theatre so he could surreptitiously check on the state of the back of her frock.

We try to stem the red tide — pads, tampons, pads *and* tampons — but we fail. So we have become very good at cleaning up after ourselves. For as long as I can remember, every 28 days I have prepared a Blood Bucket in my laundry. The bucket is red, as it happens, but it doesn't have to be. I fill it halfway with blood-temperature water (the temperature where it doesn't feel either hot or cold when you stick your hand in), and dissolve strong laundry powder in it. That's where all the knickers go for about five days. They also get rubbed with a cake of miracle-working laundry soap, and are left there to soak until the whole thing is over while I go and eat chocolate and shout and cry. Around about the time I stopped needing the Blood Bucket (hysterectomy), Holly reached puberty, so this has been going on at my place for decades.

When it was Holly's time, I, of course, told her all the family stories and got her grandmother to join in. The story about my mother's cream wool coat, purchased at great expense with her first proper wages and ruined on its very first outing on the bus from Hataitai into town, is heartbreaking. To cheer her up, I took Holly out to get her ears pierced and buy shoes. She'd been wanting to get her ears pierced for ages, but I'd made her wait so we would have something to do to celebrate her reaching womanhood. A good time for piercing, I'd said, as you'll be bleeding anyway. And the shoes because, well, obviously … shoes. Holly plans to continue this new tradition when the time comes.

Eucalyptus oil
This is another thing I always keep in the laundry — a little bottle of eucalyptus oil. You can buy it for not very much at the chemist. It is brilliant for getting pen ink off leather handbags, mysterious black marks off shoes, and tar off the soles. Dip a cotton bud into the oil and rub gently until the mark disappears.

It is also superb for removing adhesive labels off pretty much anything, particularly price tags on the soles of shoes, or those stupid clear-plastic stickers under the instep that say whether something is made of leather or synthetic material. Put some eucalyptus oil on a cotton wool ball, and dab at the sticker until it lifts off. Methylated spirits works, too, but eucalyptus is less likely to take the colour off with it. This is a fabulous way to remove any evidence, once you kick your heels up, that you might have got your sexy, funky shoes on the cheap. If they don't say *Made in China*, they might have been made in Italy, right? This matters because, well … shoes.

CHAPTER 4

MIDDLE AGE

Here's the thing every middle-aged woman wants to say in a firm, clear, loving voice to every young woman: 'I have been you. But you haven't been me — yet. So I know some extra stuff that you don't know. So you should listen to me. Quite hard.'

This is a tricky concept for a young brain to wrap itself around. Sometimes I think that if a girl properly absorbed the idea that a woman is just a girl living inside an older body, her brain might explode with the truth of it.

IT IS ONE OF MOTHER NATURE'S HILARIOUS LITTLE JOKES THAT WE ONLY AGE ON THE OUTSIDE.

And it is not just that we have been you, it's that we still think we *are* you. On the inside, we all think we are 18 years old.

Honestly. We are that same person we always were — the one you are now. It is one of Mother Nature's hilarious little jokes that we only age on the outside. That's why, in those moments when we forget the world is watching, forget our responsibilities and our place and our decorum, we hitch up our skirts, wave our arms about and dance. It is also why I've stopped telling people what my age is: you can see, when they hear the number, something change in their eyes as they readjust their assumptions about who you are, and their expectations about how you should be living your life. On the inside, we are all margaritas and stilettos. Looking at us from the outside, the world shakes its head and mutters, 'Not so much the margaritas and stilettos, lady. More Metamucil and Crocs. Stop dancing. Go knit.'

But here's a thing. I really love being middle-aged. I feel better about myself than I ever have — fewer insecurities, less self-doubt, more confidence. I worry less about offending people on the one hand, or pleasing them on the other. I am blissfully aware that if people don't like who I am or what I say and think, there are literally billions of other people on the planet they can spend their time with.

Writer and poet Alice Walker talks eloquently and often about telling ourselves about 'having the right to be this self'. It seems such a simple thing, but properly embracing that idea feels powerful. Not long after I turned 50, I built a shrine — quite literally — in my office to Stroppy Women. There are photographs of my heroes like Lucille Ball and Carol Burnett, alongside Wonder Woman and Annie Oakley figurines, plus a very democratic range of religious iconography featuring the female stars of Buddhism, Hinduism, Catholicism and Louisiana voodoo. Inspired by thinkers like Alice Walker, I've put Post-it notes on the shrine reminding myself of things: 'This Is Who I Am'; 'This Is What I Look Like'; 'This Is What I Do'. When I'm working and need a bit of courage or a smidge of motivation, I look over my shoulder and there it all is.

Songwriter and poet Leonard Cohen said something that has stuck in my head for a while now. In *I'm Your Man*, Cohen tells his biographer, Sylvie Simmons, that he believes the world conspires to silence everyone — to be normal, passive, to fit in — so that by the time we reach 50, we have either stopped talking or started shouting. Me, I've started shouting.

Women in particular, I think, grow into themselves as they age. We become clearer about who we are, and feel better about our place in the world and the contribution we make to it. We even start to feel good about how we look. Which is ironic, because around about the time we finally start to feel good about how we look, we actually start looking quite shit. But fortunately, we're too tired to care.

So, while I love being middle-aged, there are, you know ... *moments*. Like before a gig when I get out of the shower, wet hair, no makeup, and look in the mirror and think, 'Oh, good lord ... this'll be a project.' But you push on through with the eyeliner and hair-straighteners, because people are going to have to look at you, right? You don't want to frighten them. Or spend the whole night saying 'No, actually I'm quite well. No, no kind of treatment. Honestly,' as you point at your face, 'this is as much as I could be bothered doing right now.'

That's another thing young women won't understand, with their firm, smooth skin and their bright eyes and their hopes

WOMEN GROW INTO THEMSELVES AS THEY AGE. WE EVEN START TO FEEL GOOD ABOUT HOW WE LOOK. WHICH IS IRONIC, BECAUSE WE ACTUALLY START LOOKING QUITE SHIT. BUT, FORTUNATELY, WE'RE TOO TIRED TO CARE.

and dreams. (Yeah, all of that will fade.) Young women look fabulous before makeup, with makeup, and after makeup. But the middle-aged amongst us know that once we have constructed that gorgeous face just in front of our actual face, there is a moment during the evening when the whole thing will slip, somehow. It will melt, or blur, or run, or smear. Now, we don't know *when* that's going to happen, we only know that it *is* going to happen. Which is why we carry a compact, with a little mirror, so we can check regularly for the right time to undertake running repairs. This is, in fact, how you know you are middle-aged. Middle age isn't a number, or a particular birthday — it is suddenly needing to carry a compact. The one I carry is an antique; it used to belong to my grandmother and it's very pretty, with enamel flowers on the lid. Occasionally, I pull it out to check for running repairs and give myself a fright, because, in the wrong lighting, the compact appears to still have my grandmother's face in it. I'm not even sure how that works. At which point, I just give up and put it away. Like I say, too tired to care.

But really, we only start looking a bit shit in conventional terms, in the context of a society that worships youth. And you can find real joy in this business of no longer caring.

I have this crazy theory about why we worship youth and find ageing less attractive — and a lot of it has to do with architecture. It is an idea that struck me on my first visit to Europe in the mid-1990s, and I get more certain with every visit back. If you are from one of the young countries — New Zealand, Australia, Canada, America — the first thing you notice about Europe is that it has a lot of old stuff. History, and so forth. It's all over the place. History is fascinating — lovely to look at and feel part of, and it provides a sense of perspective that makes you feel important and insignificant at the same time.

MIDDLE AGE ISN'T A NUMBER, OR A PARTICULAR BIRTHDAY – IT IS SUDDENLY NEEDING TO CARRY A COMPACT.

In the Portuguese city of Lisbon, I visited two churches built side-by-side. They were referred to locally as the 'old' church and the 'new' church. The old church was built in the twelfth century, and the 'new' one was built 100 years later. The way the locals said 'new' was kind of sniffy and disparaging, like they were implying the paint might not have dried yet, and that if you wanted to see something with a proper story to tell, you might want to nip next door. Coming from a country that knocks its CBD down every 30 years because it is evidently past its use-by, you quickly get the idea that 'old' is a very relative term.

And in the glamorous cities of Paris and Vienna, I was struck by two things: the way they treasured and nurtured and revered their older buildings; and the way they treasured and nurtured and revered their older women. I chatted with 'women of a certain age' in Vienna who — unless it was a trick of translation — totally agreed with my theory. Yes, they said, it is our duty to preserve and protect the buildings that have seen so much and tell us about who we are and where we have come from. And, they said firmly, it is our duty to preserve and protect the women who have done, and do, the same. Dress well, smell good, keep the paint fresh, make sure the lighting is flattering, but don't be banging up any new façades, they argued. A sixteenth-century castle should look like a sixteenth-century castle, not a Surfer's Paradise condo. These were women who looked like they wouldn't have a bar of Botox or Hollywood-style surgery, but who made trips to the day spa for facials and pedicures like we make trips to the supermarket — weekly, and with a sense of necessity, not luxury. Pay the power bill, get your hair done. Tick.

Back then, I tried to sell my 'women and buildings' idea to some of the local women's magazines I write for, but, while they said they liked the theory, they weren't buying the story. Doubtless, that kind of copy wasn't going to sell a lot of products on a facing page shouting 'New! Improved! Age-defying! Look younger!'

Those women-of-a-certain-age in Europe weren't interested in looking younger. For them, it was about looking your age and good. And not ignoring an important part of the equation: beauty equals what you started with, plus time. That 'new' Lisbon church probably looked quite pretty in 1245. And 770 years later, it's bloody gorgeous. Partly just because it's still here. Magnificent.

That European better-with-age attitude leads to a fair amount of everyday self-acceptance amongst its citizens and its visitors. After admiring centuries-old buildings with their worn stone steps and collapsed foundations, you can grow quite brave about getting your kit off at the beach. In my early forties,

I spent three delightful days frolicking topless on the Algarve Coast. I had never frolicked topless on a public beach before. Around here, we stop frolicking, topless or otherwise, around the time we hit puberty and become increasingly aware — and not in a good way — that our body tells a story. A story about age, children, surgery, our genetics and our lifestyle. After 40, you are a walking autobiography. So we tend to slip on a pleasant dust jacket to protect our real story from random eyes, sit very quietly, and leave the frolicking to the young and very young.

BEAUTY EQUALS WHAT YOU STARTED WITH, PLUS TIME.

But not on the Mediterranean Coast. When you visit those beaches, all the books are out. I saw a veritable library of women in Faro, volumes of them — plump, stretch-marked, pendulous, dimpled, sagging, wrinkled and wobbling. Wandering about blissfully, not only without 'beach wraps' to protect the world from the evidence of what life has done to them (and what they have done with their lives), but without their bikini tops. *Mon Dieu!* as they might say on the Riviera, but don't.

Can I tell you how liberating this is? To completely relax under a sun with an ozone layer, although still SPFed to the max, and not suck it in, cover it up or tense an ounce? Swim and read and waddle off to the bar (yes, they sell wine at the high-tide mark — it's very European in Europe) without hearing the word 'waddle' resound in your head? Meanwhile, back home, 13-year-old girls swim in board-shorts and T-shirts because they don't look like a girl in a glossy magazine, and their mothers and grandmothers don't swim at the beach at all, because they're embarrassed that they've become a book. That's what happens when you are older than most of the architecture in your country.

I made a promise to myself back then that I would continue to swim and frolic, and I've kept it — within the by-laws, of course, which means the top stays on. Being a woman in her fifties in her togs on a public beach already feels like an act of social disobedience. For civil disobedience, I occasionally conceal a little chilled wine in my water bottle and toast the women who inspired me on the Algarve Coast.

BEING A WOMAN IN HER FIFTIES IN HER TOGS ON A PUBLIC BEACH ALREADY FEELS LIKE AN ACT OF SOCIAL DISOBEDIENCE.

So I am embracing middle age, and I want my daughter to look forward to it — or at least not be frightened that it's on its way. On the downside, each day when you look in the mirror, you don't look as good as you did yesterday. But on the upside, you look better than you will tomorrow. Which is also the downside. On another upside, once the communists stop taking over the summer house (my favourite euphemism for menstruation) you can start wearing white slacks. On the downside, hardly anyone looks good in white slacks. But middle-aged women wear them heaps, just because they can.

There will be (spoiler alert) some things you will have to do a little differently, like you can't just stumble out of bed any more and head out to a café, because it takes at least an hour for the features on your face to shuffle back into their rightful place. And your eyebrows disappear and the colour goes from your cheeks. But this is all cosmetic — for which there are cosmetics, right? Brush on some blusher, draw those eyebrows back on, and stick your face into a headwind. You'll be fine. You are so full of wisdom and experience that what you say will fascinate people so much that they'll hardly notice your face. Honest.

I do a bit of television, mostly for the fun of having my makeup done on a regular basis by a professional. Best recent tip from a makeup artist is that, once you've filled in your eyebrows with a pencil, take a tiny brush and smooth the pencil lines out along the direction of the natural hairs. It will stop it looking like a clown has just drawn a picture on your face with a Vivid marker.

Birthdays can be a challenge. Not just for the middle-aged — I've met 29-year-olds who freak out about getting old, which is both adorable and a bit ridiculous from where I'm sitting. But everyone's life crises come at their own times. For me, the birthdays that end in zero are the easy ones. These tend to involve large gatherings with party-poppers, or hedonistic getaways to exotic locales. It's the birthdays that end in an eight or a three that give me the most trouble — the ones just a bit before or after the milestones. You can dance on a milestone. It's the other years that irk and irritate like a rough pebble in your dancing shoe.

Some of this is maudlin self-indulgence. First-world grief for the attributes the first-world values — that loss of youth in a culture that worships it. Determinedly contrary, I either feel or fake impatience with my own and other people's complaints about sagging and drooping and greying. 'Embrace the crone!' I sing on my good days. 'You have wisdom, you are still here!' And I properly believe me. But I'll admit that more than once the Black Dog has turned up a few days before one of my birthdays, panting and slobbering, demanding to know what I have done so far, and what else I plan to achieve in the ever-decreasing time left. Questions asked with a sneer rather than genuine curiosity, and designed to elicit panic.

There is some point — different for everyone — when you become aware that the birthdays behind you are likely greater in number than the birthdays to come. And that there are things you had planned to do which now look *unlikely*. That you are Running Out of Time. The Birthday Black Dog turned up while I was writing this — unbidden, unwelcome, badly in need of a bath. Barked like mad, and set his fangs in my shin. We growled at each other for a few days, and he refused to let me out of the house. And then I remembered that we've been here before, the dog and I. And that these days he doesn't stay very long. He's a weekend house-guest rather than a flatmate. What sends him away, eventually, is music and dancing and other people's voices. Which I might not feel like, but he likes even less. So we do champagne and cake, and invite people over and make a lot of noise, and at some point I throw a stick and the Black Dog chases after it and doesn't come back.

That's one of the great things about having had a lot of birthdays. You know how they go. Starts with a dog, ends with a cake.

My lovely friend, Lesley, is eight years older than me, which means she is a handy canary down the mineshaft of middle age. Always just ahead of me on the journey through life's stages, she reports back with wit and wisdom on how the land lies, and what I might expect next. A few years ago, she let me know that when we reach 50, we suddenly become Invisible In Shops. Those cool young things — particularly the ones at the makeup counter with designer nails and eyeshadow combinations that work only on the very young and drag queens — just can't see us any more as we wait politely for someone to explain the difference between the anti-ageing lotion and the anti-wrinkle cream. Lesley, not a natural fan of shopping (it is her one flaw) was so disheartened after being ignored for ages that she gave up and went home, lotion-less. With her courage screwed up, she returned on another occasion and managed to nail down a painted waif to ask whether she should be going for the 'anti-ageing' or 'anti-wrinkle'.

'Oh my gosh,' said Waif, 'you're much too late for the anti-wrinkle!'

Maybe if she'd served her on her previous visit, they might have caught it in time.

'OH MY GOSH,' SAID WAIF, 'YOU'RE MUCH TOO LATE FOR THE ANTI-WRINKLE!'

Two things. First, someone should get all the shop girls together and tell them that the people most able to spend ridiculous amounts of money on things that smell nice and make you feel good are women over 50. Mostly that's because their daughters have left home and are buying their own smelly feel-good things with their staff discount, meaning we can confidently buy the really expensive stuff now and not risk having it filched by a kid who doesn't actually need it.

Secondly, if we really are invisible in shops, we can start nicking stuff. I propose we all get together, hire a bus, and head down to the Smith & Caughey's makeup department where we can shoplift to our hearts' content. We will never have to pay for a lipstick again.

And this whole ageing thing is ... relative. The truth of that will be confirmed by your relatives. For my most recent birthday, Dad chose a card for me that said: *To a special daughter. With every step you grow more beautiful. With love on your birthday.* I said to him, 'That's lovely, Dad. It's bullshit, but it's a really nice thought.' He looked amused. He is 85. Doesn't look a day over 80.

CHAPTER 5

YOUTH

I am never sure whether this is useful thing for a young woman to know or not, but let's run it up a flagpole and see who salutes.

Youth equals power. As a young woman, you will never be more powerful than you are right now. And — this is another one of Mother Nature's little jokes — you will never have less of an idea about what you'd like to do with that power.

Ask your mum if I'm right. Is she nodding? There you go.

The reason young women have so much power is because the world is largely run by men. These men think you are beautiful and wonderful, and they will do almost anything for you to make you happy, because what they would really like to do is shag you. Mostly in their dreams, right? But also literally, at some deep, primal, unconscious level. Massive generalisation, sure; but there is enough truth in it to make it worth saying out loud.

I have occasionally thought that we could end the need for the feminist struggle if we got all the pretty 18-year-old girls together to say to all the men in the world, 'Please give us equal pay and maternity leave and the right to control our own bodies! Go on, pleeeease!' and then bat their eyelashes. There'd be workplace crèches and 100 per cent safe contraception and vast numbers of women on every company board before you could say 'Gloria Steinem'. But playing on your sexuality to wheedle equality out of them would be like using your third wish to wish for three more wishes — it's against the laws of Nature and physics, and the universe would explode.

Also, and this is more important to understand, the fact that men think you are gorgeous and want to sleep with you is not nearly as impressive or exciting as it might sound. Here's the thing: men will put their penises into almost anything. Seriously. Somewhere around puberty — maybe earlier — the male of the species begins to experience the world through his penis. Or, at the very least, he experiments with putting his penis into all kinds of places. Just to see what it feels like. According to my research — part observation, part conversations had over a few drinks — there comes a time when the young male of the species will look at a new thing and immediately wonder: 'What would that feel like on my dude?'

During a particularly robust game of Truth Or Dare not so long ago, I was given a glimpse into the range of things that various men of my acquaintance have put their penis into. A bowl of mashed potato. A vacuum cleaner ... while it was turned on. Down the back of a couch — that firm bit between seat and back. And (one particularly courageous young man) into an eftpos machine. This is not the kind of information men volunteer, but, asked point blank, very few will deny it. With any conviction.

LATER ON, YOU WILL HAVE
A LIST OF ALL THE THINGS
YOU WOULD LIKE TO DO
WITH THAT POWER FOR
YOURSELF AND THE WORLD.
AT WHICH POINT YOU WON'T
BE SO YOUNG ANYMORE,
SO NOT SO POWERFUL. YES,
MOTHER NATURE, HA HA.

What does this mean for us? Certainly this: never be too impressed that a man wants to put his penis into you. Specifically, if you are feeling a bit down about yourself, don't ever try to cheer yourself up by going out and finding a man who will sleep with you. That he will sleep with you doesn't mean you are special. It merely means *you were there*. And always remember he would be just as happy with a pizza.

So, as a young woman, you have a lot of power. Later on, you will have a list of all the things you would like to do with that power for yourself and the world. At which point you won't be so young any more, so not so powerful. Yes, Mother Nature, ha ha, ha ha ha. In the meantime, all I can suggest is that you try to only use your power for good. You are a Jedi of youthful sexuality. Don't go over to the dark side.

Around the time I was writing my comedy show, a magazine asked me what I would say if I could send a letter back in time to me when I was 16 years old. This is what I wrote:

Dear 16-Year-Old-Me

I think of you often. I like to imagine that that 16-year-old girl still exists in a small corner of my middle-aged soul. You were in your final year of high school in a small town, a little nervous about launching yourself into the unknown, but also excited and determined to leave and start your life. About the only thing you were properly afraid of was living an ordinary life. You needn't have worried.

Right now, you are trying very hard to think of the right way round to do things — university English, polytech journalism, or drama school. Your problem is you want to do everything, but you don't know which to do first. You will discover that the order doesn't matter — you will end up doing everything at some point. Regardless of which door you choose, other doors seem to stay open for later. You can stop worrying about doing the 'right' thing, and just choose the thing that thrills you. Your instincts are good.

Boys confuse you. They seem so certain of everything, while you are sure of nothing when it comes to relationships. You spend a lot of time bewildered by their ability to cast themselves as the lead actors in every one of life's scenes. Much later, you will realise that this is all bravado. Deep down inside every man there is a small boy waiting for someone to tell him off and send him to his room. I'm not saying you should do that, but it is a useful thing to know.

You worry a bit about being uncool. Your passion for op-shop clothes hasn't caught on yet, so the nana cardies and pensioner shoes you find charming draw some criticism. Go harder with that — you're finding your own style. Though I think you could maybe start plucking your caterpillar eyebrows sooner. And the whole smoking thing is a mistake. Don't do that.

You will learn some things the hard way. You get your heart broken more than once — twice in fact, by just one boy, early on — and there are a couple of times when you end up in such a mess you can't see a way out. But there is always a way out.

You are a people-pleaser, which is lovely, but sometimes it gets you in trouble. You marry twice out of some odd need to satisfy convention or to have a crack at conventional life. But you are at heart (and you already know this) a Fringe-dweller. Eventually, you will find your own place on the fringes of conventional society to set up house. The family you create will look nothing like the kind of family anyone would put in a TV commercial, but it will work perfectly for you. You will get married on a whim in Las Vegas, which will surprise you at least as much as everyone else.

The thing I most admire about you at 16 is your sense that anything is possible. Sometimes you will achieve things because you don't know yet how difficult they will be. You will do the impossible because you think it is possible. Hold onto that for as long as you can. Later on, I will imagine being you so that I can find the courage to try new things.

It may be useful to know these things: always count your drinks; the bubble skirt is never a good idea, ever; and don't go to bed with your mascara on.

Other than that, you know all the things you need to right now. Trust yourself more and carry on. It is going to be fun.

Much love always,

Me

It is a lovely thing to do, to take a moment to stop and really picture the young person you were and send her kind thoughts.

Like I say in the chapter on middle age, we are all still the same person on the inside. Or, as I say in this letter, the original girl still lives in a corner of our soul. Quite often these days I think of time as not a linear thing — with the past way back there and finished, and the future off in the distance, yet to happen. Instead, I like thinking of time as a continuum with everything happening at once so we can whisper messages to our past and future selves. Now and then, in the present, you get a strong feeling that you are on the right path, making the right choice, doing the right thing. In the part of my brain that approves of magical thinking, I like to believe that this is Future Me letting me know it turns out right, whispering down the years, 'Yes, that's the one! You got it!' Maybe what we think of as 'following our instincts' is about taking advice from that voice. Whether that's a crazy or not, it doesn't do us any harm, ever, to send kind thoughts to ourselves.

THE ORIGINAL GIRL STILL LIVES IN A CORNER OF OUR SOUL.

CHAPTER 6

'DOES THIS CHAPTER MAKE ME LOOK FAT?'

We've been lucky, Holly and I, in that body image has never seemed to be an issue for her. She has always felt really good about how she looks, loving her body for the way it can dance and move, and celebrating it with the way she dresses. It is one of the things I've adored and admired about her group of friends, the way they'd all come over to our place to get ready to go out, spend hours intricately painting their already gorgeous faces so they'd look like Nicki Minaj (or like Nicki Minaj's makeup — no one knows what Nicki *really* looks like), and then clearly forget to put their pants on before leaving the house. You could tell how confident and how at ease they all were, tottering off in their tiny little midriff tops and that teensy bit of fabric they'd wear round their bottom bits which I always referred to as a 'quim cover'.

I like to think I helped encourage Holly to have a healthy attitude towards body image. My basic philosophy is that if you are recognisably human-shaped, you're fine, have another pie. Like, as a benchmark, if you were, say, shot, and the police came and drew a chalk outline around you and then took your body away, and people saw that chalk outline and could tell it had been a person lying there previously, then you are within the parameters of an acceptable body shape. If, however, people looked at the chalk outline and wondered if perhaps a very large, sprouty potato had been lying there, or a Sputnik had landed, then maybe it is time to back away from the buffet. This is clearly not as refined as the Body Mass Index system of assessing healthy weight, but the BMI is increasingly poo-pooed in many quarters. You will find less evidence documented against my Chalk Outline Test if you go sticking it into Google.

Over the years, I have gone through phases of unconsciously piling on the beef, as they say, and then suddenly realised it was time to put down the pie and back away from the buffet. It's like a ripcord was pulled and I just automatically inflated. Although I can't pinpoint the moment this begins, I can be entirely specific about when I've suddenly been made aware of it. Once was in my late twenties when I bumped into a friend I hadn't seen for ages. 'Michèle!' she shrieked. 'How wonderful to see you! And how exciting! You're having a baby!'

I wasn't.

Here's a useful bit of advice. Never assume a woman is pregnant unless she tells you she is. Never. There is no way out of that kind of *faux pas*. No amount of 'But *Sally* said you were … I mean, you don't *look* pregnant … to *me*,' or 'It's just that you're *glowing*,' is going to get you out of that one. All it can ever mean is that she's looking a bit fat. Always wait for the possibly

IF YOU ARE RECOGNISABLY
HUMAN-SHAPED, YOU'RE
FINE, HAVE ANOTHER PIE.

pregnant person to bring the subject up herself. Even if you can actually see the baby's head *crowning*, even then I'd recommend going for something subtle like 'Would you perhaps like me to boil some water and rip some sheets?' Trust me on this one.

I have a new benchmark now for knowing when I am overweight. I do a lot of yoga, and it is my belief that when you are doing a shoulder-stand — *Salamba Sarvangasana* — you shouldn't be suffocated by your own tits.

SUCCESSFULLY LOSING WEIGHT IS A LOT LIKE ANNOUNCING A DIVORCE: BY THE TIME PEOPLE START SAYING SUPPORTIVE THINGS, THE HARD WORK IS ALREADY OVER.

Which is why, in the last little while, I took myself in hand and lost 12 kilos. This may sound more impressive than it is. I'd put on 5 kilos when I stopped smoking, and I was already 5 kilos over ideal, so really I maybe only lost two. And I put those back on over Christmas, so, actually, it is entirely possible nothing happened and I don't know why we're talking about it.

Successfully losing weight is a lot like announcing a divorce: by the time people start saying supportive things, the hard work is already over. Mostly, people want to know 'how you did it'. Because I think we are all waiting for the magical day when we ask someone for their diet tip and they say 'a teaspoon of cinnamon' or 'licking kittens' — just one painless thing we can do that miraculously releases our inner thin person like a handsome prince bursting out of the Beast.

But there's no point in any of us swapping diet stories. Everyone finds their own solutions: exotic teas, eschewing carbs, going all protein and no veges, or all veges/no protein, or one of those esoteric ones like the diet where you only eat white food, or stuff that begins with the letter 'k'. In the end, it all boils down like a simple low-fat, low-salt reduction to this: eat less, exercise more. Snore.

So there's no point in telling you how I lost weight. In general terms, it was about no longer feeling like it was my responsibility to honour all the food in the fridge by consuming it; and it turned out to have more to do with what I *did* eat (fruit and vegetables) than what I *didn't* eat (cake and chups).

But I can tell you how I got chunky this last time. It wasn't about 'comfort eating', seeking solace in vast secret bowls of potato and gravy. I didn't wrap myself in a blanket of sponge cake or bury myself sorrowfully in chocolate. And I don't think food is wicked and therefore binge on it when I want to be evil. When I want to be evil I talk about people I don't like, or buy expensive shoes. Healthy stuff like that.

I don't actually like overeating. But sometimes my politics made me do it. I am a fierce believer in equality and democracy. So whenever I bought a bottle of wine to share (who am I kidding? *bottles*), I would assiduously ensure I drank my equal share. Dinner at my house consisted for years of three identical plates — despite the fact that one of us is a Mac truck to my Mini and therefore requires more fuel to run him, and another of us was dancing eight hours a day and still growing taller.

One of us didn't need one-third of the lasagne. But democracy made me do it.

And feminism. My generation are the daughters of women who took the burnt chop and the broken biscuit. This was despite the fact (or because) they'd cooked both chop and biscuit: they still put their needs last. My sisters and I, we will have none of this! Work like a man, eat like a man, I say. With my mouth quite full.

There is an allegory I like about two children. One of them is very active and adventurous and she goes through two pairs of shoes each winter. The other is very dainty on her feet and only needs one pair. If their parents treated them equally, then either one kid would have more shoes than she needed, or one would be barefoot for part of the year. What they really need is not equal treatment but different treatment to achieve equality. Sufficient shoes. Or chops. Or Cherry-sherry Trifle. And now I'm hungry.

WHAT THEY REALLY NEED IS NOT EQUAL TREATMENT BUT DIFFERENT TREATMENT TO ACHIEVE EQUALITY.

Also, there is no such thing as too many shoes. But you get the point.

Not everything about losing weight is fabulous. The women's magazines will only tell you about the happy bits. There are sad bits, too. One of my happiest moments was buying my first new bra after losing 12 kilos. It was immediately followed by a sad bit. There was a sale on in a lingerie store, so I got them to fit me with a pretty new bra. Bra makers tend to make their prettiest bras for women who have very little bosom. This means that the women who need bras most end up with industrial-strength scaffolding with all the aesthetic appeal of a stationary forklift, while women who hardly need bras at all get the frills and lace. It's a thing.

Anyhoo, I got properly fitted by a professional for a new bra and discovered it was an entirely different size from the ones I had been wearing every day for a very long time. Completely different numbers and letters involved. This bra felt amazing, like I was wearing *it* rather than that it was wearing *me*. So I skipped home — no jiggle — and tried on all my other bras. Clearly, I had been getting dressed each morning without looking down.

In A. A. Milne's *Winnie-the-Pooh* there is a story called 'In Which Eeyore Has a Birthday and Gets Two Presents'. Pooh and Piglet discover it is Eeyore's birthday, and they have forgotten to get him anything. So Piglet races home to get a red balloon left over from a party, and Pooh goes home to get a jar of honey. Running back, Piglet trips over a rabbit hole and the red balloon bursts. And Pooh gets a little peckish on his return journey and fancies a little something, so he stops to eat some honey and, before he knows it, the honey pot is empty. So that's what they give Eeyore — a broken red balloon, and an empty honey pot. Eeyore, of course, couldn't be happier. He spends his birthday putting the broken balloon into the honey pot, and taking it out again, and putting it back in, all day.

That's what my boobs looked like in the bras that didn't fit. Broken balloons in honey pots. It was excruciatingly sad.

So I went back to the lingerie store that had the bra sale and bought half a dozen more of the new bra. And I was as happy as could be. Which is the lesson here: if you get your bras fitted properly, your boobs will once again look like puppies snuggling in baskets.

We live in an era that generally favours thinness rather than the other thing. The fashion industry prefers to hang its designs on models who look as much as possible like a coat hanger, because, they say, clothes look better on 'skinny people' rather than your average woman, size 12 to 14. The less body you have, apparently, the better their stuff looks. Consequently, those mannequins you see in shop windows are 23 per cent thinner than the average woman. And those dummies will look better in what they're wearing than you ever will. There are two ways to read this.

Option A: Fashion designers are quite shit at their job. That's if you assume that their job is to create clothes for people to wear. They clearly haven't quite mastered the task of making clothes for people who are human-shaped. They're also crap at making shoes for people who walk, swimsuits for people who swim, or bras for people with actual boobs. They can't multi-task with the practical and the pretty. Not achieved. Should try harder.

Option B: Fashion designers aren't actually in the business of creating things to be worn; they're making something to be photographed. Art, not clothes. A two-dimensional thing that looks best in the picture rather than in the flesh. I think we could live with that if we were just talking about *haute couture* — the kind of runway stuff few of us could afford to buy anyway. But when chain stores are presenting clothes that look best on mannequins whose ribs stick out, we're in trouble. Serious trouble. Anorexia is one of the top three health issues for young women. Window displays and fashion shoots that make women think they need to be skinny to look good in clothes are a significant part of that problem. Because when we buy a frock, what we're trying to buy is the look. When the frock looks better on the shop dummy, we're quick to assume the problem is our body, not their design. Our sisters and daughters are constantly being set up to fail.

But there is hope. This is actually a battle we could win. We've changed our attitude over recent decades about attractive body weight. It used to be that plumpness was aspirational because it suggested you could afford food and leisure. Now thinness is aspirational because it suggests you have time and money for diet and exercise.

This is not about judging 'plump' or 'thin' as 'right' or 'wrong', but observing that we are entirely capable of evolving our ideas about beauty. With better intentions, we can get to a place where a variety of body shapes, sizes and skin colours can be read by our collective eyes as beautiful. Changing those fashion dummies would be an effective place to start. Assuming they want to change. We should ask them. The fashion designers, I mean.

While the fashion world celebrates thinness, this isn't what happens in my head. My experience of living in my body suggests that being the kind of skinny that is celebrated must take a lot of effort, time, planning and self-focus. So when I see chunky people, I think, 'She looks busy. She probably takes great care of other people and is a good and kind person.' Also, I've become aware that I'm a bit suspicious of thin people. Any kind of prejudice is wrong, and I'm working on myself to get over it. But I've noticed I don't instantly warm to tiny little skinny things.

WITH BETTER INTENTIONS, WE CAN GET TO A PLACE WHERE A VARIETY OF BODY SHAPES, SIZES AND SKIN COLOURS CAN BE READ BY OUR COLLECTIVE EYES AS BEAUTIFUL.

A friend asked me the other day if I would like to meet her friend Kate. And I looked over at Kate, who appeared waif-like and a bit hungry. I said, 'No, not really. I can't really see the point. I don't think we're going to get on. I doubt we'll ever be friends. I mean, what would we do together? Skip a meal? Life is too short to hang out with people who have clearly spent their whole lives saying "No, thank you, I don't eat dessert; I don't actually like sweet things. And I don't drink: it's got a lot of calories. What I like to do is get up very early in the morning and go for a jog. To the gym. Also, I had a grape last Thursday and I'm still full." I want to hang out with people,' I said, 'who have clearly spent their whole lives saying "Yes, please, I'll have two."'

Though, of course, I was wrong. Kate turned out to be lovely; she just has a really fast metabolism. Measuring someone's value — your own or anyone else's — by the kilo is a really stupid idea.

CHAPTER 7

SEX

If there's one thing I thought I'd be good at as a mother, it was going to be talking about sex. As educated, open-minded parents, a lot of us thought we'd be good at this. But it turned out to be much harder than we thought.

I had all the right resource material stashed away, ready for the moment when Holly starting asking questions. I was keen to get in first, before she heard about sex from some random kid in the playground who might have filled her head with nonsense about touching bellybuttons or deliveries from storks.

Holly was at intermediate when she showed some curiosity for the subject. I pulled out my copy of Peter Mayle's excellent *Where Did I Come From?* (Carol Publishing Group, 1973), and we read it together one evening. Afterwards, I asked her what questions she had.

'Do you and Jeremy do that?' she asked. Jeremy at that point had been living with us for about five years.

I told her yes, that pretty much all grown-ups who love each other do that.

'Well, I don't think you should,' she said. 'It's too soon.'

I didn't share her judgement call in this specific instance, but I liked the way she was thinking. Sex wasn't something you should rush into.

There are huge challenges in talking to our kids about having sex. Because for the first many years of our child's life it is our job as parents to keep them safe, and keep the world away from their private bits-and-pieces. So it is hard to let go of that instinct and suddenly turn around and cheerfully talk about them inviting someone into their private bits-and-pieces.

Let me be clear: it's not like I hadn't put serious thought into it, and it is not like I didn't have some experience in the field of sex education. Back in 1990 I fronted a video for the Department of Health called *Choice Not Chance*, which was aimed at 13- to 17-year-olds. It's a very upfront video which focuses on contraception and preventing sexually transmitted diseases (STDs). I was chosen to be its face because I'd spent the three years before that hosting children's TV shows — *What Now* and *The Video Dispatch* — so they felt I was a good person to be talking to teenagers. I'd also had a passion for promoting the 'safe-sex' message since my earlier years working as a journalist for the Education and Information Unit of the Health Department, so the two things came together nicely.

In *Choice Not Chance* you can see me — curly bobbed hair, lime-green shirt with shoulder pads — talk frankly, straight down the barrel of the camera, about sexual intercourse, and interview a range of kids about sex, pregnancy and STDs. At one point in the 19-minute video, I expertly roll a condom onto a substantial wooden penis before launching into a hearty promotion of the use of spermicide. It's all very dignified — I'm still pretty proud of it — and I won a Special Recognition Award from the ITVA for my work in it in 1991.

The *Choice Not Chance* video was part of a comprehensive education resource for use in secondary schools — there is a book and worksheets and so on to go with it. It is still used in some schools now. Including at my daughter's school. Yes, that's right. In 2006, Holly's teacher gave her the option of sitting that class out quietly on her own in the library. She said no, she'd seen it and was happy to watch it again with her classmates. Afterwards, she said the most embarrassing thing about the video was my hair.

It has been interesting to watch it again more than two decades later. I am pretty sure part of its efficacy was to make sex so matter-of-fact, so everyday and unexciting, that none of the kids would want to do it. That's not a bad approach, I'm still thinking. Because what most parents want to do is encourage their kids to wait to have sex for as long as possible — until they are physically and emotionally ready to handle how big a deal it is. And until maybe they're flatting. Or at least, no longer sleeping under a My Little Ponies duvet just down the hall.

So maybe what we need to do, Mum & Dad Investors, is reveal a little something of the truth about ourselves to our kids that they don't yet know. That people our age — middle-aged and older — love sex. Really love it. It's our thing. And we have heaps of it. We're doing it all the time. We love it even more than we did when we were their age, because at this point we can be certain that sex won't result in any more kids. Also, we've been doing sex for so long that we've really clocked it. Next level. We know all the moves. *Dirty* sex. We know stuff that's so dirty it's not even in the porn. You bet ya. Sex? Us old people *own* it. So, kids, picture that next time you're considering having sex. You're welcome.

Should do the trick.

One of the awkward things we're dealing with now is that kids are (a) having sex earlier, and (b) leaving home later. We can't draw so much on our own experience to navigate these waters. I vividly recall the day in 1979 when my parents drove me, fresh out of high school, spotty, virginal and eager, away from our small town to take up residence an hour-and-a-half away at a university hostel in the big city.

Halfway there, we stopped for lunch (there is a photograph of my mother taken there — she looks, as always, elegant and composed but terribly sad, like a glamorous movie star on the last day of a film shoot), and then she took me to a book shop. We browsed the Women's Section (not a lot of bookshops have these any more) (also, there aren't a lot of bookshops), and my mother chose some books for me. One of them was *The Hite Report — A Nationwide Study of Female Sexuality*, which had caused something of a stir when it was published a couple of years earlier. Shere Hite had interviewed 100,000 women aged from 14 to 78 about what they did and didn't like about sex. And they had answered her questions with incredible honesty — possibly for the first time in history — about orgasm, masturbation, intercourse, pleasures and frustrations.

It was a brilliant thing to do. It meant I learnt a lot about sex — long before I had any actual sex — from the experiences

SEX? US OLD PEOPLE OWN IT. SO, KIDS, PICTURE THAT NEXT TIME YOU'RE CONSIDERING HAVING SEX.

of other women, through their voices, and with dignity and kindness. It wasn't pornographic, but it was erotic, and tremendously empowering.

I LEARNT A LOT ABOUT SEX FROM THE EXPERIENCES OF OTHER WOMEN, THROUGH THEIR VOICES, AND WITH DIGNITY AND KINDNESS.

And then my parents dropped me off at my hostel, made sure I was warm and safe and knew where to get food, and drove home. And I muddled on with my new grown-up life, popping home for weekends now and then to give them glimpses of my best, shiniest self, full of political opinion and the extraordinary wisdom you have when you are 17 and know everything.

It ain't like that now. Our kids never leave home. Adolescence starts around age 10 and ends somewhere around 27. The stuff we were doing at about 18 when we left home and were away from our parents' gaze is commonly happening now when they're 14 and we're still packing their school lunch. We're driving them to Family Planning because they're not old enough yet to have a licence.

For us, experimenting with sex happened alongside learning to be responsible about other things — rent, washing, grocery shopping. Having sex was part of becoming a grown-up. In our heads, sex and adulthood and independence happened simultaneously. Now, they're having sex while they're living on our pocket money and still earning gold stars for helping out a bit around the house. To us, that seems weird.

Parents deal with it in different ways — some welcome their kids' sexual partners into their home, working on the theory that they're going to do it anyway, so it might as well be somewhere safe with clean sheets. I've noticed that parents with bigger houses feel better about this approach, comforted that they won't necessarily bump into young Romeo in the bathroom or hear anything they'd rather not. Those of us in smaller, cheek-by-jowl accommodation sometimes prefer to take an old-time American military approach — don't ask, don't tell, do it somewhere else. Like around at his place.

So what we have tended to focus on, then, is the *mechanics* — the Safe Sex — condoms and other forms of contraception. And what we might have forgotten to talk about is the stuff I found in *The Hite Report*: that sex should be satisfying, and fun, and respectful, and, most of all, kind. Delicious and exciting like a wordless conversation between two bodies and souls. But that's enough from me. We're all blushing. Over to you now to have a conversation with each other about Kind Sex.

CHAPTER 8

WHEN SEX ISN'T ABOUT SEX

In November of 2013, a story about a group of young men having non-consensual sex with intoxicated young women exploded in the New Zealand media. On a Sunday evening, we learned from a television current-affairs programme that a group of young men had, for two years, bragged on social media about having sex with young women and girls they'd specifically targeted at parties because they were drunk and either semi-conscious or unconscious. It was reported that these young men would take photos and videos of their activities, and then they would 'shame' the girls by identifying them on their Facebook page. The young men regarded this as a kind of sport, and even gave themselves a team name: the 'Roast Busters'.

The whole story was deeply disturbing, and created a firestorm of controversy — it was one of those moments when the whole country was talking about the same thing. Parents were horrified and afraid for their daughters. Initially, people expressed frustration that New Zealand's laws seemed to leave police powerless to take action against these young men without complainants coming forward. A few days later, that frustration turned to anger when people discovered complaints had indeed been made by some young women but had not been actioned by the police. And anyone with personal experience of rape and sexual assault, plus anyone capable of empathy, felt some degree of trauma and tremendous sadness hearing all these stories. It was, I wrote in the *Sunday Star Times* the following week, a tough week to be a woman or someone who loves them.

It remained a tough year. Twelve months later, New Zealand Police announced they would not be laying charges against any of 35 'persons of interest' identified during the case, because they believed they were unlikely to achieve a conviction. Twenty-five young women believed to be victims of this sexual offending had declined to make formal statements, although seven other young women had. Police said they were disappointed not to be able to take the case to court, and left the door open to further action. There is no time limit on reporting sexual offending. Many women don't reveal the trauma of their youth until they are much older. There was a clear message from police that they would assess and investigate any future disclosures on this case. It was never over for the young women involved. It is likely that it is also not over yet for the alleged rapists.

The Roast Busters horror ignited a wider conversation about rape culture, which has managed to shed a little light as well as a lot of heat. We have learnt some things, and we keep learning more. As parents, we are starting to understand that there has been a shift in cultural norms. Our sons and daughters live in a world that is very different from ours, and is invisible to us in many ways.

As I said in the chapter on sex, we might have been talking to them about the mechanics of sex (the 'how'), but not the ethics (the 'why'). Tricky subject, I reckon, to discuss with your own teenager — sexual pleasure, respect, love, eroticism, mutual desire, kindness. Instead, our kids are getting their sexual cues from pornography. And not the porn that men my age nicked back in the day from their dad, or borrowed from their mates. Young men now have access, through the internet, to *all* the porn. Much of which is violent, cruel and hateful.

OUR SONS AND DAUGHTERS LIVE IN A WORLD THAT IS VERY DIFFERENT FROM OURS, AND IS INVISIBLE TO US IN MANY WAYS.

And the bragging that used to be behind the bike sheds and shared only as far as the town border, forgotten about in time, can now be uploaded on video via the internet for the whole world to see, where it stays forever. You might always be what you did — or had done to you — when you were 13. And semi-conscious.

So this is a useful part of the conversation about rape culture: that there is something we haven't done and could do better for our sons and daughters. To tell them to practise not just 'safe sex' but also 'kind sex'. Take a deep breath and have that 'sexual ethics' talk.

But of course, when grown-ups start talking about young people and sex, not everything that gets said is enlightening. Talkback radio hosts and their callers — rarely numbering among the greatest thought leaders of our time — indulged in a fair bit of victim blaming, moving the spotlight almost immediately off the perpetrators, and instead asking a lot of questions about the victims. What was she wearing? Had she been drinking? Why was she there? Was she a virgin before this? All versions of 'Did she behave in a way that made her vulnerable to sexual assault?', which itself is a version of 'What did she do that made this happen?' Nowhere, at any point, were any of these kind of questions aimed at the men. We still have no idea what they were wearing, whether they were sober, or anything about their sexual history. And I'm really not sure we needed to know these things either, because none of them are relevant to an act of rape.

Let's say some things, though, about how women dress. I have spent much of the past few years wishing my daughter would put more clothes on. She and her delightful friends dress in a way that, to my middle-aged eyes, looks kind of slutty. Doubtless, my mother said the same thing about me, and hers about her. Every generation has two sartorial aims: to not dress like their mothers, and to dress like each other. It says everything about fashion, and nothing about behaviour.

This might be hard for a middle-aged man — with or without access to a microphone or a newspaper column — to understand, so I will write it clearly: a tiny skirt does not mean she wants to shag you. You know what it means when she wears a tiny skirt? That she wants to wear a tiny skirt. That's all. And to men of all ages, let's say this really clearly: if you want to have sex with her, ask her, not her clothes. And then listen to what she says.

And seriously, it is insulting to men to suggest that women can dress or behave in a way that invites rape or mitigates its criminality to any degree. Do we really think that a short skirt arouses men to such a level of sexual excitement that they can't stop themselves forcing their penis into someone? If that's all it takes, should any of them be allowed out, ever? You would have to wonder why women aren't being constantly sexually assaulted at cocktail parties, or at the beach, or working out at the gym. You would also have to wonder why the elderly and infirm and babies are also victims of rape.

Most men are good and kind, with excellent judgement, self-control and a sense of humanity. We need to be clear to everyone that non-consensual sex is never okay, men need to be told they can't get away with it, and women need to be believed.

I still find it gobsmackingly outrageous that, when confronted with evidence of sexual assault, the first thing someone wants to know is what the victim did to cause it. Instead, the first question in my head when this horrific scandal broke that Sunday night was: 'Why do these young men hate women?' Because it seems clear to me that if your thing is to get young women drunk, gang-rape them, and then put that information on Facebook, you must seriously hate women.

According to people who have a lot of expertise and experience in dealing with rape and sexual assault, rape is not about sex at all. It is about power through violence and control. In which case, it may be useful if we think of rape not as a 'sex' crime, but as a 'hate' crime. Something you do to someone for whom you have no respect, no empathy, and whom you target because they belong to a different social group — in this case, a different gender. In which case rape could accurately be described as a hate crime against women.

RAPE COULD ACCURATELY BE DESCRIBED AS A HATE CRIME AGAINST WOMEN.

Imagine for a moment that these 13-year-old people being assaulted, victimised and humiliated were instead Jewish, or black, or gay. Best guess is that there would be a lot less 'Had they been drinking and what were they wearing?' When someone is attacked because of their race or beliefs or sexual orientation, we give no credence to anyone who says 'Could they maybe look less black when they go out?' or 'What was he expecting, wearing that yarmulke?' or 'Those gays are always so well-groomed, they're just asking someone to make them look dishevelled.' Most of us are pretty good at spotting attacks based on racism, religious hatred and homophobia. We need to get just as good at recognising assaults by people based on gender, and call it what is.

Most of all, we need to know what we can do. The most useful thing I've read in recent times is by a university health educator in Massachusetts who works in the field of sexual assault prevention. Dr Emily Nagoski says that telling women not to drink so they won't be a target of sexual assault simply doesn't work on a practical level — the blame-the-victim politics

YOU KNOW WHAT IT MEANS WHEN SHE WEARS A TINY SKIRT? THAT SHE WANTS TO WEAR A TINY SKIRT.

of it aside. But what really does work is viewing sexual assault as not just something between victim and perpetrator, but as something that involves witnesses. Dr Nagoski says that in those early moments of a predator stalking and finding prey, it is our job as bystanders to step in and do something to interrupt the flow of violence and prevent the assault before it happens. One girl (or boy) on her (his) own is easily outnumbered, but include the bystanders and suddenly the numbers are on her (his) side.

'IT'S ABOUT DOING SOMETHING,' DR NAGOSKI SAYS, 'AND SOMETHING IS ANYTHING THAT ISN'T NOTHING.'

Dr Nagoski gives simple examples, like offering the potential victim a glass of water in another room, or distracting the potential perpetrator by engaging in conversation — for example, asking him the time, or has he seen Brian — or finding any way to separate them from each other. 'It's about doing something,' she says, 'and something is anything that isn't nothing.' Which makes sense, right? And it's another conversation we can have with our daughters and sons — being a witness and an interrupter — along with that conversation we need to have about kind sex.

CHAPTER 9

MEANWHILE, IN A PARALLEL UNIVERSE ...

It is fair to say that I bang on a bit about a woman's right to be safe in our neighbourhoods, and the madness of blaming victims of sexual assault. It's something I care about, what with being a lady and a mama, and knowing lots of other lady-people and so forth.

In fact, I'd suggest all women think about this at a conscious or unconscious level every day. So just in case anyone thinks that women are constantly running around half-dressed and half-cut with nary a thought to their personal safety, let's take a moment to think about what all women do every day to keep themselves safe.

Here's a tiny story. One Thursday I spent part of a sunny afternoon looking for an appropriate car park. There were several spaces tucked down an Auckland side street in walking distance from where I needed to be. But I knew, without thinking about it hard, that this wasn't a road I could confidently walk down seven hours later when my gig finished. Too quiet, too dark, too isolated. Instead, I spent a long time searching for a space on the main thoroughfare under a streetlight, outside somewhere that would be still be open at 10pm.

ALL WOMEN CAN THINK OF PLACES WE DON'T GO, OPPORTUNITIES WE MISS, CAREERS WE DON'T PURSUE. IT BECOMES PART OF WHO WE ARE.

It is a small thing, but it is daily, this constant vigilance. It becomes automatic and unconscious, but, if you press us, then yes, all women can think of places we don't go, bus stops we don't wait at, trips we don't take, events and opportunities we miss, jobs we don't do and careers we don't pursue. We lock our cars when we get in them as well as when we get out, and walk with keys between our fingers. We dress, not just for style and comfort, but at times also for the ability to run. Second nature. It becomes part of who we are.

This is daily, tangible evidence of this thing people refer to as 'rape culture' — the idea that sexual violence is linked to the culture of a society in which the prevailing attitudes and practices normalise, excuse and tolerate violence against women. Not all men are comfortable with that phrase. Innocent people don't like to be labelled or blamed. We get that. And of course not all men are rapists. But here's the weird thing: it is a woman's job to assume that all men are, until proven otherwise. 'What do you mean you were on that street? In that park? In that bar? Did you not assume that every man there would be a rapist?' This is how we are told to think.

And yes, men must be vigilant, too. There are dangerous places where they might be robbed or punched. But these are perhaps not as ubiquitous as the places where bad things happen to women. And a man is not encouraged to think of every stranger as a brutal thief. But women are required to imagine that all men might do them harm and take the appropriate measures. And none of this is doing any of us any good.

So what I like to do to give my lady-brain a holiday from all this is imagine that, in some parallel universe, things are different. Not necessarily different-better, just different-different. I find it amusing, and sometimes illuminating, to imagine boots on other feet. For example, I like to imagine that, in Opposite World, there is a men's group who are up in arms. 'We're up in arms,' a male spokeswoman would say. 'We are tired of the constant criticism about the way we dress, as though what we wear says more about us than our behaviour or what comes out of our mouths. It's just a shirt and trousers. We all wear them. It makes us feel part of a group.'

However, conservative members of the matriarchy say it is easy to misread the social cues presented by the shirt/trouser combination. 'We're not saying they're all bad eggs,' a spokeswoman said, 'but it's a simple fact that 99 per cent of men who are up to no good wear a shirt and trousers while they're doing it, so it's fair to assume that when a man is seen wearing a shirt and trousers, he is up to no good.'

Also of concern to men's rights activists is the suggestion that men should no longer be allowed to socialise. However, lots of talkback hosts say it's just logic. 'A lot of women like to wear skimpy clothes, drink cocktails and dance. It's their way of letting off steam and enjoying themselves. Unfortunately, men are easily confused by this behaviour, and trouble ensues,' one said. 'We thought about asking the women to stop it. I know! We realised how ridiculous that sounded, too. So now we're just discouraging men from being in social situations.'

When asked if this stance needed to be formalised, conservative members of the matriarchy said it was best left to social pressure. 'I don't think we need a law to make this happen. I mean, we're not Iran.' This is a reference to the Muslim practice of blindfolding men. Women's beauty is thought to be so powerful that men may only see a woman's face if they're married to her or closely related, so men's eyes must be covered whenever they are outside the home.

'It's not a big deal,' an Islamic matriarch insists. 'In fact, a lot of men find that not having to look at things is liberating. And it's not like they're not allowed out. They can go wherever they want, so long as they're accompanied by a female relative so they don't bump into things. And of course, they can't drive. This isn't sexism, it's purely practical. They're blindfolded.'

Back home, male activists believe the central issue to achieving equality is an economic one. 'How can we ever feel like full, respected members of society when men earn, on average, 12 per cent less than women?' a male spokeswoman said.

But the head of the Employers Association says it is perfectly reasonable that men should earn less. 'I'm not saying men don't work hard. Often they're just as capable as women. However, at no point do they actually create new workers. Women do. They make whole new human beings. Wages and salaries need to reflect that. Maybe in some parallel universe we'd do things a different way. But I can't imagine it,' she said.

Meanwhile, in yet another parallel universe, Road Safety NZ (RSNZ) is announcing a new approach to reducing car crashes. 'What we've decided to do is encourage normal drivers to stay off the roads, out of the way of drunk and dangerous drivers,' RSNZ spokesperson Brian Little says. 'We particularly want them to keep off roads at night and at weekends when the risk is higher. Though we're also aware that bad drivers cause crashes on, for example, Wednesday mornings, so we'd advise your average driver to stay home then, too.'

Mr Little describes the 'Stay Home, Stay Safe' campaign as a sophisticated, multi-layered approach which they hope will become part of our culture. 'We have tried for years,' Little says, 'to get drunk and dangerous drivers off our roads with little long-term success. We got the idea for this new approach from the extraordinary success of Rape Culture, where women are blamed for putting themselves in the way of rapists. We feel that kind of approach could work quite well here, too.' To be known as 'Crash Culture', the RSNZ says people in vehicles hit by drunk and dangerous drivers will be asked a lot of questions. 'Were they driving in a high accident area? It may have been the shortest route from A to B, sure, but we'll be suggesting maybe they should have gone around the long way. We want people to think about that.'

Little says RSNZ has always done a little 'victim blaming' in terms of what people were wearing — seatbelts, car seats and

'WHAT WE'VE DECIDED TO DO IS ENCOURAGE NORMAL DRIVERS TO STAY OFF THE ROADS, OUT OF THE WAY OF DRUNK AND DANGEROUS DRIVERS. IF YOU ARE OUT DRIVING AT NIGHT, YOU ARE PRETTY MUCH ASKING FOR IT.'

helmets — but they're keen to extend the blame to the victim's character and behaviour. 'If you are hit by a drunk driver, we will investigate your driving history. What sort of driver are you usually? Have you driven erratically in the past? Have you had a parking ticket? We will also ask why you were out in your car at that time — the purpose of your trip, who you were seeing, the context — to see if your intentions contributed to someone driving into you. If you were off to a meeting of a feminist collective, for example, and a drunk driver crashes a red light and speeds through an intersection, we want to know what led you to being the car that was hit, as opposed to somebody else.'

Little says we all need to start thinking that part of being a responsible driver is about staying home. 'If you are out at night, you are pretty much asking for it. But if we leave the roads just to the drunk and dangerous drivers, we will all be much safer. If innocent drivers aren't out there, too, they can't be hit, right?'

Has RSNZ perhaps jumped the shark? 'Maybe a little,' Little admits. 'But it's been so effective with the lady-thing it has become almost unconscious, so we thought it was worth a crack.'

CHAPTER 10

DRUGS AND ALCOHOL

Raising a glass ...

While I would never advocate modelling the wrong kind of behaviour as a failsafe form of aversion therapy, it seemed to work at our place. Holly has shown nil interest in smoking and very little attraction to drinking — her glass of champagne on Christmas morning always goes flat long before she gets anywhere near the bottom of glass number one, and invariably it can be found, largely untouched, somewhere under the wrapping paper when we're tidying up on Boxing Day. She has no patience with drunkards, and, when she worked part-time behind the bar at our local comedy club, had little reticence about cutting people off. She served drinks, not drunks, like the sign said. Around home, she was adept at giving people entirely judgemental side-eye whenever someone — home team or visitor — appeared to be a bit skew-whiff.

This is not to say she has never fallen off her stilettos, but it really isn't her thang. I am pleased about this. Many of the adults in her life have addictive personalities — myself included — and

I'm grateful her addictions so far seem to be restricted to dancing, shopping and putting 'like' into sentences that really don't need it.

I recall a Comedy Festival Gala — the annual big night out for people of my ilk — which Holly also attended before she was legally allowed to drink. She has been coming with me to my comedy gigs since she was a baby. In the early days, I'd pop her — asleep in her car seat — behind the bar and try to time my set to finish on a sure-fire big gag around the time she was due to wake up. We were reasonably in tune with each other; back when I was pregnant with her I had embarked on a national tour of *Exposed*, a three-woman music and comedy show, and I noticed then that, even *in utero*, she knew how to behave when a show was on. She'd be a calm and placid little fetus when I needed to focus on what I was doing, and wait until the show was over to do her somersaults. Although I also noticed that, during one particularly small, quiet solo bit I had on stage, she'd jam her face against my belly as though she wanted to see out into the audience, too. Holly has always looked at home on stage, as though it is an entirely normal place to be. I blame the mother.

And she's always been enthusiastic about watching me on stage, too. So for years she would frock up with her mama for the Comedy Gala, and the other fancy-pants comedy nights I'd do each year on Mother's Day, when she would sit in the audience with her grandmother, and she has been at every opening night of each of my solo shows throughout my career. So it wasn't unusual for her to be at the Gala, and not crazy for me to give her a celebratory glass of champagne to hold.

But this one year — maybe she was 16 or 17 — I noticed she was actually drinking the champagne, and yet the glass always seemed to be full. That was odd. Turned out, of course, that all my colleagues (who think of themselves as her comedy uncles and aunts) had decided amongst themselves that she was old enough to properly join in, and so had been making deliveries of subsequent glasses of champagne without running it past me first.

'Is that,' I said in my best Mother-Voice, 'your second glass of champagne?'

'No, Mother,' she said firmly in her best Daughter-Voice (she always calls me 'Mother' when she's about to win a point), 'it's my fourth glass. I'm doing what you taught me: I am counting my drinks.'

'See this?' I said to the guilty and nervous uncles and aunties gathered. 'This girl is raised! Life lesson learned. Achieved with Excellence. Good girl.' And then I called her a taxi.

The drink-counting tool is tremendously useful. I still find, on the very rare occasion that I wake up in the morning with a vice-like pain in my temples, white noise in my ears, toxic bile in my tummy and a lack of will to live — symptoms known collectively as 'the hangover' — it is because at some point in the preceding evening I have lost track of the number of drinks consumed. Silly girl. It is sometimes the most youthful thing about me.

The hangover is a terrible thing, as vile and miserable as all the movie sequels of the same name. Alcohol is a sneaky depressant. When it arrives in your system, it tells you that you are wonderful, glorious and bulletproof, that everything you say is brilliant and that you look gorgeous in that skirt. But as it leaves your system, it convinces you that you are the world's biggest twat who says stupid and insulting things, that no one likes you and, moreover, you will never amount to much. You will, the next morning, want to reach for the phone, call the world, and apologise to it for being, you know, *you*. This is a phenomenon known as the Booze Blues — proper, chemically-induced depression and self-loathing. You will hate yourself so much that you will think something made of lard and salt is the only thing you deserve to eat. And then you will hate yourself a little more. Ignore these Booze Blues. Breathe through them. Understand them for what they are: just a whole lot of evil toxins in your system. Sit tight, drink some juice, and trust that not all of your regret is based on actual events. Next time, count your drinks. And stop at a very small number.

THE HANGOVER IS A TERRIBLE THING, AS VILE AND MISERABLE AS ALL THE MOVIE SEQUELS OF THE SAME NAME.

While I would never argue that we don't have a problem with 'binge drinking' in our culture, I might argue — for the sake of comedy — that we should be realistic about what a 'binge' actually is. Until recently, we had an organisation in New Zealand called ALAC, the Alcohol Advisory Council. Now they are not necessarily the people you might assume they are, based on the name. I got it terribly wrong at first.

I rang them up. 'Hi, there,' I said. 'Is that the Alcohol Advisory Council? Excellent. I'm cooking lamb for dinner. What goes best with that? Would you suggest a pinot noir or a cabernet sauvignon? Perhaps a syrah?'

'What is wrong with you, lady?' their imaginary call-centre staff member asked. 'Are you pissed?'

'No,' I replied, 'I haven't been drinking at all yet, but I would like a little something to go with my roast. What alcohol do you advise, Alcohol Advisory Council?'

Yeah, that's not what they do. What they actually do is tell us that if you're a woman and you have three or more drinks over the period of a day, you are having 'a binge'. Or if you are a man and have five or more drinks, then technically you are binge drinking. Which, to my mind, is overstating it. Three drinks isn't a 'binge', is it, ladies? You could just as easily describe that as 'lunch'. A binge, to my mind, is where you go out for a glass of wine at lunchtime and wake up three days later in Oamaru. Wearing a cheerleader's costume. And married to a shearer called Barry. Now, *that's* a binge. Trust me. I know someone who did that.

Pretty regularly, we, as a community, lament our Antipodean drinking culture — the genuine bingeing, risk-taking and violence — but, although we find it easy to identify the problems, we find it pretty hard to visualise solutions. The best we manage is the clamp-down: less access, shorter bar hours, higher prices — a kind of 'prohibition-lite'. Not quite America in the 1920s, but raising our glass in that direction. This is despite knowing that prohibition-proper was hardly a resounding success, and that it did little to change attitudes or behaviour in a positive way, and was successful only in making bootleggers and dealers in other illicit substances very rich.

Each time I visit a place where drinking is woven into the culture — Paris, New Orleans, Palmerston North — I wonder if the solution might be the opposite of the clamp-down. 'Unclamping', if you like. New Orleans, for example (my favourite place on the planet), is a town where everybody drinks all the time, though you rarely spot anyone actually drunk except on Bourbon Street, which is populated entirely by tourists — out-of-town beginners and amateurs — who treat every night as though it's just before closing time on a Friday in Hamilton. Sure, you see the occasional drunkard, serious casualties of alcoholism, but they are no more common than at home, and are treated by that community with patience and kindness.

So here's a suggestion I concocted once over a Bloody Mary at breakfast time. (Note: By 'breakfast time' I mean it was mid-afternoon and I had just woken up and the Bloody Mary *was* breakfast.) This demonstrates the first part of the plan, which is that we should start drinking earlier and at a leisurely pace, maintaining a pleasant buzz throughout the day but without entirely losing track of it. The Bloody Mary is a superb choice, involving a fair portion of your five-plus daily vegetable requirements. It's like soup. There are also fresh juice stalls in New Orleans which routinely offer shots of vodka or tequila the way juicers at home suggest wheatgrass. One of those at morning tea and you can really *carpe* the *diem*.

Second point: maybe we need more bars rather than fewer. In a town like New Orleans, which has a plethora of small bars, nowhere is cramped or crowded, so you are unlikely to be jostled or left waiting impatiently to have your order taken. Also, more bars frequently spaced means you are always in walking, not driving, distance of home.

THREE DRINKS ISN'T A BINGE,
IS IT, LADIES? YOU COULD
JUST AS EASILY DESCRIBE
THAT AS 'LUNCH'.

MAKE BARS THE HEART OF THE COMMUNITY, WHERE SOMEONE WHO LOOKS LIKE YOUR AUNT IS ASKING FOR HELP WITH THE CROSSWORD.

Third, the drinks should be cheap so you don't feel obliged to down every last drop because you've just paid $15 for a middling pinot noir; and there should be a takeaway 'go-cup' option so you can wander off to another spot when you feel like it rather than that terrible guzzling we do when the rest of the group says that it's time to go.

Fourth, we should make these bars the heart of the community, where someone who looks like your glamorous ex-showgirl aunt is reading the newspaper and asking for help with the crossword. There's less chance the lads will misbehave when she's in the room. A calm oasis with jazz in the background rather than deafeningly loud dreary hits from the 1970s, so your soul is soothed and the world feels like a place that understands you. And all bar staff should address patrons as either 'honey' or 'baby' to engender a sense of care and respect.

And finally, we need to adopt the philosophy stated clearly in a sign behind every bar in the Quarter: *Be Nice, Or Leave*. It is a rule strictly enforced by bar staff and adhered to by all clientele who wish to remain on the premises. Though, even if ejected, they are free to take their drink with them and sip it quietly on the pavement while they think about what they've done.

I totally understand that a plethora of small bars, live jazz, and Bloody Marys for breakfast is not everybody's cup of spiced tomato juice and vodka. A different kind of person to me might admonish us to 'try teaching our children that they don't need to get a buzz on to have fun', and start setting a good example ourselves. But here's the thing: this drive to 'get a buzz on' is hardwired into human beings. Every culture has conscientiously sought out a fruit, vegetable, plant or leaf that, when appropriately prepared, will alter the state of mind. Euphoria, sedation, hallucination — you name it, we'll find something for it in the garden. This sort of carry-on (fermenting grapes, chewing nuts, doing whatever you do to potatoes to make vodka) has been part of life since the dawn of time. It is entirely possible that, shortly after Adam and Eve bit into that first apple, they turned the rest of it into cider. It's what we do.

SHORTLY AFTER ADAM AND EVE BIT INTO THAT FIRST APPLE, THEY TURNED THE REST OF IT INTO CIDER.

But it's not *all* we do. And I think that's the trick. While all these little bars are the beating heart of a place like New Orleans where the drinking happens all day, and gently, the city offers other things to go with it. On the day of the Bloody Mary breakfast I also visited a 293-year-old cathedral and chatted to a nun, and later spent an enthralling hour with a Voodoo priestess. I ate alligator sausage one meal, and had a delicate pecan, cranberry and blue-cheese salad the next. During drinks that evening I met music great Kermit Ruffins, and we talked about our pets — he has a dog, and I have a cat, both named Satchmo after jazz legend Louis Armstrong. Not a bad day. And the next morning I felt so refreshed I got up early enough to attend a jazz yoga class I'd heard about from someone in a bar. Jazz yoga involves doing your Salutes to the Sun — *Surya Namaskar* — while a dude in a Panama hat accompanies the class on piano. Afterwards, I had a Bloody Mary.

... and moving on to drugs ...

Okay, so it is possible I'm not the most responsible person to listen to about drinking. There, I've said it now. Tell me to hush and I'd raise my glass in agreement. But I'm much less liberal in my attitudes towards drugs, because of the awful effects they have on a young, still-developing brain. Terrible idea, to mess up that lovely thing you only ever have one of, your unique and very useful mind. And I have to say, I am entirely bewildered by the youthful penchant for synthetic marijuana, the fake stuff you could for a time buy at the local dairy, which — from everything I read and heard — just made people feel sick and tetchy. Also, can I say this: if you want marijuana and are sufficiently old enough to make that choice, surely there is enough natural, organic, free-range marijuana available without anyone needing to make it synthetically? How into instant gratification, and how lazy do you have to be to buy it pre-packaged at a dairy? Why can't people just grow one little plant in the hot-water cupboard like we did when we were young and silly at university? Making synthetic marijuana seems entirely unnecessary and superfluous to requirements. That'd be like an affirmative action programme to get middle-aged white men into government. Why would you do that? Government's full of them already.

Raising Holly hasn't all been plain sailing or entirely without incident. Back when she was 15 (general note: the terrible stuff mostly happens when they are 15 — if you can live through it until their sixteenth birthday, you are largely home and hosed) there was The Party. Yep. The night every parent dreads, and that some of us have actually lived through.

I travel a lot with my work and so does my partner, although often at different times like wistful ships in the night, so we've been able to tag-team the parenting. And I've also been tremendously lucky that, since Holly was two years old, her grandparents — my wonderful parents — have lived right beside us. It has been an amazing arrangement that has given me the space to pursue my crazy career as well as enriching Holly's life and, I like to think, bringing a lot of joy and satisfaction to her grandma and granddad.

But one Friday, a lack of forward planning on my part meant that I was at the southern end of the country (Invercargill) while Jeremy was in the middle of the country (Wellington), and the grandparents were housesitting in rural splendour, babysitting their friends' dog and cat. So this perfect storm in our domestic arrangements meant that Holly was left alone overnight for the first time ever. I gave her permission to invite a couple of girlfriends for a sleep-over so she wouldn't be lonely. What could possibly go wrong?

Well, this. During popcorn and a re-screening of *Step Up 2*, one of them sent a text saying something like 'We're eating popcorn and watching *Step Up 2* at Holly's place. Come over.'

That text was — but of course — forwarded to a few more people and, in true Amway spirit, by 11pm there were at least 50 very loud, drunk teenagers in the driveway who forced their way onto the deck and into our home. Our neighbours, bless them, called the police.

Before the cops arrived, this swarm of pubescent locusts drank every drop of alcohol in the house — and we had quite a lot of stuff — except for the red wine, which, one could only assume, would have confused their youthful palates. They ate all the processed food in the pantry and fridge, but tossed fresh fruit and vegetables off the deck for sport, along with my flower pots. They kept their shoes on (where were their manners?) and permanently ruined the carpet. They left an unholy mess. By the time I got home the next day, it smelt like a rural public bar after a flood and before the smoking ban — all wet wool, mud and nicotine. On the way out of the house, in one final assault on our property and privacy, someone had slipped into my office and stolen my computer, taking enough time about it to pack it away neatly in my brand-new laptop bag.

I was furious that all of this had happened. Over the next days and weeks I mentioned to Holly quite a few times that this was Exactly What I Had Warned Her Against. I was also deeply relieved that it was confined to property damage and that no one had been hurt. And as we spent the next days discovering just how much was missing, I was also caught somewhere between outrage and amusement that they had taken things they couldn't possibly appreciate. Gone were the magnum of good French champagne and the bottles of rare white port we'd been saving for a special occasion. (Like a sixteenth birthday, which seemed so far away at this point.) We found the empty bottles discarded in the driveway where some of them had paused long enough to drink these aperitifs and digestifs. For the love of God, could they not have waited to chill the champagne? And perhaps stolen a flute from which to drink it? In some part of my brain I would have felt better if it had been stolen by a thief in a smoking jacket with a cigar.

Then there was what they didn't take. The cheque books (this was 2008 when some of us, ahem, still put the electricity payment in the post), which were sitting by my computer, doubtless left because the thief didn't know what they were. Forging signatures on stolen cheques is a lost art, sigh. And they took none of the hundreds of CDs (so what's wrong with my musical taste?) and film and comedy DVDs stacked obviously and neatly in alphabetical order in the living room. Clearly, you don't carry away what you can download. Ah, young people.

So, a disaster set in motion by an ill-advised text. Although as much as texting created the problem, texting was also part of the solution. The house might have still stunk like a riverside brewery after a tidal moon, but, by the time I arrived home, the broken glass had been swept up, bottles and butts binned, flowers re-planted, and a brave attempt had been made at shampooing the carpet with dishwashing liquid. First thing in the morning, my daughter had organised a working bee with her classmates, using the same social networking system that had started this hell — by text. Not everything about the way our kids connect with each other is a disaster. Some of it undoes a disaster.

CHAPTER 11

HOW TO STOP YOUR TIGHTS SNAGGING

One of the things that makes me glad to get up in the morning is the chance that I will learn something new. I relish those moments when someone passes on a little bit of wisdom, or a new skill, and you wonder how you ever got so far through life without knowing this particular thing before. So this bit is not so much something I forgot to tell my daughter, but something the world had forgotten to tell me. Very happy to pass this on so you don't suffer in the same way.

I had one of those times recently — useful wisdom imparted — when I was out shopping in Christchurch. I adore shopping in Christchurch. I adore Christchurch. I haven't lived there for years, but I still know it well and I write a weekly column published in the region's newspaper, *The Press*. I lived in the city for a year when I was finishing my university degree in 1983 (English Literature and Drama, plus a fair bit of political activism), and lived there again for a couple of years while I worked on the children's TV show *What Now* in the late 1980s. So the city holds a special place in my heart, and I get back there to work and visit friends as often as I can. And to shop.

I believe shopping is more enjoyable when you are away from home, because it is easier to spend money on frivolous things the further you are, geographically, from your mortgage. And my excuse this time for diving into a swanky department store was that I was in dire need of new tights. Not just supermarket tights, but something special, I felt. Possibly tights that were a little bit magic. This was during my chunky period and I was finding that the usual tights were gripping my soft middle bits so tightly the waistband was visible through my clothes. I appeared to consist of two sections with an obvious seam where my top half had been joined to the bottom half, like a badly made doll. Were there, I asked the nice lady in the shop, some magical tights that wouldn't make me look like a beanbag wearing a rubber band?

SHOPPING IS MORE ENJOYABLE WHEN YOU ARE AWAY FROM HOME, BECAUSE IT IS EASIER TO SPEND MONEY ON FRIVOLOUS THINGS THE FURTHER YOU ARE, GEOGRAPHICALLY, FROM YOUR MORTGAGE.

She very kindly showed me a range of top-of-the-line, less-tight-topped tights with a soft, wide, forgiving waistband.

They felt like velvet, or suede, or kittens. You could tell, just by looking, that when you put them on they wouldn't squeeze you or judge you; they'd just wrap themselves unconditionally around you and stay very put. I knew I had to have them; that they must come home with me and become part of my life, despite the — oh, good lord — price tag, which was roughly nine times the price of those mean, judgemental tights at the supermarket. The tremendously kind and sensitive lady, reading my face and my mind, assured me they would last for a very long time. At least 10 times as long as the supermarket variety, she estimated, which would make them, ultimately, a bargain.

'And of course, you know how to stop your tights snagging?' she asked, with a rhetorical air. I wasn't sure I did.

'Something about not putting them on while you're wearing jewellery, and avoiding the furniture and pets?' I ventured.

'Body lotion,' she said.

So this is the thing she told me: once you've put your tights on — fancy or supermarket or whatever variety — you take a small blob of body lotion, rub it between your hands, and smear it over the legs of your tights. It leaves an imperceptible layer of slitheryness between your tights and the world's snag-making things, and makes it ever so unlikely that the fibres will be caught by anything and pulled out of place.

Which is exactly what I have done whenever I have put on any pair of tights ever since. My tights never snag. La la la. I still have the original pair I bought from this paragon of women's accessories three years later.

Yes, I *know*. Why weren't we taught this at school? It would have been so much more useful than many of the other things we were taught. Heaps more useful on a day-to-day basis than, for example, calculus.

Which leads me to another thing they should be teaching at school — feminism.

CHAPTER 12

WHY YOUR MOTHER
IS A FEMINIST

For some reason that I can't quite fathom, women like me have forgotten to talk to our daughters (and our sons) about feminism. I know this is a pretty universal oversight because I've asked around, and all the other mothers have done a double-take, acknowledged the omission and looked panicked, like they've suddenly realised they'd forgotten to switch off the hair-straighteners back at home. And weirdly, we've forgotten to talk about feminism despite the fact that it really matters to us, and that it is something we thought about deeply when we were first making our way in the world, and still think about every day. Perhaps we've assumed that: (a) our children would simply absorb the information from us by osmosis; or (b) that feminism was so self-evident, we didn't need to talk about it explicitly, with actual words and stuff.

But it turns out neither of those things is true. Which means that we frequently find ourselves in an exhausting *déjà vu*, revisiting the same arguments we had 30 and 40 years ago. Oh, for the love of God. If I had a dollar for every time I've thought 'Didn't we sort this back in the 1970s? I'm pretty sure we all got the same memo,' I'd be sufficiently flush to adequately fund a women's refuge all by myself.

'DIDN'T WE SORT THIS BACK IN THE 1970S? I'M PRETTY SURE WE ALL GOT THE SAME MEMO.'

So let me tell you about My First Feminist Experience. I would have been about four years old — certainly a pre-schooler — growing up in the small town of Levin. I have, over the years, made a lot of jokes about Levin. I mentioned as much at the beginning of a speech I made at a fundraising debate back in Levin a few years ago. At which point a visibly angry man in the audience shouted back at me, 'Yeah, we know. And we don't like it.' So I won't revisit any of those stories here. Let's just say that all fringe dwellers who come from small towns — those who don't play netball and tend to swim a little against the tide — have a complicated relationship with the place they grew up in. If you're the kind of person who is only going to connect with, say, 10 per cent of your neighbours and you have only 10 neighbours because it's a very small village, you're going to get pretty lonely and spend a lot of time reading *Little Women* and Maurice Gee short stories in your bedroom by yourself.

My mother insists it was a fabulous place to bring up a family, with lots of opportunity for a creative and social life. She would say that: it was my parents' idea to move to Levin from the relatively large metropolis of Wellington shortly before I was born, exactly for this 'great place to raise a family' scenario. And to be fair, although I left Levin for Wellington very soon after the last bell rang on my last day of school and I have rarely been back for 30-odd years now, at night when I am asleep it's our family home and the surrounding neighbourhood in Levin which still form the backdrop to my most peaceful, least anxious dreams.

And whatever comedic nose-thumbing I might have engaged in about the town, it was a tremendously happy childhood. My parents and I, and my big brother Stephen (two and a half years older than me), lived in a lovely house on a quarter-acre section, surrounded by lots of other lovely houses on quarter-acre sections not far from the local primary school. Our family raised chooks for the eggs, and knew them all by name — Sandy and Little Chook and so forth — and had a ginger cat called Kitty, who got on pretty well with the chooks. We grew our own vegetables in the back garden, and I encouraged the chooks to eat the ones I didn't much care for, like silverbeet. They were extremely obliging.

My parents, John and Donna, owned a factory called A'Court Industries, which made mostly shirts and blouses and, later, tracksuits. My father (long-retired now) was an experienced garment manufacturer who knew all about cutting cloth and organising his 40 or 50 machinists, and my mother also went to the factory every day where she did the books and paid the wages. On Thursdays — known forever in our house as 'Wages Day' — my mother would be so busy putting the exact amount of notes and coins into little brown envelopes with each worker's name on it, and licking them shut, that she wouldn't have time to make 'a proper lunch' for us all at home, so we'd have a Bought One. Either stuff from the local bakery brought home to us during her break, or, when my brother and I were both school age, a lunch order. A lunch order was this glorious thing you would register for at the start of the school day and pick up at the beginning of lunch. Your name would be called out by the big kids (they would have been 11 or 12, and giants in my eyes), who were in charge of huge brown cardboard trays with the kind of food that on any day other than Wages Day was off-limits. Mine was always a meat pasty, a cream doughnut, and a fizzy drink. Take that, Heart Foundation. I don't recall fruit being an option. After school, we'd take the empty Fanta or Coke bottle to the school dairy and swap it for a not insubstantial bag of lollies. Aniseed wheels, Imperial mints, and glow-hearts. It always seemed a special kind of miracle to me that even the thing that was left over from that sweet, greasy lunch — the glass bottle — could be turned into yet more sweetness for the walk home.

Every Friday afternoon my mother would take Stephen and me to pick up our grandmother, who lived a few blocks away, and we'd all go to the supermarket and then on to the Levin Public Library, where Stephen and I were allowed to choose three books each. A greedy reader, I always marvelled that the books were free to take home and didn't cost me any of the pocket money my brother and I were given each week 'for being good'. (Dishes, putting away, generally not being frightful.)

In summer, we'd often spend my father's one day off at Waitarere Beach, where he'd smear himself in coconut oil and

Stephen and I would swim or dig for toheroa, and my mother would look glamorous and never get her hair wet. In the school holidays, my parents would put Stephen and me on the bus or train to Napier, for a week or so with our Great-aunt Ruth (we called her Russie) and Great-uncle Frank, who spoilt us with homemade blackcurrant jam and scones, and bottles of pop kept in a crate in the garage — Creaming Soda always first choice. In summer there was freshly squeezed orange juice from the garden, endless days at the local Olympic Baths, and visits to Marineland to watch the dolphins frolic, in those blissfully ignorant years before we understood it made them so unhappy. In winter, my brother and I raced slot cars at a place called The Hive on Marine Parade, and on frosty mornings Russie would warm our undies by the blow heater before we put them on, while we'd stuff our faces with toast and her famous marmalade. One year, when I was maybe eight, Russie and her sister-in-law, my Great-aunt Eileen, entered me in the Miss Junior Hawke's Bay Beauty Pageant. I won, despite being a good foot shorter than the willowy blonde who came second (there was a photo of us in the local newspaper), and Russie was so excited that she banged her sun umbrella up and down instead of clapping.

MY BROTHER AND I LIVED THE SAME LIFE AS EACH OTHER, WITH THE SAME RIGHTS AND RESPONSIBILITIES, THE SAME EXPECTATIONS AND OPPORTUNITIES.

I was quite grown-up before I realised that these heavenly holidays with Russie and Frank were likely as much about giving our hardworking parents a break as were they were about us. But I still reckon we got the best end of the deal.

I mention all this because nostalgia is delightful and quite bonding (every reader my age is now wondering what the hell happened to Creaming Soda as a flavour), and also to draw you a small picture of who we were and how we lived. Mum and Dad both worked, and my brother and I lived the same life as each other, with the same rights and responsibilities, the same expectations and opportunities. I danced, did drama, made toffee, and mowed the lawns. He learned guitar, built the model slot cars that we raced in the holidays, worked in the vege garden and showed enthusiasm for cooking. Stephen and I stuck up for each other outside the house, and swapped music and books at home. When I moved to Wellington, Stephen was already there making a space for me, and we worked together on the university student newspaper, *Salient*, and marched together against student fees and the Springbok Tour.

But that's all in the future — back to being a pre-schooler, and my feminist awakening. There I was, maybe four years old, and hanging out with Stephen and the other kids in our neighbourhood. The six of us were playing a game of Cowboys and Itchybums, which was a pretty sophisticated mash-up of tag, hide-and-seek and bull-rush. Some hiding up trees, some chasing over fences, some throwing a tennis ball at each other, and a lot of shouting 'You're it!' I was always pretty small but fairly fast, and occasionally pretty darn accurate with the ball. On this particular day I hit Russell, one of the neighbour kids, quite hard on the side of his thigh with the ball, in the 'dead leg' area that makes your limb go momentarily limp. Pure fluke, not planned. God's honour. But, you know, shit happens when you're playing Cowboys and Itchybums.

Russell started crying and, as we were playing that day at his place, went inside and told on me to his mother. She came out into their driveway, wiped her hands on her apron and fixed me with a fierce look. 'Haven't you got any girls to play with? Go home to your mother! The boys don't want a girl hanging around.'

All these years later, my face still feels hot with hurt and humiliation. Up until that moment, it had not occurred to me that I was different from my friends. In fact, if you'd asked me who was the odd one out in our group — Stephen, Brian, Greg, Warren, Russell and me — I would have told you it was Russell. Not because he was a ginger (maybe a little of that, but not much), but because he was such a cry-baby mummy's-boy who whined whenever he was 'It'. This was genuinely the first time I had realised that I was 'a girl'. Or, more importantly, that some people are boys, and other people are not. And that people might treat you differently because of it.

So I went home. And my brother came with me, because he is a good person. And we told our mother what had happened. And she's a good person, too, and she said that if I wasn't welcome to play at Russell's house, then neither of us would play there. And then we probably went to the library and got some books and forgot about it. Except I didn't ever forget it. And my brother still remembers it clearly, too.

SHIT HAPPENS WHEN
YOU'RE PLAYING COWBOYS
AND ITCHYBUMS.

Of course, we kept on playing Cowboys and Itchybums, just not at Russell's place. Eventually, he must have moved away, because I remember Brian and Warren and Greg all the way through school, but Russell seemed to disappear from our adventures. I hope he has found a life that fits him. Like maybe being a candidate for the Conservative Party.

So that was it: the moment I became aware that the world was a slightly different place for girls. It was the first but by no means the last time I've felt this way. And it is still a shock and my face gets hot whenever someone says some version of 'But you can't do that — you're a girl.' Like I say, being a girl wasn't an issue in the loving, private world of my home and family. But now I should probably tell you a little about the wider world I was born into.

CHAPTER 13

WHAT WAS IT LIKE IN THE OLDEN DAYS, MUMMY?

I was born in 1961. And yes, I can feel you doing the maths and thinking, 'Good lord — Metamucil and Crocs!' Fair call. Though I can still sip a margarita while sashaying about in stilettos when the occasion presents itself, so my earlier point from Chapter 4 stands.

Back in 1961, New Zealand was at the height of its post-war baby boom. We were getting record prices for beef and wool, and there was a sense of freedom and plenty, although that would shortly be tempered somewhat by the threat of nuclear war, then the actual Vietnam War, and a Cold War between East and West that carried on until I was old enough to vote. In general terms, it was a time of huge opportunity with great social change on its way — you could smell it in the air. But in New Zealand, the 1960s with their free love and hippie ethos didn't really arrive until the 1970s, and a lot of very conservative and conventional attitudes were still firmly in place. So one or two arguments were being had in the workplace, around the dining table and in Parliament about what those changes would be.

At the time I was born, there was no such thing as equal pay. A woman standing next to a man and doing exactly the same job was paid less for it, simply because she was a woman. There were two assumptions to justify this: one, that she would be less productive than him because she was girly; and two, that she needed less money than him because it was a man's job to support the family and she only needed to buy nylons and lipstick. Which she wouldn't need if she didn't go to work. Ta da! Oh, and three: that if you had to pay women as much as you paid men it would cost employers more to run their businesses, so they'd have to put prices up to cover it and the economy would collapse, and the sun would stop rising.

I remember my mother, otherwise a very sensible person, arguing this point at our dinner table. As an employer, she understood that equal pay for women would mean that she and my father would have to increase the hourly rate they paid to their women machinists to be in line with the rate paid for the equivalent kind of work that men did. Which they would have to cover, she explained, by increasing the price of a shirt. When all producers did that it would raise a thing called 'the cost of living', and before too long it would be impossible for women *not* to work, because families wouldn't be able to survive on one income.

I must have been about 10 years old at the time, and therefore I knew everything. I argued back that I believed two things were true: one, I couldn't imagine not wanting to work, so having to join the workforce sounded fine to me; and two, it was the principle that mattered more than the economics. It was just fundamentally unfair to pay a woman less than a man, simply because she was a woman.

My mother, a very intelligent person, was right of course that it would become nigh-on impossible to afford to be a stay-at-home mum, but I haven't changed my mind in the intervening decades: when it comes to economics versus principle, I'll back the principle of social justice every time. This is why I will never be prime minister.

Women in the private sector eventually won the right to be paid the same as men in 1972, not long before I got my first weekend job.

When I was born, women were not only economically worth less than men, they were valued differently in other ways, too. Throughout the 1960s, on our newly invented televisions, it was unwritten broadcasting policy that only men would read the news, because women didn't carry enough authority. No one would believe it if it was women telling them important stuff. Instead, ladies did something pretty with the weather. Forecasts didn't matter so much, because it was always wrong anyway, and really you just wanted someone pretty to look at while you heard about a cold front coming in. And that pretty thing should be a lady.

Women were allowed to be TV continuity announcers, though. The continuity announcers' job was to back-announce the last programme and tell viewers what was on for the rest of the evening, the way a pre-recorded voice promotes the evening

A WOMAN DOING EXACTLY THE SAME JOB WAS PAID LESS FOR IT, BECAUSE SHE ONLY NEEDED TO BUY NYLONS AND LIPSTICK. WHICH SHE WOULDN'T NEED IF SHE DIDN'T GO TO WORK. TA DA!

line-up now. Back then, it was live and they sat behind a desk and smiled at you. For 10 years, there was a particularly popular and lovely woman on our screens, Marama Martin. In my memory — and memories are sometimes unreliable — I swear I can recall the night when it was revealed that Marama would be taking some time away from the camera because she was about to have a baby. And she stepped out from behind the desk to prove it. No one had known she was pregnant in the preceding months because (I'm sure this is true) they had built a special desk to fit around her growing belly to hide it from viewers. There was an implication (and certainly a prevailing attitude out there in the world) that women in an obviously fecund state shouldn't be popping up on the screens in our living rooms. Perhaps because you could — gasp — guess at what they had been doing to cause it.

WHEN IT COMES TO ECONOMICS VERSUS PRINCIPLE, I'LL BACK THE PRINCIPLE OF SOCIAL JUSTICE EVERY TIME. THIS IS WHY I WILL NEVER BE PRIME MINISTER.

Speaking of which, the oral contraceptive pill had just been invented shortly before I was born, and made available through family GPs shortly after. (I was, I note, the last child in my family.) This was the first reliable contraceptive ever invented in the history of people, enabling women for the very first time to have some real control over when they got pregnant.

But, importantly, 'the Pill' was legally available only to *married* women. The concern was that, if unmarried women could get the Pill, they'd be having sex all over the place, leading to moral decay. It wasn't until the 1970s that a woman who wasn't married could legally get the Pill. The New Zealand Family Planning Association — seeing how many unmarried women wanted to control their fertility, and how many married women were embarrassed or otherwise unable to ask for the Pill from their family doctor — provided the Pill quietly under-the-counter to women who asked for it, regardless of marital status. Which is why Family Planning lost its licence from the New Zealand Medical Council for several years, and didn't get it back until the law changed in 1978.

And there weren't too many other contraceptive options. Just condoms, diaphragms and celibacy, really. The IUD and the contraceptive injection hadn't been invented yet. In New Zealand, all abortions were against the law regardless of who you were, your health, or how you got pregnant. If you wanted to terminate a pregnancy you had to fly to Australia, or risk a 'backstreet' abortion in a place that wasn't a medical clinic and was performed by someone who may or may not have known much about what they were doing. And who might not have washed their hands.

A support group called Sisters Overseas Service sprang up when abortion became legal in Melbourne in 1969, and then in Sydney in 1971. New Zealand women would be flown across the Tasman to terminate an unwanted pregnancy with personal and financial support from SOS. One of the many things I admire my parents for is that, from time to time, when one of the women who worked at their factory became pregnant (no reliable contraception, remember) and didn't want to continue the pregnancy, they would help make arrangements and advance her wages so she could get to Australia. It wasn't the only thing they did out of their sense of social justice — Dad would also intervene when he knew about incidents of domestic violence, and I was aware of more than one late-night run to whisk a woman away from a dangerous situation and deliver her to another staff member for safe haven, long before women's refuges were established. But it's that thing of understanding that abortion was against the law but that the law was an ass that impresses me about my otherwise entirely law-abiding parents. Eventually, in 1977, the Contraception, Sterilisation and Abortion Act was passed, and women stopped having to fly to Australia as their only option.

The law was an ass in other ways, too. At the time I was born and right up until 1989, it was illegal to supply contraceptives or talk about contraception with anyone under the age of 16 — illegal just to *talk* about it, unless you were a parent or an especially approved person like a doctor or someone the school principal and board of trustees had vetted. Illegal, too, to supply contraceptives to the under-16s; you couldn't buy condoms at the supermarket, you would need to make an appointment at a clinic. Remember the *Choice Not Chance* video I made in 1990? That was the Health Department responding immediately to the law being changed in 1989, when suddenly it was no longer against the law to freely give information about contraception to people under the age of 16. It must be said, though, that many enlightened GPs and educators had been quietly flouting the law over the years, and providing information and contraception when it was clearly needed. There was also a fair bit of rubbering up bananas with condoms, though this was done in the context of preventing sexually transmitted diseases, rather than presented as a method of contraception. Sometimes I'm surprised there isn't a whole generation of people who think they won't catch herpes if they cover their fruit in latex.

I have to write this really loudly: *when we talk about contraception, we are not just talking about sex.* Contraception is about a woman's right to self-determination. It's about choosing the kind of life you want to have, and the kind of person you want to be. For one thing, women don't always get to choose when they have sex. But they should always get to choose when they have a baby. Having a baby changes everything. It alters the path of your life in a profound and irreversible way. It opens doors and closes others — sometimes for a little while, sometimes forever. If a woman cannot control *when* she has children, and *how many* children she has, she is not free. And we all deserve to be free.

WOMEN DON'T ALWAYS GET TO CHOOSE WHEN THEY HAVE SEX. BUT THEY SHOULD ALWAYS GET TO CHOOSE WHEN THEY HAVE A BABY.

So yes, the world was a slightly different place for women than it was for men when I was born. Single women, for example, weren't allowed to work in bars: the idea of putting 'available' women in a room where men were drinking and their wives weren't nearby was thought unwise. Married women, on the other hand, weren't allowed to go to Teachers' Training College. Why would a woman need a career when she had a husband to support her? Best leave those spaces to men and the single ladies. That sort of thing.

This kind of carry-on wasn't just happening in New Zealand; it was a worldwide thing. In many countries, like France and West Germany, women weren't allowed to get a job without their husband's permission, and they couldn't own property — a woman wasn't allowed to own a house. And throughout the world — this one seems mad now — rape wasn't a crime that was committed against the victim, it was regarded as a crime committed against the father's or husband's *property*. In 1707, English Lord Chief Justice John Holt described the act of a man having sexual relations with another man's wife as 'the highest invasion of property'. Because legally, that's what a woman was: something that belonged first to her father, and then to her husband.

And marital rape wasn't a crime at all: the assumption was that if you had married a man you had permanently consented to sex and had no right to say no at any point, even if you were separated and no longer living together. Legally, that didn't change in New Zealand until 1985. Sigh.

But let's not get despondent! That might have been the wider world I was born into with some crazy rules and attitudes, but it wasn't a terrible place. Remember the chooks and the aniseed wheels and my great-aunt's marmalade? Not to mention the Creaming Soda. Ah, halcyon days. But this other stuff is certainly part of our story as women and workers, wives and mothers, and we need to tell these stories, because those rules informed attitudes to society's view of women — what we were worth, and how we should live. So for more about that, let's take a jolly romp through the history of feminism. Not that we feminists would have called it that in the 1970s and 1980s …

CHAPTER 14

THE HERSTORY OF FEMINISM

We were pretty hot on reclaiming words in the 1970s and 1980s, us feminists. As we launched ourselves into the workforce and fought for equal pay and job opportunities, we believed titles like 'chairman' and 'spokesman' were a subtle way of excluding women from taking leadership roles. A concerted campaign was launched against 'man-made language'. While some argued that 'man' was an all-encompassing term, women like me argued 'Not so much, Barry — a woman is not an honorary man, dude. When you maintain that "man" is both gender-specific *and* gender-neutral, yet "woman" is only gender-specific, it implies that "man" is the default mode. Which makes me infer that "man" is normal, and woman is "other". I'm not having that, Barry.'

So new terms like 'chairperson' were invented, although it took a while for them to feel comfortable in people's mouths. A lot of people's mouths might have got comfortable more quickly if they hadn't also been engaged in simultaneously sniggering behind their hands about what those daft girls wanted now.

Alternative titles such as 'chairwoman' were tried in some quarters, but hardliners like me believed we should find words that weren't gender-specific in either direction. 'Chairperson' started to enter the lexicon. These days, wherever possible, I like to make it even simpler by referring to the person in charge of the meeting or the board as 'the chair'. (It doesn't work quite so efficiently for 'spokes', sadly. But 'representative' often suits.) I still think words matter, and I bristle when I hear a workplace has been 'manned', and can be found muttering 'staffed' in that cute way I have. 'Manmade fibres' are 'synthetic'; a 'manmade' lake is 'artificial'. I have always resisted being described as a 'comedienne' and prefer the gender-neutral 'comedian' or 'comic'. It suggests there is a standard one, and then a lady-version, or that men are normal and women are the variation. Plus, I'm not sure why we need to signpost someone's gender in their job description — we don't do it for a doctor, lawyer or teacher, right?

WHILE SOME ARGUED THAT 'MAN' WAS AN ALL-ENCOMPASSING TERM, WOMEN LIKE ME ARGUED 'NOT SO MUCH, BARRY – A WOMAN IS NOT AN HONORARY MAN, DUDE.'

And because so many of our ancient chronicles focus on what the blokes did rather than the adventures and contributions of the lady-people, we feminists had a bit of fun with the word that described it all: 'history'. In a strictly linguistic sense, 'history' isn't a running together of 'his' and 'story', but, you know … Could have been. So we invented 'herstory' to cover the stories back along our matriarchal line. It made a point, ruffled some male plumage, and was a delightful feminist joke. People (men) like to say feminists don't have a sense of humour. Hah. That one still tickles my fancy.

IN A STRICTLY LINGUISTIC SENSE, 'HISTORY' ISN'T A RUNNING TOGETHER OF 'HIS' AND 'STORY', BUT, YOU KNOW … COULD HAVE BEEN.

It wasn't always about finding new ways of saying things — sometimes it was about re-popularising something old. As a title, 'Ms' first turned up in the seventeenth century as a convenient alternative to 'Miss' (an unmarried woman) or 'Missus' (one who was married) when you wanted to formally address a lady whose domestic situation you weren't aware of. (Salutations for men — 'Master' and 'Mister' — were based simply on age rather than marital status, so 'Ms' provided a useful equivalent for a grown female person to the masculine 'Mr'.) 'Ms' was reclaimed by feminists in the 1970s as a way of addressing a woman without making reference to whether or not she 'belonged' to a man. At the time, many of us were unaware of the 'Ms' history — we just knew it as the title of the hugely popular *Ms* magazine, which did an effective job of re-establishing 'Ms' in common usage.

And we have, in a very short period of time, achieved radical change in our language. We don't have 'policemen' any more, we have 'police officers', and people who were once 'stewardesses' and 'air hostesses' are 'flight attendants'. 'Farmers' wives' are now correctly referred to as 'farmers', which seems fair, given that what most women do on farms extends further than knocking up some scones and roasting lamb. Not that there's anything wrong with scones and roast lamb, my word.

I'VE BEEN AT A WEDDING WHERE BOTH BRIDES, FRESHLY MARRIED TO EACH OTHER, THREW A BOUQUET EACH – WHICH DOUBLED THE CHANCES OF EVERYONE ELSE GETTING HITCHED NEXT. AH, PROGRESS.

And at the end of wedding ceremonies it is the husband and wife who kiss, rather than the oddly non-parallel pairing of 'man and wife' (he was a person; she was described in relation to that person). Even more evolved, in New Zealand some ceremonies conclude with the husbands kissing each other. I've been at a wedding where both brides, freshly married to each other, threw a bouquet each — which doubled the chances of everyone else getting hitched next. Ah, progress. All of it makes me smile.

So let's go back even further and take that jolly romp through the Herstory of Feminism. My personal view is that we can trace feminism back to the 1750s. There are other perspectives — some people point to medieval witches, or Greek goddesses, or pre-historic matriarchs in hunter-gatherer times when the gatherers (the women) took charge of organising communal life. But I can see a clear link between the feminism I grew up with and live daily, and the English 'Blue Stockings Society' in the mid-eighteenth century.

The Blue Stockings Society was an informal group of women who got together in London to form a literary discussion group. They read books, and talked about the ideas in those books. Before long, it turned into a social and educational movement. It is hard for us to appreciate how revolutionary this was — for women to go over to Lizzie's place and read and talk about literature, and occasionally invite a writer to come and speak. Women were not allowed to go to university at this point in history, and a gentlewoman's interests were supposed to be limited to needlepoint, knitting, playing cards and gossip. That's not me playing down their expected interests for comedic effect — that's pretty much the full list.

According to legend, the Blue Stockings got their name because when they gathered together of an evening, instead of frocking up and wearing their best black silk stockings, they wore their ordinary, workaday blue wool stockings — an outward statement about being less interested in physical appearances and more concerned with things of the mind. It was about what they thought and said, rather than what they wore. Which was, trust me, all tremendously shocking at the time, and many of these otherwise privileged ladies were shunned by polite society. Little girls caught with their noses in books were admonished to go play outside lest they turn into one of those hideous Blue Stockings whom no man worth his salt would wish to marry. ('I say, hear, hear!')

I think they sound adorable, and quite fancy the idea of having been one. I even have a pair of blue tights in my drawer which I pull out on suitable occasions. (Applying a light layer of body lotion each wear, of course. See Chapter 11.) When my lady friends and I are hotly dissecting some new movie or tossing around some idea we've read somewhere, I like to give a silent nod back down the last 260-odd years to my first feminist sisters. We're still talking, girls!

So yes, this whole feminism thing was started, essentially, by a book club. Which just goes to show every misogynist old bugger was right when he said, 'The trouble always starts when you let the bitches learn to read.'

THIS WHOLE FEMINISM THING WAS STARTED, ESSENTIALLY, BY A BOOK CLUB.

Then feminism became a proper social and political movement in the late nineteenth century. We look back now and, with the benefit of hindsight, call each phase in the development of feminism 'a wave'. I like to picture that in my head as a bunch of the sisters waving cheerfully down the years, but for others I'm sure the image of the wave is more akin to something tidal and quite drowny. Whichever vision you conjure, there is general agreement that the First Wave started in the 1870s and kept going for about 50 years.

The First Wave: fighting for our rights

Our First-wave Feminists were the suffragettes — or in New Zealand, the suffragists. The difference between the two is that suffragettes took direct action (often physical protests that put themselves or property in harm's way), while suffragists were pacifists who took a 'ladylike' approach (lobbying politicians, writing letters to the editor, calling town-hall meetings and distributing quite a lot of leaflets).

The major focus for this First Wave in New Zealand, Australia, the United States and Great Britain were the legal obstacles to gender equality: the right to vote; and the right to own property. In the eyes of the law, women weren't quite proper people — they not only had no say in who governed them, they weren't really allowed to govern themselves. Their lives were wildly dependent on men. If, for example, your husband died, ownership of the family home would pass from him to the next male in line — his father, his brother or his son. He couldn't leave the house to you, because women weren't considered capable of owning property. Where you lived as a widow (or the daughter of one) was left up to the largesse of whichever male person took over control of the house and land — if you had some. But it couldn't be you. Property couldn't be owned by 'property'.

So the suffragists (pacifists) and suffragettes (aggressivists) fought for the right to be proper, legal people who could have a say in how their countries were run, and also the right to own stuff. But while changing these laws was the major focus, they also battled for hearts and minds to effect social change.

They talked about a woman's right to control her body and fertility — not in terms of contraception which was effectively non-existent, or abortion which was largely frowned on — but in terms of marital consent. Women were suggesting that they would like to have the right to say no to sex with their husband when they didn't want to get pregnant. Given how often pregnancy and childbirth killed women and babies, you might have thought men would have been happy to hand over the decision-making about the right time to have sex to their wives but … Not so much. The power in the bedroom had for centuries been vested in the lap of the husband, with the risk of pregnancy left in the lap of the gods.

These first feminists raised their voices about other issues for social progress, too. They allied themselves to movements like the abolition of slavery in the United States, and the temperance movement (which called for total or partial abstinence from alcohol) in America, Britain and New Zealand. Alcohol was identified as one of the things — along with social attitudes — that fuelled violence against women, made things complicated in the bedroom, and led to poor decisions about financial matters by the men who controlled all the property and wealth.

Taking a deep breath and raising their voices got easier, of course, once women whipped off their corsets. And can I just say that I love it that what women wear becomes a part of every feminist movement, whatever the era. 'Feminism? But what shall I wear?!' Yay us and our frocking up (or down) for the cause. In the late nineteenth century it was the corset that was tossed around as the symbol for the restrictions on women's lives. As early as 1873, American feminist Elizabeth

Stuart Phelps wrote this, probably in purple ink and a fair hand: 'Burn up the corsets! Make a bonfire of the cruel steels that have lorded it over your thorax and abdomens for so many years and heave a sigh of relief, for your emancipation I assure you, from this moment has begun.'

Another fashion side-note for your reference: the suffragette colours were green for hope, white for purity of purpose, and purple for dignity. They look pretty great together (think of an emerald, pearl and amethyst broach), and they suit most skin tones. It could be fair to say that in the late nineteenth century and early twentieth century, green, white and purple were the new black.

Corsets off, the ladies fought an amazing battle for legal and social change. There were heroines all over the world who wrote to and visited each other to give and receive support. In New Zealand we had our much-loved suffragist Kate Sheppard, immortalised now on our $10 note. In Britain, there was the fabulously militant suffragette Emmeline Pankhurst, imprisoned many times for chaining herself to railings and allegedly setting fire to the odd thing here and there, and who led prison hunger strikes. And poor little Emily Davison, killed from injuries sustained from King George V's horse at the Epsom Derby as she tried to throw the suffragettes' green, white and purple flag over the beast as it thundered by. (The horse, not the king.) And in America, Susan B Anthony, whose birthday on 15 February is still celebrated as a public holiday in some states. (Not as universally popular as the day before, but much less commercial.)

New Zealand, we are proud to say, was the first nation where women won the universal right to vote — 1893, exactly

100 years before my daughter was born. It sent ripples around the world and provided women in other countries with a great surge of hope, although it still took a while before the rest of the planet caught on.

Women in Australia won the right to vote in 1902. Unless, of course, you were an Indigenous woman, in which case you weren't allowed to vote until 1962. It is amazing to me to think that change happened within my lifetime. In America, white women had to wait for a world war to come and go before they could all cast their first vote in 1920. In many states, African-Americans and Native Americans struggled with the right to vote for decades to come, and many still feel barriers are thrown up to prevent them from voting even today. In Great Britain, universal suffrage was granted after quite a lot of Charleston-ing had been done — 1928. And there were some significant late adopters — French women didn't get to vote until 1944. *Liberté, egalité et fraternité* were guy-things until then, *apparentlé*. And Switzerland turned out to be a bit bloody neutral on the subject of women's rights: no ladies allowed at the polling booths until 1971. Clearly behind the times, which is odd for a nation which is famous for its clocks. Still, Swiss chocolate! Am I right, ladies? Yeah, nah … not really.

LIBERTÉ, EGALITÉ ET FRATERNITÉ WERE GUY-THINGS UNTIL THEN, APPARENTLÉ.

Strongly religious countries have been the most tardy: Bahrain, for example, granted women the right to vote in 2002.

The Vatican City — a nation in its own right — doesn't allow women to vote. Only cardinals can cast a vote for the Pope, and women can't yet be cardinals. Or even priests. Certainly not the Pope.

At the time of writing, Saudi Arabia has promised to give the girls a chance to get involved in democracy in 2015. Even so, they'll still be dependent on the men in their family to give them a lift to the polling booth, because women in Saudi Arabia aren't allowed to drive. That's because, according to a dude in Saudi Arabia who knows all about this kind of thing, driving a car hurts women in the ovaries. When I say 'dude', I mean Sheikh Saleh Bin Saad Al-Lohaidan, who is a judicial adviser to an association of Gulf psychologists.

You may at this point be confused about some things. I can help you, but only with three of them. First, make sure you read 'Gulf', not 'golf' as I did when I first read about it. We're talking about Persia, not the game. These aren't the therapists who talk Tiger Woods through his swing or advise him how to keep it out of the rough. Gulf psychologists are a whole different thing.

Second possible confusion: the sheikh is their judicial adviser so, best guess, a lawyer rather than a doctor. Which leads us to the third fuzzy bit: the assumed medical implications for the female reproductive system of driving a car. 'If a woman drives a car, not out of pure necessity, that could have negative physiological impacts,' Al-Lohaidan has been quoted saying in international media. He goes on to say that 'functional and physiological medical studies show that it automatically affects the ovaries and pushes the pelvis upwards'. This leads to kids being born with clinical problems, apparently, although the sheikh was unable to cite any specific functional and physiological medical studies to back this up. To be fair, I'm not a doctor either and I don't know how they're driving their cars in Saudi Arabia. But I suspect you'd need to fold yourself like a hairpin while wearing a crushingly tight seatbelt in a vehicle made of pure carcinogens with a very oddly placed stick-shift in order for tootling about in the family sedan to have any negative effect on your lady-parts. Also, I am also pretty sure the toughest thing you can put your pelvis and ovaries through is the whole baby-making thing. So really, less offspring, more road trips would be the way to go if you really want to keep your reproductive organs properly pristine.

THAT'S WHAT YOU DO WHEN YOU VIEW WOMEN AS FRAGILE, BUT ALSO MYSTERIOUSLY POWERFUL AND CONSTANTLY ON THE VERGE OF EVIL. SCARE THEM INTO SITTING STILL, FRIGHTEN THEM OUT OF INDEPENDENCE.

But at the heart of this kind of story — or possibly at its uterus — is an attempt to frighten women. That's what you do when you view women as fragile and therefore in need of protection to maintain their purity; but also mysteriously powerful and constantly on the verge of evil. Scare them into sitting still, frighten them out of independence. If you don't want women to drive (presumably because you want to know they'll be wherever you put them last), the best thing to do is make them afraid of driving. Because, although women aren't allowed to drive in Saudi Arabia, there is not actually a specific law that prevents that. It is generally agreed there is nothing in sharia or Islamic law that supports banning women from the wheel of an automobile. But (this is clever) only men are granted driving licences. So women caught behind the wheel are simply fined for driving without the licence they're not allowed to get. Sometimes they've been detained and put on trial on charges of political protest. Naturally, the good women of the Gulf plan collective protests each year when they just, you know, get in a car and drive. The protests are never easy to organise — their websites are usually blocked inside the kingdom — but it still works. You know how women talk. I like to think about these Saudi women and their ovaries each time a national or local body election rolls around. It is one of the many reasons — love of democracy, Kate Sheppard, my absence of corset — that gets me out to vote.

But by and large, most women in most democracies get to drive, vote and put their name on a lease or a mortgage for the family home. That's thanks to the First Wave of Feminism, which carried women along for 50 years or so as laws and attitudes changed all over the world.

And then the ladies settled down for a bit. There was the Great Depression and a Second World War, and a helluva lot of darning to do, air raids to deal with, and jobs to get on with while the boys were away fighting to protect the democracy that most women were now allowed to take part in.

The Second Wave: Universal Womanhood

The Second Wave of Feminism kicked off in the 1960s and lasted a good 20 years. These were the 'Women's Libbers' — a slightly pejorative, cutesy title given to the women who wanted to be 'liberated' from prescribed roles and expected behaviours. As so often happens in a protest movement, the Women's Libbers owned the title spat at them by their taunters, embracing the label as they sang along lustily, arms in the air, pits unshaven, to Helen Reddy's anthem 'I am Woman'. These are the women I grew up with and the ones I couldn't wait to join as soon as I was old enough to not shave my legs.

This Second Wave was, it's generally agreed, a delayed reaction to post-war domesticity. Here's what happened. While the men were away fighting in World War II, women had taken up the slack — filling jobs in factories, single-handedly running the home, taking more responsibility in business, generally (and actually) wearing the trousers. They got a taste of financial independence, had a crack at doing jobs not conventionally open to women, and experienced a new sense of being out in the world, working and socialising alongside other women. They doubtless discovered skills and interests that hadn't been available to them before, and learned one or two things about their ability to be self-reliant. When the men came back, women were expected to stop what they were doing and go home. And they did exactly that throughout the 1950s — they went home and had babies, spawning the Baby Boom that still shapes today's world. (I'm talking Michael Bublé Christmas CDs, Robert de Niro comedies, a penchant for renting a place in Provence for a year, and other obsessions almost entirely funded by the Grey Dollar.)

But throughout those outwardly idyllic baby-booming 1950s a fair bit of resentment was building up in the kitchen. Eventually the lid blew off the pressure-cooker over three big issues: work, sex and violence.

Women who were young, unmarried or childless were still a major part of the workforce. In the early 1960s, these women glanced over at the bloke next to them, saw his hourly rate and started asking for the same. And not just equal *pay*, but also an equal *opportunity* to do the fancy job he was doing. Next thing you know, these working women also started taking the issue of equality home, suggesting for the first time in human history that, since they were both working, perhaps men and women should share the domestic responsibilities of cooking, cleaning and raising kids. Outrageous. Married women at home cottoned onto the idea, too. The old aphorism that 'Man may work from sun to sun, but woman's work is never done' started to seem less like something you'd embroider on a cushion, and more like an issue that needed sorting.

It was a remarkable shift in thinking. These delightful feminists — remember, I became one of them at the age of four — were talking about women demanding the same rights and opportunities as their brothers in the grown-up world of Cowboys and Itchybums. It was like they all woke up from the same dream with the same idea. There must have been a fair bit of nattering about it in the office lunchroom and a silence falling when Steve wandered into the room. You know how men think when women get together we're always talking about them? Sometimes, we're actually talking about equal pay and that.

And as they all came around to the same idea, they developed a big, beautiful vision: these Women's Libbers could see they shared the same experiences and had a common goal. They came to believe in a Universal Female Identity which crossed the barriers of race, class and sexual orientation. We were all sisters under the skin! No matter what else you were, you were a woman! And women were wonderful! Tougher and stronger than anyone had suspected, and about to claim our power alongside all the other women just like us! We had found sisterhood! And sisterhood is powerful! It was a movement that involved a lot of exclamation!

Like the First Wave, this Second Wave joined forces with other movements for social change, literally holding hands in the streets with those who fought for American civil rights and gay rights, and against the Vietnam War. And it reached out to defend women from violence — this is the era in which the first women's refuges were established, safe-houses for victims of abuse. The idea that behind closed doors a man could do whatever he liked to his partner and children was challenged — a challenge that went to the very heart of the legal and social presumption that a wife and child were the 'property' of the man in their lives, to whom he could do as he thought best.

Some of that kind of thinking still exists in pockets of every neighbourhood. But it has changed enough for our mouths to drop open when we hear stories like the one I've heard from within my circle of women friends about the wife who went home to her parents, eyes black and face blue after a beating from her new husband. 'You can stay for a couple of days,' she was told, 'but after that you'll have to go back. He'll be needing clean shirts for work.' We are shocked enough by that kind of response to know there's been a shift in the way most of society thinks.

And there was sex, firmly on the feminist agenda: not just in terms of reproductive rights, contraception and abortion, but also in terms of sexual freedom. First Wave feminists had demanded the right to say 'no'; Second Wave feminists also wanted the right to say 'yes'. The recently invented contraceptive pill made this possible for women for the first time. Sexual exploration had always been part of men's lives, but forbidden for women through fear of pregnancy, and by social disapproval. The Pill dealt to a large extent with the pregnancy risk, so the battle was on for access to that pill, and for a change in attitudes about how women should behave.

A quick side-note about something that has always intrigued me and anyone else who is into, you know, logic: men had always been encouraged to sow their wild oats, and women had always been encouraged to remain virgins until marriage, so I've always wondered who the men were supposed to be sowing their wild oats *in*. Some tiny group of tremendously busy harlots, one imagines. It sounds exhausting. You could argue we should all help out.

But back to our Universal Female Identity. Consciousness-raising groups were formed, based on the idea that sexist ideology was so ingrained that women needed to sort of 'unlearn' it and 'raise our consciousness' by talking to each other. At CR groups (yes, there were enough of them around for them to need a handy acronym), women were encouraged to tell our stories and become aware of how the world saw us, and, more importantly, how we saw ourselves — to develop an understanding of the oppression women experienced and then use that as a springboard for political action.

WHO KNOWS HOW MANY LIVING ROOMS AND HALLWAYS IN THE 1960S AND 1970S BOASTED A MASSIVE OIL PAINTING OF THE LADY OF HOUSE'S VAGINA. 'MY, WHAT A LOVELY ORCHID,' DINNER GUESTS MIGHT SAY.

We were encouraged to appreciate the feminine (hitherto less popular and celebrated than the masculine), and get in touch with our womanhood. Sometimes literally. There were consciousness-raising groups which in part involved women getting together and looking at their own vaginas with a hand-mirror. Which might seem kind of crazy, but you need to understand that these were women who might have never looked at their own lady-bits before. For centuries — nay, since the dawn of time — people have been encouraged to think of women's bits as dirty and wrong. Now, women were happily admiring the qualities of their quims, appreciating the form of them, admiring the uniqueness of each one, and occasionally painting them symbolically on canvas. Who knows how many living rooms and hallways in the 1960s and 1970s boasted a massive oil painting of the lady of house's vagina. 'My, what a lovely orchid,' dinner guests might say. 'You don't often see them that pink and frilly.' And your gracious host-woman would blush prettily and open another bottle of Cold Duck.

For the same reason, women were encouraged to taste their menses — not each other's, that would be weird in a random group, just their own — to break through the accepted belief that a woman's period was a sickness and that the blood was dirty. Again, not something we all need to do on a regular basis but it won't do you any harm to experience it once. After thousands of years of being told that what our body produces each month is evil, it takes a big action to make the pendulum swing back the other way before we can find equilibrium.

Consciousness-raising groups were still a thing when I was at university in the early 1980s, including the hand-mirror/ menses bit. You don't see that so much these days. About the only time you'll see a whole room full of twats now is at an ACT Party conference. I'm sorry my daughter missed out on this part of the feminist movement, though — it was very sisterly. But I am glad we don't have to tiptoe around periods or be fearful of vaginal examinations, and that we only use euphemisms for vaginas now because it's fun.

It does worry me, though, that we've become judgemental about our vaginas, applying the 'youth equals beauty' rule to this body part, too. Labiaplasty is a thing now — trimming your lips surgically to return them to their un-lived-in state. May the goddesses save us all from ourselves. Let me say this very firmly: a grown-lady's vagina is meant to look like a flower, not a moneybox. Put the scalpel away.

'Women's Lib' became a media event on 7 September 1968 at the Miss America beauty pageant in Atlantic City. There, 400 women gathered to protest against the event because it objectified women, presenting them as something to be judged on appearances according to male-devised standards of beauty. Thinness, hairlessness, symmetry, coiffedness, swimsuitedness, and the correct amount of paint. The protesters outside the pageant gathered around metal drums, which they dubbed 'freedom trash cans', and symbolically threw into the cans a whole lot of products which were made for and marketed only to women, or which were designed to instruct women on who they were to be. They called them 'instruments of female torture and enforced femininity'. So into the cans went curlers, hairspray, makeup, high-heels, girdles and corsets (Elizabeth Stuart Phelps was smiling down), false eyelashes, *Cosmopolitan* and *Playboy* magazines, mops, pots and pans, and one or two bras they'd brought along with them.

It was the bras that made the news. The headline the next day read *Bra-burners Blitz Boardwalk!*, and reports said that, inspired by anti-war protesters' burning of Vietnam draft cards, these protesters had set fire to their lingerie. The women who were there that day insist there was no fire, but 'Women's Libbers' became known as 'bra-burners' from that moment on. The Second Wave was official — it had found its symbolic item of clothing.

Australian singer and songwriter Helen Reddy wrote the song to go with the movement in 1971, and when the United Nations declared 1975 International Women's Year, they also made 'I Am Woman' the campaign's official song. The feminist firmament was full of stars: writers and thinkers like America's Gloria Steinem, Rita Mae Brown and Betty Frieden; New Zealand's Sandra Coney and Marilyn Waring; and Australia's Germaine Greer, whose take on the Second Wave was firmly focused on women's liberation rather than equality with men. Don't be like men, Greer suggested — aim higher. Greer visited New Zealand in 1972, and was arrested at a public rally for saying 'fuck' and 'bullshit', which was fucken bullshit but excellent publicity — it made the TV news I was watching as an 11-year-old and led me and many others to go looking for her books.

But the stars weren't just these stars. My memory of that time is that it was a wildly democratic movement which encouraged ordinary women — our mothers, our grandmothers and ourselves — to pitch in with ideas of her own. There were events like the United Women's Conventions, open to any woman who wanted to turn up and talk about the issues that affected her life. Everything was on the table, because 'the personal was political' — who made the tea at work, who cared for the kids, what women wore, healthcare, sex, sexuality, housework, support for solo mothers … All of it. A movement that, at its best, embraced all women and all issues under that umbrella of Universal Womanhood.

And a lot did change. The Equal Pay Act was passed in 1972; the domestic purposes benefit (DPB) was established in 1973, in large part to make it possible for women to leave violent relationships and for single women to support their own families; the Contraception, Sterilisation and Abortion Act became law in 1977; and more women began to be elected to

Parliament thanks to the Women's Electoral Lobby, which was established in 1975 to encourage women into public office.

Also, heaps of it was fun. I recall 'pub liberations', where large groups of women would take over male-only bars for the night — the kind of pubs where the music would have stopped if a woman had walked in by herself. There were many of those kinds of bars, this pre-dating the kind of hostelries where women would be welcome to socialise with or without men. We had a fine time draining their stocks of gin and tonic, and taking over the pool table.

And there were Reclaim the Night marches, often held in direct response to a sexual assault in a public park, after which the police and other grown-ups would advise women not to venture into that area after dark for a while. It was a powerful thing to instead turn up with a few hundred of your closest girlfriends and some candles and march *en masse* into the grassy darkness and sing and chant and feel like, just for an evening, you owned the world and could go anywhere you pleased so long as you were in the company of your sisters, because we made it safe for each other. It was a summer sport, certainly, but I found the whole thing tremendously liberating.

But by the late 1970s and into the early 1980s, things began to fall apart. The unity of the Second Wave was showing serious cracks. That all-embracing, seductive vision of a Universal Female Identity was seriously challenged as the differences among women became as important as their similarities. Women, it turned out, wanted different things. Some feminists wanted women to play a fuller role within society. Socialist feminists wanted to fundamentally change that society. Some lesbian feminists argued that lesbianism was as much a political choice as it was a sexual orientation, and focused on creating a separate community. More divisions emerged along race and class divides. In other words, the bitches started fighting.

My arrival at university coincided with all that splitting. CR groups fragmented into lesbian separatist collectives, Marxist-Leninist cells, Maori sovereignty hui, and some nice, straight, middle-class young women focusing on how to become prime minister or chairperson of the board. I was one of the Marxist-Leninist activists, dubbed 'a feminist puppet of the white male left' by pretty much everyone when I stood for Women's Rights Officer in the Students' Association. The lesbian-separatist and I split the left vote, and a pretty girl who played hockey, went out with a rugby player and didn't believe that sexism existed won. It was a salutary lesson.

What happened at Victoria University was, in microcosm, what was happening in the worldwide movement at the time. Ultimately, I believe, two big arguments caused the power to ebb from the Second Wave of Feminism. In simple terms, it went like this. Many feminists believed that pornography and prostitution were oppressive of women. That they objectified women, presented them as objects of male desire, which diminished their humanity. But many other feminists believed that pornography and prostitution were valid expressions of a woman's sexuality, and women should be supported in their involvement in both industries as workers and as consumers. Really, this was just a lightning rod for all the other arguments feminists were having amongst themselves. But that issue remained symbolic of the split, and couldn't be reconciled.

The second reason the Second Wave lost momentum was because we had championed a very dangerous idea. We had argued that women were not only *equal* to men but — ooh, watch yourselves, sisters — that we were *better*. That we were kinder, maternal, more nurturing, and peaceful. And that if the world was run by women, we would do it magnificently and by consensus. If women ruled the world, we promised, it would be a better, safer, gentler place and there would be no more wars. And then Margaret Thatcher turned up and blew it for the sisters by proving that none of that was true.

IF WOMEN RULED THE WORLD, WE PROMISED, IT WOULD BE A BETTER, SAFER, GENTLER PLACE AND THERE WOULD BE NO MORE WARS. AND THEN MARGARET THATCHER TURNED UP.

Thatcher was elected prime minister of the United Kingdom in 1979, and led the Conservative government until 1990. She was the first woman to take such a powerful leadership role in a Western democracy, ever. What did she do with her decade? She crushed the unions, closed the mines, threw thousands of families into poverty, battled hard against gay rights, and started a war.

You will find people who will say admiring things about Thatcher — her focus, dedication and political ability — but not in this book. I cannot overstate how much she took the wind out of our sails for a full decade. For me personally, as an advocate for feminism, she was a stick with which I was constantly beaten. 'Women—' I'd begin. 'But Thatcher,' they'd respond. She took our dreams from us and made our lives hell. We came to hate her.

'The feminists hate me, don't they?' Thatcher said in the early days of her political career to her adviser, Paul Johnson, who wrote about it in *The Spectator* in 2011. 'I don't blame them. For I hate feminism. It is poison.'

So that's pretty clear. Just in case anyone missed it, though, in a lecture she gave in 1982 as British Prime Minister, Thatcher said this: 'The battle for women's rights has largely been won. The days when they were demanded and discussed in strident tones should be gone forever. I hate those strident tones we hear from some Women's Libbers.' Not so big on the sisterhood, then, Maggie?

MARGARET MEAD REPLIED, WARMLY, THAT OUR VOICES MIGHT SOUND A BIT SHRILL, BUT YOU'D HAVE TO EXPECT THAT SINCE WE HADN'T BEEN ALLOWED TO USE THEM FOR SO LONG.

When I hear her say that about 'strident tones', I think of the wonderful cultural anthropologist, Margaret Mead, who died the year before Thatcher was elected. Mead was asked in an interview something along the lines of 'How come

Women's Libbers all sound like shrieking harridans?' She'd replied, warmly, that our voices might sound a bit shrill, but you'd have to expect that since we hadn't been allowed to use them for so long. My mum heard the interview and told me about it. We shrieked and giggled together like gleeful banshees.

Thatcher, so often characterised as the grocer's daughter who succeeded in a man's world, showed no outward interest in giving a leg up the ladder to, or breaking the glass ceiling for, any women behind her. A fierce individualist, she believed it was up to everyone to make their own way, and there was no common cause that we, as women, needed to fight together. 'There is no such thing as society,' she said. 'There are individual men and women.' Which is precisely the opposite of everything women had been arguing for the previous 20 years beneath the banner of Universal Womanhood. So there she was, the most powerful and famous woman in the world speaking directly against everything feminism stood for, and going on to embody the exact opposite of what we had promised from a woman leader. Sigh. It was enough to make a girl weep hot tears of frustration all down the front of her gender-neutral overalls. And we did.

It wasn't all dire. Radical feminists might have had the fervour knocked out of them with the Thatcher-stick but, as so often happens, mainstream society was catching onto feminist ideas and embracing them. The New Zealand government, not always a hotbed of radical thinking, launched a mid-1980s campaign through its Employment and Vocational Guidance Service called Girls Can Do Anything, which openly encouraged women and girls into the kind of occupations usually thought of as 'men's work'. Building, plumbing, engineering — work in sectors that generally paid better than industries populated by women.

However, the campaign affirmed what was already happening around the country rather than leading a charge, although there were still pockets of resistance. More than one auto shop argued that women couldn't be mechanics because they'd be uncomfortable around the nudie pictures on the workshop walls. Because you couldn't, you know, take the pictures down just so a lady could have a career. Mate, you can't drain a radiator without glancing up now and then and looking at pictures of titties.

I recall a news story about a plumbing company that didn't want to take on female apprentices because they didn't have a separate ladies' loo. No, seriously. Even at the time, it begged the question: what sort of plumbing outfit were they that they couldn't bung in another dunny somewhere before lunchtime on any given Tuesday? Clearly not the right spot for an ambitious young pipe-diver to learn her trade, anyway.

In general terms, though, the world was embracing the notion that girls could do anything. And before too long we were pretty much doing *everything*. Job, kids, baking, aerobics, community work ... Which turns out to be fairly tiring, and none of us is quite sure that this is what we planned. Still, it's nothing that pay equity, paid parental leave, reasonable access to childcare, safe and reliable contraception, freedom from violence, and a fairer division of domestic responsibilities can't fix, right? More on that soon.

The Third Wave: honouring diversity

Once again, the wave ebbed and the ladies took a breath, but a shorter one this time. The Third Wave of Feminism began in the early 1990s, post-Thatcher, in response to — and acknowledging — all those divisions that had reared up at the end of the Second Wave. If the previous swell had been about a Universal Female Identity, this Third Wave was all about honouring diversity. Women, we agreed, are not a homogenous bunch. We want many different things, and if the point of feminism is to stop telling women what they can and can't do because of their gender (and it is), then feminism should embrace all the choices without getting all judgy.

So this Third Wave actively rejected any prescribed ideas about what a feminist should want, or what she looked like. You could keep wearing your pointedly sexless dungarees and overalls (my flatmate Fee and I referred to ours in the 1980s, quaintly, as our 'over-ies', geddit?), or, if you were of a mind, you could mince about in a mini skirt. It's your call, sister. You could join the army or become a domestic goddess — guns and muffins were both valid pursuits. You could be a passionate member of Greenpeace, or a dedicated fan of *Sex and the City*. You could be a working mother, or a stay-at-home mother, or not a mother at all.

I find it hard to define the Third Wave with absolute clarity, because it was, in essence, about not wanting to define or limit what feminism is. Also, these were the years when the baby ate my brain. (See Chapter 1.) But the major forces that carried the movement forward are pretty clear: it was a youth movement driven internationally by three groups — Queer Culture in all its rainbow shades, Women of Colour, and 'Girl Power'. Naturally, it was Girl Power and its twisted sister, Ladette culture, that captured the imagination of mainstream media, because young women empowering themselves into tube tops and chugging down quite a lot of lager made good visuals. 'Dear me,' I tut-tutted, at home in the 1990s, stuffing organic vegetables into the Moulinex for my daughter (who, as soon as she was old enough, batted that rubbish away and reached for a mince and cheese pie), 'I totally defend your right to make your own choices, but did you have to choose to dress and behave like skanks? Someone get those girls a cardy.'

YOU HAVE THE RIGHT TO TWERK, BUT WE ALSO HAVE A RESPONSIBILITY TO EXPRESS OUR VIEWS TO EACH OTHER ABOUT WHETHER TWERKING SERVES US WELL.

The past 20 years of feminism have been confusing, and not just for old-school feminists like me. It can be bewildering when Miley Cyrus describes herself as 'one of the biggest feminists' and yet … twerking. So let's say this: an essential part of feminism is not being told how a woman should behave, what she can and can't do in work and in life. But let's also say this: another drive for feminism was always about women fulfilling their potential and being the best people they can be. So you have the right to twerk, but we also have a responsibility to express our views to each other about whether twerking serves us well.

I can celebrate Girl Power (though, crikey, a lot of the music was awful), and I totally get Slut Walk events as protests against sexual assault, when women take to the streets dressed however they want, to make the point that rape and sexual assault can never be excused or explained by what a woman wears. When you know our history, it is clear that Slut Walks are natural descendants of Reclaim the Night marches, which in turn owed a lot to British suffragettes chaining themselves to railings. In fact, you could probably trace the Slut Walk provenance right back to outrageous women wearing those inappropriate blue wool stockings in the 1750s if you were of a mind. And I am.

But Ladette culture — the booze, the violence, the recklessness — was a weird distraction. In my secret dreams, I suppose, I had hoped that feminism might have seen us all progress by now to a point where men were behaving like the best of women rather than women sometimes behaving like the worst of men. There's still time. It is also worth taking a moment to remember what we said at the beginning of this chapter: that feminism was started by a book club, by women who wanted to talk about big ideas that elevated all humanity. The best thing we can do for our daughters, then, is to tell them what those earlier waves were fighting for. We all need to know our own history. Herstory.

When people talk about us living now in a 'post-feminist' era, I take a leaf out of Germaine Greer's 1972 playbook and call 'bullshit'. To my mind, each of these waves of feminism is part of an evolution. We are sitting right now on the soft, low back of the Fourth Wave and I have a feeling in my bones that is going to be a glorious ride …

CHAPTER 15

WHY MUMMY THINKS YOU SHOULD BE A FEMINIST, TOO

Do we still need feminism? Now that the ladies have got equal pay and the Pill, surely it's done its dash? We're all equal and there's no such thing as sexism any more, right? (You might want to go back and make sure you have read Chapters 8 and 9 properly.)

I find it very sweet when people suggest that no one needs to be a feminist any more. That's a bit like saying 'Now that slavery has been abolished, does anyone really *need* to be black?' Okay, not exactly, but you don't become black because of slavery. It's who you are. And being a feminist is not just about winning the right to vote. Feminism is about being a person who doesn't want to take shit for being a woman.

My favourite current feminist is the English writer and social commentator Caitlin Moran. She says there's a simple test to work out if you should be a feminist. Put your hand in your pants. Do you feel a vagina? Do you want to have control of that vagina? Then you need to be a feminist.

Here's another really useful question: can I have a career and a family? Have a little think about that for a minute. Not about your *answer*, just think about the question. And now ponder this: every woman who considers a career asks herself that question; very few men do. This tells you everything you need to know about whether we have achieved equality yet. Like we said in the 1970s as we put down our razors and stopped shaving our legs: if the boys aren't doing it, it's not equal.

IF THE BOYS AREN'T DOING IT, IT'S NOT EQUAL.

A hairy side-note: the not-shaving of legs and armpits was a big deal back in the day. Hairy legs were an act of social disobedience — a shocking affront to accepted standards of femininity — and also a handy marker to let you know who else was part of the sisterhood. 'Hello, Alice, I see from the state of your legs that we're probably going to get on.' Now that men have embraced their own grooming obsessions we've evolved past it being an issue. I held on to the not-shaving for a long time, though, particularly the armpits. That was until one fateful day in 1989 when a supremely creepy dude told me he liked my hirsute underarms because they looked like two vaginas. Though he didn't say 'vaginas'. I've been shaving my armpits ever since.

Here's another way of answering the question about whether you need to be feminist. Women in New Zealand earn on average, over a lifetime, 12 per cent less than men. That's because the industries women work in are often less well paid than the industries dominated by men, and also because of the time women need to take out of the workforce to make new people. This means for every dollar He earns, She earns 88 cents. Now, I don't want to just be about the problems; I want to offer some solutions. So what I believe we should do to deal with this inequity, sisters, is actually *do* 12 per cent less.

This means that, if you are working a 40-hour week, for 4.8 hours each week you should do nothing. Just drift off. Stare into space. Take it in one chunk and give yourself a half-day. Or spread it out over the working week. Roughly an hour a day of humming, meditating, staring out the window or otherwise disengaging from being productive. You're not getting paid for it, ladies, so don't do it. If anyone notices, simply explain you are having your 'Lady Time'. This will confuse them. Most people think that sort of carry-on happens once a month. It's once a week, sisters. Take it. It's yours.

You could also apply the 12 per cent rule to individual tasks. If your job involves answering the phone, only answer it 8.8 times out of every time that it rings. If your job entails responding to emails, delete 12 emails out of every 100 without reading them. And if you are required to do filing or any alphabetising of any kind, choose three letters of the alphabet that you will have nothing to do with. 'M, P and S? Sorry, Andy, I don't do those. I'm ignoring 12 per cent of the alphabet. You're not paying me for 12 per cent of my work, so let's call that fair.'

Take the problem home: remember, this is how women have always managed to effect social change, by making the political issues personal ones. At home, only pay 88 per cent of your share of the rent or mortgage. If you are cooking dinner and it happens to be meat and three vegetables, don't cook one of the vegetables properly. 'Potatoes ridiculously hard? Yeah, that's not bad planning, darling, it's a political statement.'

If you are ironing his shirts — I'm sorry, what? Why are you doing that? It's the twenty-first century, ladies. He does his *own* ironing. Seriously, I can't help you because I don't know who you are. But, okay, don't iron the sleeves. And if you have three children, ignore one of them 25 per cent of the time. That's easier than it sounds. You know how people say you have a favourite child? That's not true. But you *do* have one you really can't stand. Make it that one.

If anyone complains, tell them that, if you're earning nothing 12 per cent of the time, they can get what they pay for.

♣

Clearly, we need fresh new feminists to keep fighting the good fight for pay equity, and for all the other issues we're going to address in this new Fourth Wave, which is rising up and breaking through even as we speak. Around the world, young women are once more forming themselves proudly into feminist collectives, and people like me are finding our voices again. Three years ago, while speaking to a group of nurses, I was introduced by the Chair — an old Second Wave friend — as 'a strident feminist'. I had forgotten how good it felt to have that said out loud. I've put it on my CV.

Let's take a look at this new wave the way we've looked at the others, then: what it is reacting to, the issues, the Grand Vision, who the stars might be and, of course, what we are going to wear.

I reckon the renewed interest in the women's movement is a delayed response to the feminist backlash of the 1980s and 1990s. Remember that 1985 campaign Girls Can Do Anything, and how successful it was because suddenly we seemed to be doing *everything*? Job, housework, kids, their homework, cooking, chauffeuring, household accounts, DIY, world's best lover … We were exhausted. Still are a bit. Hence the rise of Coffee Culture. But I digress.

This 'superwoman' exhaustion was translated by some (I'm not pointing fingers, but let's just say it might have been people who hadn't been into feminism all that much in the first place, because it wasn't about them) into the assertion that feminism had Ruined Women's Lives. 'See,' these people said, 'you women are all equal and that, with your laws and jobs and stuff, and you're still not happy! Feminism doesn't work!'

Lots of women were so tired they couldn't argue any more. Hence a bit of neo-conservatism from the 1990s onwards, rediscovering quaint social traditions like wearing pink and taking your husband's name and getting back to baking, and lots of 'I'm not a feminist' hoo-ha right down the line to today's Women Against Feminism nonsense in social media.

Except, friends, we aren't tired, confused and overcommitted because feminism was a stupid idea. The reason we're exhausted is that WE HAVEN'T FINISHED YET. We don't earn enough, we don't get enough paid parental leave, childcare

IF YOU'RE EARNING NOTHING 12 PER CENT OF THE TIME, THEY CAN GET WHAT THEY PAY FOR.

is too expensive, we still don't have 100 per cent reliable contraception, we've never entirely cracked that equal sharing of domestic duties thing, we're dealing daily with misogyny, the glass ceiling works as a skylight but we need a door and a solid staircase leading up to it, we still can't use public transport after dark, we have to be constantly vigilant about sexual assault from strangers even though we're more likely to be attacked by someone we know, and if we *are* attacked we have to prove it's not our fault ... And globally we're the *lucky* ones.

These aren't problems created by feminism; these are problems that feminism can fix. Plus, finding each other, sharing our stories and speaking up, we're rediscovering, is already making us feel better. So Mummy thinks you should be a feminist and we should get on with this together. First up, we need to remind ourselves that what we are asking for is not unreasonable. That's a really good phrase to keep in mind.

I have a friend and colleague who is an excellent negotiator. Not as in 'Step away from the edge, buddy,' but in terms of striking deals and signing contracts. Which is probably why he was one of my few colleagues who had for years made a properly decent living. So, more than a decade ago, we asked him to be our representative at a crucial meeting that changed the face of our industry.

As professional comedians appearing in a televised comedy showcase, we suggested we should get paid for our appearance. It seems mad now that we weren't getting paid (since cameras, sound, makeup, director, producers, all the crew were), but at the time the people in charge of budgets gave myriad reasons for expecting us to perform for free — mostly based on the idea that appearing on the telly would make us famous, which should be enough reward in itself. We'd tried sensible counter-arguments for years, using whiteboards and flowcharts to show how 'fame' didn't show up in our bank accounts, so we couldn't use it to buy food or pay the rent. I believe there was also a memo in which someone wrote down the definition of 'professional'. To no avail.

This time around, our negotiator, dressed better than the rest of us and not smelling of public transport, stuck pretty much to one line throughout a long meeting: 'What we are asking for is not unreasonable.' To each of their various descriptions of how the sky would fall in if they had to change the way they did things, he would calmly repeat 'What we are asking for is not unreasonable.' In the end, they absolutely agreed that what we were asking for was pretty reasonable.

That mantra often plays in my head as I watch various debates play out, none more so than in New Zealand's recurring debate over extending paid parental leave from 14 weeks to 26. Our current 14 weeks puts us alongside Algeria and Malta on the 'here's how we value a good start in life' register. I try to mutter the 'not unreasonable' mantra in the same calm way my friend would say it, but it's hard when you hear a spokesperson from Business New Zealand allege that women would forget how to do their jobs if they stayed home for six months and, moreover, it would be bad for women because it would discourage employers from hiring women of childbearing age. To which I say: 'Step away from the edge, buddy.'

Many jobs are like riding a bike, and in more complex industries good employers are constantly engaging their workforce in training and retraining anyway. Also, best of luck with running any industry without using the talents and energy of women under 50. Although I do quite fancy the idea that women over 50 will suddenly be really, really popular.

Given paid parental leave is taxpayer-funded rather than paid for by individual employers, I'd imagine a smart boss would jump at the chance of retaining a skilled and experienced employee once her baby is weaned. There is a wealth of reasons for supporting families for the first six months of a baby's life — putting kids first, long-term savings on healthcare, social welfare, education and crime costs, and generally putting a child-proof fence at the top of the cliff rather than funding ambulances to wait at the bottom.

SING IT WITH ME: WHAT WE ARE ASKING FOR IS NOT UNREASONABLE.

But the crux of it is this. Most women have babies — this has always been true. Most women also work — and this is a relatively new truth. Yet we continue to arrange the workforce as though women aren't in it. We need to stop pretending that it is odd that someone who has a job also has a baby. Because, actually, this is what we do. We need to adjust the labour market to fit that, and get on with supporting mothers while they do it. Sing it with me: what we are asking for is not unreasonable.

We know it in our hearts, just not in our pockets. Catch a business leader at just the right time and he will tell you, wet-eyed, that being there when his child was born was the most significant event in his life. In a private moment, the head of a multinational company will confess that being a mother is the hardest, most rewarding job she's ever had. As a society, we all sing along with Whitney — yes, we really do believe that the children are our future. Pretty sure you're humming it right now. Sorry about that. It'll fade out.

We've all agreed that raising children is really valuable. Except, oddly, we don't value it with our usual currency — money. Not much of it, anyway, and not for long. Many other countries have got their heads around the idea that half the workforce are women, and most of them need to pop out of the office to make a new human being at some point, and that this doesn't make them weird. New mothers in the UK get 39 weeks' paid leave to get things off to the right start, and in Sweden (it's always Sweden) it's 16 months.

So there's nothing more valuable than good parenting, raising our kids right, giving them the best start, blah blah — unless you're asked to value it in monetary terms. Again, I don't want to always be about the problem, and want to find some solutions. Maybe what we need is another way to reward parenting that is transferable on the open market. I suggest launching the Kidcoin — a bit like the Bitcoin in that it doesn't really exist and no one can properly explain it. Think of the Kidcoin as a virtual currency in which you take precious moments — like your kid's first smile, their first sleep-through-the-night, a really successful burp or their first word — and trade them in at the bank for Kidcoins to pay your mortgage, or swap them at participating retailers for nappies and wet-wipes. That should buy parents another few weeks of time with their newborns, which is invaluable in terms of those long-term payoffs in improved health, education and social outcomes. Many of which really *are* quantifiable in actual dollars. We could also consider extending the Kidcoin to later life events, so that all those paintings from kindy, certificates for participation, Mother's Day cards and finger marks on the walls can be put aside as your retirement savings.

So pay equity, workplace flexibility and paid parental leave are the Fourth Wave's legislative aims, I'm guessing, along with effective and accessible contraception, and abortion by choice. And some serious thinking and talking about internet privacy and security, now that sexual violation occurs in the virtual world as well as the physical one. Hearts and minds issues? Violence against women, LGBTQI rights, and a lot more consciousness-raising about rape culture and victim blaming. That would do for starters.

Every good wave of feminism needs a grand vision. Most likely something truly great will develop over time, but I'm happy to offer one to be going on with. I've had it lying about since the 1970s and I'm buggered if I know why I didn't articulate it before. I think it was another one of those bits of feminism that I thought were self-evident or would be absorbed by osmosis, but when I finally put the words together and said it out loud on stage it seemed to resonate with my daughter, and all the other mothers and daughters. So let me tell you about the Feminist Dream.

As the feminist daughters of feminists, we envisioned a future for our own daughters that was rich in choice and possibility, with satisfying work, motherhood (if and when she was ready), and a relationship based on equality and shared tasks.

And they could do those things in any order, but they would always choose independence and dignity. They would embrace their sexuality and explore it. Abortion would be safe, legal and rare. And freely available contraception would mean that every child would be a wanted child, and they would be raised to be the best that they could be.

Also, it would be awesome if they could ride unicorns and wear sparkling gowns woven from angels' joyful tears. But that would just be a bonus.

FEMINISM IS ABOUT FREEING WOMEN FROM PRESCRIBED ROLES, AND ALSO FREEING MEN FROM THEIR PRESCRIBED ROLES. WHICH LIBERATES US ALL.

Who will the stars be? All of us. By which I mean men, too. Just as I think it is straight people's job to go in to bat for gay rights, I reckon the boys can have a turn at talking to the other boys about feminism. Which is exactly what we can see happening, particularly in social media, which will play a huge role in the Fourth Wave. Being a man speaking up for feminism is a bit like being an interpreter. Your first language might be Man, but you can speak a bit of Woman. So you translate a bit of Woman to your Man friends. The thing you wouldn't want to do is, at any point in the conversation, turn around and mansplain to the Woman how she might speak better Woman. *Comprendez?*

Feminism is incorrectly characterised as 'man-hating'. Feminism isn't *about* men. It's about women. It's about women not wanting to be treated as 'other', and it is about all of us challenging sexism and rejecting misogyny, wherever and whoever it comes from.

Feminism is sometimes expressed as being about women doing all the things that men do. But really, it should be about freeing women from prescribed roles, and also freeing men from their prescribed roles. Which liberates us all. So it *is* a little bit about men. But not nearly as much as some of them think. And only in a good way.

And what shall we wear for the Fourth Wave of Feminism? Let's just see what we've got lying about that's clean.

CHAPTER 16

MRS HUSBAND

According to parenting manuals which no one has time to read because they've got kids, one of the essentials of being a good parent is 'consistency'. Have an idea, attitude or rule, and stick with it come hell or high water. Bedtimes, mealtimes, household chores, rewards and punishments, acceptable language and behaviour. While I haven't been a complete ning-nong about structures and boundaries, I haven't managed consistency in at least one area of our lives — my feelings about, and engagement with, the custom of marriage.

Depending on how you view these things, I'm either an expert at marriage (I've had three of them) or a failure at marriage (I've had three of them). You might variously say I've 'flip-flopped' on my marriage policy, or been 'flexible', or maybe I've allowed my ideas to 'organically evolve'. Not a lot of clarity, then, in my role-modelling of wife-hood for Holly. Though good modelling, I think, on the essence of relationships being about finding someone in the world whom you can always count on to be kind to you, and to whom you will always be kind. And I like to think I've demonstrated willingness to work hard on creating joy. And that an example has also been set about removing yourself from situations that are ultimately unsafe and unbearable. But in terms of the whole dress-like-a-meringue and legal-contract thing? Jeez, Mum, could you pick a team? Let me untangle the knotty issue that tying-the-knot has been for me, then, and see if we can weave something useful out of the wool left over.

Back when we were being youthful and rebellious, my peers and I consciously and actively eschewed as many of the societal conventions as we could get our hands on. We wouldn't go to the school ball (they, in fact, stopped being held), we didn't let our parents throw us a twenty-first, and we barely turned up for our own graduation ceremonies. These were all archaic traditions up with which we would not put. We would, thanks very much, choose our own milestones (I threw myself a party when I turned 20) and find our own ways of celebrating achievement (my university graduation photo was taken by my photographer-brother and features me with my mortar-board at a rakish angle, sitting in a cemetery on a gravestone — can't quite remember what we were going for thematically now, but it was all very hyper-gothic).

And I swore I Would Never Get Married. I didn't swear that I wouldn't fall in love and live with someone — I was always a romantic bohemian at heart: all truth, beauty, freedom and love — but I wouldn't *marry* them. We were acutely aware of the historic legal and social meaning of marriage: that a female person was the legal property of her father until she married,

I'M EITHER AN EXPERT AT MARRIAGE (I'VE HAD THREE OF THEM) OR A FAILURE AT MARRIAGE (I'VE HAD THREE OF THEM).

at which point she became the legal property of her husband. Hence the tradition of being 'given away' by the father on her wedding day, and changing her surname to the husband's to signify that he'd taken over the title on this particular chattel. Bear in mind, too, that we were still living in the era when a married woman lost not only the surname she'd lived with all her life on her wedding day, but in formal situations she lost her first name, too, and became Mrs Husband. When Barbara Smith married Tom Brown, her mail would forever more be addressed to 'Mrs T. Brown'; 'B. Smith' was gone forever. The letters in our letterbox all came for 'Mr & Mrs John A'Court'. In an act of political protest, whenever I wrote letters home from university I would address them to 'Mrs & Mr Donna A'Court'. My poor father no doubt found this all very odd, but probably sighed and added it to the growing list of my oddities, like my penchant for second-hand clothes and my refusal to drink his South African wine because of apartheid.

'Living in sin', as it was so attractively described — a phrase that suggested something a lot more hot and frothy than the general reality of two young people huddling together over beans-on-toast in a manky flat — was only just catching on when I was a gel. I remember Loys, our neighbour and my second mother, describing a couple who were to come to dinner as 'not actually married but, you know, nice people'. That passed for liberal in my small home town. When I was at university and my boyfriend and I moved into a flat together, my father took an unheard-of day off work and drove to Wellington with my mother and an empty suitcase to retrieve me from this den of sin and take me home to the family cat and my single bed.

When they arrived, I made bran muffins and terrible instant coffee and spent the whole afternoon pretending I didn't know the real reason for their visit, and eventually they went home again without me, Dad with one more thing to put on the ever-growing Oddities List.

So the not-getting-married was a social protest. It didn't, for most of us, mean a lack of commitment or a rejection of couplehood and monogamy; it was more a loudly stated choice to leave both Church and State out of our romantic relationships. Then somewhere around my late twenties the resolve weakened. Why? Parties. Some of my friends were getting married, finding their own unique and delightful ways of publically expressing their love and commitment. Dresses in all colours, no longer compulsory white (which was supposed to signify virginity, as if, and anyway it wouldn't suit me — I'm a Winter); cakes made of ice-cream; writing your own secular and gender-blind vows. It looked like fun. I wanted a party! I looked over at who I was dating at the time and booked a venue.

TERRIFIC PARTY: IT JUST SHOULDN'T HAVE BEEN A WEDDING.

The whole thing was disastrous and mercifully brief. Not the wedding — it was spectacular and lasted all day, and is still one of my favourite dos, bringing together friends and family from various cities and pockets of life. At the centre of it there was a grand mountain of profiteroles filled with cream and drizzled with toffee, in lieu of the traditional fruit cake which

I hate. Terrific party: it just shouldn't have been a wedding. A year later, the marriage was over. It was a good thing I'd dug my toes in (but of course) about keeping my name, or there would have been a lot of suddenly useless monogrammed towels.

So the first marriage was about wanting a party, and the second marriage — resisted for years through the early romance, pregnancy and parenthood — was about bowing to pressure. 'Kids need their parents to be married for stability, and it upsets your nearest and dearest that you are not,' said people who weren't themselves our nearest and dearest, and who, it turned out later, were basing this reading of the situation on diddly-squat. It was also, on my part, a shot at fixing a relationship that was beginning to break. Not a rare occurrence: we all have friends who have lived together for years, then suddenly got married, then just as suddenly split. That's not how I explained it to myself at the time, of course — or to anyone else. That would be a weird wedding invitation. 'Things are a bit crap between us, but we thought having you around for a party and us signing a contract might help. Come along and save us. No pressure.' What I did say to anyone who asked why I was suddenly wanting to get-my-bride-on was that filling in forms had become problematic. Faced with 'marital status' boxes — Single? Married? Divorced? — I didn't know which one to tick, as none of them seemed appropriate to my situation. Not the worst reason to buy a wedding licence, but not the best either. Things properly fell apart shortly after, and Holly and I hunkered down and muddled on through, loving each other fiercely and continuing to make each other the most important person in our lives.

So there I was, someone who had never had wedding dreams — I can honestly say hand-on-heart that at no point in my life have I dreamily visualised what My Big Day would look like — now twice married and twice divorced. I was more surprised than anyone at how things had turned out. And doubly convinced that marriage as a social and legal convention didn't suit me at all, *and* firmly resolved never to do that again. That and never washing another man's socks or ironing his shirts became Promises to Self. When I eventually met Jeremy and we started talking about maybe possibly having a future together perhaps, I was upfront about not being able to have any more children, and also about the no-washing, no-ironing, no-marriage manifesto. He was 100 per cent on board.

Over our first dozen years together, we put a lot of thought into not getting married. It's something the world requires you to keep thinking about. I remember listening to a lovely radio interview a few years ago with a woman who lived in a small place and who did interesting things. The specifics of her family's location and pursuits aren't what I remember, although my impression was that it all sounded very jolly. What caught my ear was when the interviewer asked something about her husband. Before she answered the question, there was a brief pause. 'We're not actually married,' she said. Then there was another beat before she added: 'Though after eight years, two kids, a mortgage and running a business together ...' She didn't need to finish the sentence — we hear you, sister. She probably didn't need to get hung up on providing a legal definition of her relationship either. But I also liked it that she didn't let the misnomer slide.

In New Zealand, one in four couples aren't married, yet the default assumption is that people who arrange themselves in families either *are* married, or *should* be. If it turns out that they're not, the next assumption is that they forgot, or haven't got around to it yet, or — at worst — aren't really all that committed. To some minds, a relationship is not real if you haven't celebrated it publically. I quite fancy applying that philosophy to birthdays: if you don't have a party, you don't actually get a year older. If you planned it carefully, you could be forever 22.

But we should acknowledge that some couples put more thought into *not* getting married than other people put into marrying. There are those who consciously choose not to involve lawyers in their romantic life, or who are averse to religious tradition and social convention, or who find joy in constantly 'opting in'. No doubt there are one or two people who are simply bitten and shy. For me, all of the above applied. After that second divorce I was psychologically allergic to ever being described again as someone's 'wife'. I couldn't bear to say the word or visualise the role. For me, the W-word needed to come with a trigger warning.

Although words are also a problem for the not-married/not-single. 'Partner' is easily confused with a business arrangement, and 'de facto' sounds — to bohemian ears — as pompous as the holy state of legal matrimony you're eschewing. 'My better half' often comes across as both patronising and creepily passive-aggressive. I tended to refer to Jeremy as 'my boyfriend' despite the fact (or maybe because) it suggested we spent a lot of time holding hands and skipping, and writing each other's names on our pencil cases. My favourite way of describing the other person in your couple comes from a novel I read a while ago which referred to her or him as your 'One In Particular'. The book was a futuristic fantasy so there's still time for that to catch on. I would love it if it did.

MY FAVOURITE WAY OF DESCRIBING THE OTHER PERSON IN YOUR COUPLE COMES FROM A NOVEL I READ A WHILE AGO WHICH REFERRED TO HER OR HIM AS YOUR 'ONE IN PARTICULAR'.

Even after we'd been together more than a decade, friends would still occasionally ask Jeremy and me for a wedding, because, you know … parties. But I was wise to that one, obviously. So we would just explain that we'd made a solemn promise to stay unmarried forever. Although with a caveat that there was no saying that we wouldn't find an Asian Elvis impersonator sometime in Vegas and accidentally get married on some ridiculous whim.

So a big fat 'no' to a family wedding, but a warm embracing 'yes' to being a family. I still don't care about the social niceties of marriage, but I'm big on Family and, no matter what else has disintegrated around us, I've always made sure Holly has been surrounded by all of that unconditional love.

My Great-uncle Frank — the one who kept the Creaming Soda in the garage for the school holidays — had a fondness for observing at family gatherings, whisky in hand: 'You can choose your friends, but you can't choose your family.' A charming wit and raconteur, this was always greeted with much hilarity, given he was surrounded at the time by the latter rather than the former. It was his way of saying that he properly loved having us all there, and not just because he had to. Usually, it was preceded by some piece of extended-family news — a loony sister-in-law's latest antics, a hopeless cousin's fresh folly, or a re-telling of some legendary family saga. What Frank meant, what we all understood, was that *some* of our relations (specifically, the ones not in the room) were crazy fools and we wouldn't have a bar of them if we didn't have to. But we had to. So at the very least, we could turn them into a good story. At which point my Great-aunt Ruth — she of the marmalade and winter undies warmed in front of the blow heater — would offer with a smile: 'Ah, blood's thicker than water.'

As a tiny child, I spent a bit of time considering this deliciously visceral image. Familiar with stubbed toes and grazed knees (Cowboys and Itchybums for starters) and my mother's valiant efforts to remove the tricky stains from my clothes, I was fascinated by the thought that this warm, sticky, indelible stuff also somehow bound us all together. It impressed me as an explanation for the fact that, no matter what idiotic thing you did, your family would always support you, take you in, and keep loving you.

Happily, not just idiotic things engendered expressions of family loyalty. Ritual readings of my brother's and my school reports always ended with Russie and my grandmother reverting to their original Lancashire accents, saying, 'Aye, there's no ducks like our ducks' — shorthand for family pride and unconditional love.

So I grew up with a sense that if you messed up, you would be comforted, and if you did well, you would be celebrated. It was wonderful to grow up surrounded by people who loved like this and who were able to say it out aloud. It wasn't that it made me think I could do no wrong, but rather that, even when I did wrong, there would still be a place for me. And more: that the chances were I'd do well, because I came from 'good people'.

Of course, it hasn't all been beer and skittles — across the generations there have been disagreements, disappointments and testy silences, and, in some of the more conventional branches of my wider family, my own career and lifestyle choices have occasionally made me feel like a lap-dancer at a church picnic. But at the very least, you can turn any of that into the kind of story Frank would have been happy to tell.

All of us have two potentially conflicting desires: one for safety and security, the other for risk and adventure. 'Family' is our safe place — the place we spring from, and can retreat to. Every board game has a square called 'Home', where players are untouchable and can take a breath between rolls of the dice. If you are lucky — or not unlucky — in the-world-as-it-should-be, the square on the board called 'Home' is also called 'Family'.

We all have, of course, more than one family. There's the one we are born into, and then there are the new families we create. One of the ways you know you are a grown-up is that moment when, filling out a form stating 'Next of Kin', the name you put is someone you have *chosen* to spend your life with, rather than your mum. Your One In Particular. We find partners and make babies and do our best to merge the old families with the new. And we create some interesting families that can look a lot different from the ones that have come before. Until Holly left home, our house held three generations: my parents have their separate place on the ground floor where they live independently; and Holly, Jeremy and I lived on the first floor. Jeremy is not my daughter's father. I'm Pakeha; Holly is Maori; Jeremy is Canadian with an Irish father. I'm a Baby-Boomer; he's Gen X; she's Gen Y. It's unlikely that we'd ever get asked to depict a family in a TV commercial. Unless they were trying to say something wacky about race and age.

But while we might not look like an advertising agency's idea of a family, that's what we are. It's an interesting thought to me that, despite all the lack of convention involved in getting us all under one roof, once there we have arranged ourselves just like a conventional family — grandparents, mum, dad and the kid. No doubt some sections of the community would be appalled with us on paper, but I'm pretty sure they'd be comforted by the ordinariness of our daily routine.

THAT'S WHAT MAKES A FAMILY — THE BANALITY OF DAILY LIFE CONDUCTED IN THE SPIRIT OF SOMETHING FINER.

When Jeremy and I were agreeing on the no-washing, no-ironing, no-wedding manifesto all those years ago, we also agreed that what we wanted was to have that one person we could count on to always be kind to us — and that we would try to be that person for each other. That's also the promise I made to Holly when she was born, and continue to say to her: that she can always count on me to love her, stand by her, put her first, and be kind to her. I wrote it in her Baby Book, said it all through her teens, and still mention it in passing pretty often now. And sure, in the general chaos of making a living, getting to the supermarket, negotiating schedules and after-school pick-ups, cooking dinner, folding laundry and paying the bills, it can be a challenge to remember to be kind at all times. But that's what makes a family — the banality of daily life conducted in the spirit of something finer.

And then, of course, as you've no doubt guessed, Jeremy and I got married. I know! On a whim, in Las Vegas. Not, I hasten to say, because anything looked a bit cracked and needed gluing, but because suddenly one day it felt like a terrifically good idea. We were on a six-week trip through the United States and Canada, celebrating my fiftieth birthday (we spent the day at Disneyland), then visiting Jeremy's family in Vancouver, Toronto and Montréal, and finishing with attending our good friends' wedding in upstate New York. One week into this trip we were in Las Vegas and decided to take a gamble on something that felt like — still feels like — a sure bet.

One morning, apropos of nothing, Jeremy said, 'I wonder how easy it really is to get married in Las Vegas?'

'Dunno,' I said. 'Find out', la la la, and went for a swim.

We were married the next day.

Later that week, once word had got out at home — my brother was so excited about what we'd done that he told everyone, including one of our State broadcasters, which very much separated cat and bag — I sent this message to our friends.

Dear Friends,

We're really pleased to let you know that, after 11 years together, Jeremy and I were married in Las Vegas this Tuesday.

Like all weddings it took a huge amount of planning — Jeremy went online on Monday and applied for a marriage licence, and shopped around for the right chapel. That done, we took a well-earned break and went to see *The Lion King* at the Mandalay Bay Theatre.

The day of the wedding started in the traditional way — Jeremy won a few hands at Black Jack in the Tropicana casino while I got a bit of work out of the way in our room before we hit the pool for a swim and a massage.

We had lunch at our regular Vegas haunt, the Salsa Cantina (Jeremy — fajitas and beer; me — taco and margarita), and then dropped by the Hawaiian markets to buy a couple of wedding bands.

Back at the Tropicana, we changed into our wedding ensembles: the bride wore cream and black Annah Stretton that she found in her suitcase; the groom wore a DKNY shirt with a Celtic belt buckle and Canadian First Nation's silk tie to honour both sides of his heritage.

We caught a cab to Old Vegas to pick up our marriage licence from the Clark County Marriage Bureau; dropped by Freemont St for refreshments (Jeremy — beer; Michèle — champagne); and then on to the chapel.

The Little White Chapel is where Frank Sinatra and Mia Farrow were married, and Mary Tyler Moore and Slash (though not to each other). The ceremony was officiated beautifully by Minister Mujahid Ramadan (everybody had wet eyes) and witnessed by Sharon from the 24-hour drive-through window. ('Do I have a witness?' 'Yes, sir!')

Then we went to Paris. Paris is a casino on the Strip. We sat on the balcony, ate pâté, drank wine, and watched the fountains play across the road at the Bellagio.

It was a beautiful day, and it feels wonderful to be married. We'll be home to celebrate some more in August. In the meantime, lots of love from both of us to all of you.

Michèle

I learned a whole lot of significant things from this drop-of-the-hat, spur-of-the-moment wedding of ours. First, it showed me how important it is to find the right way to celebrate your relationship, which will be different for different kinds of people. For us — two people who spend a fair bit of our lives on stage under a spotlight, with people staring at us as we tell our stories in public — having a wedding that *didn't* involve an audience was liberating. Neither of us had to spend a nanosecond thinking about how we appeared to anyone else, because we were the only ones there. What we'd both wanted, without articulating it to ourselves before, was not a public declaration but a very private one. A quiet, intimate moment just for us and our celebrant — not an Asian Elvis impersonator (we were too spur-of-the-moment to book one), but a beautiful man who looked and sounded for all the world like Morgan

Freeman. We even said no to the photo and video package — only one photograph of our wedding exists, taken by Sharon, the big, loud African-American receptionist over at the drive-through window, as a favour to us. Only three people on the planet know what was spoken between us. It felt like magic.

I've heard a gorgeous story about a couple getting married with the full family wedding hoo-ha, who both freaked out the day before — not because either of them had doubts, but because they couldn't bear the thought of exchanging their vows in front of everyone. So the celebrant had a brilliant idea. The next day, before the church bit, the bride and groom and their wedding party went down to the beach. The bridesmaids and groomsmen all made a big, wide circle and turned themselves outward, as though they were standing guard. Bride and groom stood in the centre of the circle and exchanged their vows just with each other, unable to be heard by anyone else over the sound of the waves. The celebrant married them there and then. The church bit followed and covered the legal niceties, but the really personal stuff was kept between the two of them. I love that story. Not everyone needs a public declaration. Some words seem more real and solid when they're the ones you can say only to each other.

Another thing I've learned is that (I would never have said this before Vegas), for us, being married *feels* different. Like a question we didn't know existed has been answered. Lots of it is to do with how much Jeremy loves being married; remember, unlike me, for him it was a new thing. He's still excited about being a 'husband' and having a 'wife'. And I've grown to like the W-word. He shouts 'Where is my Wife?!' up the stairs when he comes home, and you can hear that it is spelt with a capital W. There's a lot of 'Would my Wife like a cup of tea?' in the mornings, and we've taken to buying the most cheesy Husband and Wife birthday and anniversary cards we can find. There was nothing wrong with the way things were before Vegas, but it is — in a way I still can't properly articulate — even better now. It occurs to me that I got married the way a lot of other people have babies: it was unplanned and a surprise to everyone, but it turned out to be exactly what I wanted. Third one's a charm.

Which leads me to the third thing I've learned about marriage: everyone should be allowed to know what this feels like. I'm not suggesting for a second that marriage should be compulsory — there are other valid ways to arrange our loves and lives. But I like the idea that every grown-up could have this sparkly thing as an option. Which is why I was so proud of New Zealand when our politicians passed our Marriage Equality law in 2013, allowing gay and lesbian couples to get married in exactly the same way as the rest of us.

The news reached me that year when I was, as it happens, back in Las Vegas doing a week-long season at a comedy club. Every night, two shows a night, I'd ask my audience who else was part of the 'married in Vegas' family. There was always someone — married last year, 12 years ago, 27 years ago. I had a happy onstage chat with an impossibly beautiful young couple who had just got married that week. On another night, in the lounge post-show, I met an elegant middle-aged couple in full wedding finery — including a tiara for her — who had returned to renew their vows after 10 years. Always good to know that quickie weddings lead to these long liaisons.

I told my audiences about what was happening in New Zealand, where marriage was hot news and the first gay weddings were being celebrated around the country. You could hear the champagne corks popping from the other side of the world, and I shed a happy tear like a mother-of-the-groom when I read a story online about Warren and Tony, together for 30 years, who finally had their relationship legally celebrated and respected.

THERE WAS A SUGGESTION THAT SURELY CIVIL UNIONS WERE SUFFICIENT FOR GAY PEOPLE – SOMETHING AKIN TO SAYING THEY WERE ALLOWED ON THE MARRIAGE BUS, BUT STILL COULDN'T SIT UP FRONT.

There were — and are — of course, nay-sayers, ranging from the shouty 'Next we'll be legalising bestiality' to the quieter 'Can't those gays just shut up?' Somewhere in the middle was a suggestion that surely civil unions were sufficient for gay people — something akin to saying they were allowed on the Marriage Bus, but still couldn't sit up front.

There will be initial confusion for people who can't get their head around two people both calling each other 'my husband'. I'm going to have to catch up, too. Comedy show banter relies on quick assumptions, so when a man at a recent show volunteered he had a new baby and the baby was at home with his partner, I asked after the mother. It took a moment for me to grasp that Baby had two dads.

Change, I think, is a little like childbirth — painful, but afterwards you forget that it hurt. Until 1986 in New Zealand, gay men could be (and were) arrested for making love to each other. That, I hope, seems crazy to us now. By the time Holly is 40, I reckon we'll find it hard to imagine there was a time when her lesbian godparents, Sue and Jo, weren't allowed to have a proper wedding with the women of their choosing.

Side-note: I was involved as a supporter in gay rights protests in the years leading up to the passing of New Zealand's Homosexual Law Reform Act in 1986, because it seemed madness that two grown-up people having consensual sex should be illegal. It occurred to me, and still intrigues me now, that it has never been illegal in the Western world for women to make love to women — anti-gay laws are all directed at men. I reckon there are two reasons for that. Apparently, when Queen Victoria was asked if she would like to extend the existing anti-homosexual laws to cover women as well as men, she said she didn't think that would be necessary because 'women wouldn't do that'. An interesting perspective. Which I'd put down to no women ever hitting on Queen Vic. (Let's be honest, I've seen the pictures and she wasn't hot.) The other explanation for the absence of laws against lesbians is that the world is largely run by men and they're not so keen on legislating against girl-on-girl action. This appears to be a universal fantasy. Men, it seems, like to think of women making love to women as some kind of side-dish to a threesome in which they may be also be on the menu at some point. It's not a side-dish, though, is it, sisters? That's a whole valid eating experience all of its very own. Think of it as tapas. But with no chorizo.

To anyone who still opposes gay marriage, I'd say this. As a heterosexual woman, I've been free to make my own choices. I've been free to marry the wrong person for the wrong reasons (for the party, as a fixer, or to please other people) and also to marry the right person for the right reasons — albeit in an apparently frivolous way in a chapel in Las Vegas. In doing so, I don't believe I've done anything to undermine the value of marriage, or that I've disrespected anyone else's union. It has always been some kind of act of courage, and a statement of hope. I've been to other people's weddings and, no matter how things turn out, I think this is always true. Also, it's not like straight people are so brilliant at marriage that they don't want gay people coming along and ruining their record of success, right? Adam and Steve deserve the same chance to get it wrong or right as the rest of us.

♣

Now that we've untangled my complex marriage flip-floppery, let's go right ahead and use what we've straightened out to tie up some loose ends. In contrast to the zeitgeist of my youth, the pendulum has swung back in the other direction with regard to social convention. Weddings are hot right now (not just for gay people), as are those other celebrations like the twenty-first and the school ball.

Our daughters love a party and a frock. In between formal occasions they may wear something your nana would consider insufficient to blow her nose on, but I swear that every one of them has, on her laptop, a picture file of ball and wedding dresses she is, oh my God, just aching to wear.

I clearly forgot to tell my daughter about my assumption that 'youthful rebellion' would mean a continuation of that fine tradition of thumbing a young nose at conventions like these. Though I now suspect re-embracing the conventions *is* the act of rebellion. It certainly felt gobsmackingly odd to find myself shelling out squillions each year for high-school ball tickets, fancy frocks with matching shoes, hairdressers, manicurists and stretch limousines. There I was, a reluctant Fairy Godmother waving my magic credit-card-wand so that she shall go to the ball. The other mothers and I would proudly and tearfully wave the kids off from their pre-ball gatherings and, once the limo had pulled away, look at each other wide-eyed and murmur, 'What the fuck just happened? Who did we *raise*?' Then I'd sweep up the crumbs from the asparagus rolls (my retro food is very popular) and hope that these parties and frocks might get it out of their systems early so that they might avoid Marriage Mistake Number One — The Party. 'Even if it saves one of them,' I murmured feverishly to myself, 'it would be worth it.'

Go on, then, have a ball. And a Sweet Sixteen (there is way too much American stuff on our televisions) and a twenty-first. Whatevs. I'll give you those, but I am drawing a line in the sand at that other expression of new conservatism currently embraced by both Gen X and the Millennials: becoming Mrs Husband.

Stop that. Changing your name to your husband's when you get married is metaphorical twerking. Yeah, yeah, I know, feminism is about *not* telling women how to live. But remember, we've also agreed that it is our job as women to tell each other when we think some of us are doing stupid things, and fill you in on the reasons why. Robust discussion. I'm going first. Sit down and listen very carefully. Though I will repeat this as many times as necessary. Don your safety goggles and strap yourself in.

CHANGING YOUR NAME TO YOUR HUSBAND'S WHEN YOU GET MARRIED IS METAPHORICAL TWERKING.

Five minutes ago, back in the 1970s, it took considerable courage for women to fight against the convention of a woman changing her name on her wedding day from her birth family's to her husband's. As I said at the beginning of this little chat about marriage, before my blood pressure went up, historically the convention was about the legal definition of a woman as 'property' being passed from one man to the other, and it remained a social definition of her: that she had belonged somewhere, but now belonged somewhere else. Suddenly, you're on a different page in the phone book, and no one from your previous life can find you unless they caught your wedding notice. Anything you achieved pre-marriage is no longer directly attributable to you.

Hence the necessary exceptions, even back then, to the rule. Actors, writers, singers and dancers kept their own names — a nod at the need to protect their brand, even before we talked about 'brands'. In the wider world, movie stars kept their names and, closer to home, my dance teacher and drama teacher kept theirs. So I noticed even as a child that women who *did* things were allowed to keep on being the person they had always been, identified as their own selves rather than in relation to someone else.

I remember my mother's excited exclamations whenever she discovered that some successful woman she admired turned out to be a girl she had gone to school with. It would take some effort to uncover her identity. 'Goodness, that Stephanie Meacham doing interesting things turns out to be Stephanie Turner-what-was,' she would say with all the glee of Hercule Poirot solving a tricky murder. Indeed, Stephanie Turner, as an identity, was dead. And then my mother would have to sleuth further to find out what Stephanie's husband's initials were so she could track Stephanie down again, now she was represented only by his identity in the phone book.

I decided pretty early on, around Standard One, that I would have none of this. It seemed an odd practice and, as we've made clear, I've always fought against having to do anything that the boys didn't have to. Also, around that time, I had a crush on a charming boy called Mark Bell. As a seven-year-old pondering the abstract possibility of spending the rest of my life with him, it seemed to me then that the most difficult hurdle in our life together would be being known as 'Michèle Bell'.

Then there was Miss Pottinger. Miss Pottinger was our school's favourite teacher, and my older brother spent a glorious year in her class. Two years later, when it was my turn to have her, she had inexplicably changed her name to Mrs McCaul — to me a completely different person. My sense of betrayal was compounded when she left me before year's end to have a baby. Clearly, these 'Mrs' types were not to be trusted.

But really it was wiping your pre-marriage history, and overnight defining yourself in relation to someone else that irked (and still irks) me. I understand the arguments put forward by the neo-traditionalists. That you want to be *one* family with *one* name. But I've already argued here that 'family' is about much more significant things which have little or nothing to do with what you're called. The whanau I love — grandparents, aunts, uncles, in-laws — have a heap of different surnames, and none of us need to signpost our relationship by changing them to each other's.

Women with embarrassing surnames (Smellie, Daft, Shufflebottom) sometimes argue that they've been waiting for marriage so they have an opportunity to land something better. This smells a bit like Bad Reason For A Wedding Number Four to this expert. What if Brian Dungworth is perfect for you, but you just can't take it any more and settle instead for Bob Smith? Disaster waiting to happen. If it's the Shufflebottom you want to get rid of and you don't mind losing what you did when you operated under that banner, find your own alternative that speaks to your own history — like your mother's or grandmother's name — and breathe new life into the matriarchal line rather than hitching your wagon to a current star.

Here is my big gun in the Mrs Husband argument: if it is an act of love and respect to take your significant other's name, why is it the default position that she changes her name to his, rather than his to hers? It is rare for a man to take his wife's name and your average dude would balk at the suggestion. Which should make us ask: why the balking, buddy? If that seems an odd reversal of status, then there must be status involved. Why is it weird for him to adopt her family name, but natural for her to take his? We're back to 'If the boys aren't doing it, it's not equal', and I'm going to have to stop shaving my legs again.

Children, people argue, find it confusing if their parents have different surnames from each other and from them. No, they really don't — and if you find that hard to explain to the little ones, good luck with some of the other stuff you're going to have to deal with, like what happened to the guinea pig. That might be a fair argument if your kids called you by your surnames, but since they mostly call you 'Mum' and 'Dad' it shouldn't be an issue. Other than that, kids are pretty good at accepting the things we tell them are acceptable, like 'Mummy has her own name. Now, let me tell you about Santa.'

I appreciate that when Holly was little it sometimes took a moment for doctors' receptionists and teachers to get their head around the idea that my daughter had a different surname from mine. She was given her father's family name when she was born (as my friend Margaret likes to say: give the kids the dad's name — everyone already knows who the mother is), but it really was only a tiny moment of confusion for the person looking for the right file. And, dear God, the parent/child name differential was starting to catch on before the new conservatives began to take hold.

So what do we do with our names when we find our One In Particular? Keep them, and our history (herstory) and achievements and our network of connections, and our identity, for the love of God.

Or, if we're really wanting to share a name, have an equality-based conversation about which one it will be. Blend our names — a couple I know have invented a whole new name out of both of theirs, so if there is any wiping of history and new beginnings, at least they're doing that on equal footing. Double-barrelling is an option; though possibly not for Bill Best and Jennifer Lay, as, a couple of generations down the track, when the children of the Best-Lays marry the descendants of Sally Busch and Toby Rashe, it might start getting hard to fit all that Best-Lay-Busch-Rashe on a passport.

But don't worry about the kids. The kids will make their own choices later. What I firmly believe is that you — as the adult in the situation who is a goodly part of the way into the big job of making your place in the world — are the most important person to consider in terms of the effect this faffing about with names will have. Your children, dear reader, deserve more than one role model with a complete history and identity. Besides — here's an actual fact — there is one divorce for every two marriages each year in New Zealand. You've got enough to deal with during a marriage breakup without having to change the name on your passport and credit card. Trust me. This is my area of expertise.

Of course, there are entirely laudable motives for not wanting to carry your original family name all your life — for example, if you are a survivor of family abuse. But just don't wait for a wedding to make that change in a random way. Make your own choice. The most healing thing for person recovering from trauma is to take control of their future and make decisions for themselves.

Which is also what our double-barrelled children will do as they grow up, I suspect: drop one or the other, perhaps. And it's not that I am against name-changing *per se*. At the age of six, Holly asked her father and me if she could change her last name from his to mine. This was after the divorce, when she and I were taking our cat, Jimmy, to the vet and she realised that even the cat was an 'A'Court', and she wanted the same last name as everyone else currently living in the house. Or more specifically, that she didn't want a name no one else in the house had. This was her choice, not mine. She understood it was an option because the mother of some friends of hers had just changed back to her original name following a divorce, so the three kids had one name, the mother had another. No one felt this was weird, and I think all the kids picked up that it was something that mattered to her.

BE YOU. REMAIN YOU. QUESTION TRADITIONS, INVENT NEW ONES AND HOLD YOUR GROUND.

Holly's father and I both agreed to allow her to do it and signed the paperwork. I love it, of course, that she wanted to share my name. I also know it wouldn't have come up if her father had still lived with us. But I've always admired the tradition in other cultures of naming girl-children for their mother's family line and boy children for their father's — a way of honouring both sides of the family. And six years old seemed like a good time to make the change — there were only a few awards and certificates in the first version of Holly's name, so there wasn't so much of her own established history to lose.

So are we clear? Be you. Remain you. Bring yourself to your relationship and keep being you within it, and outside of it. Question traditions, invent new ones, and hold your ground. It is part of a woman's right to self-determination to establish and keep her own identity. Not Mrs Husband. You.

That's all. I'm done.

Okay, not quite. The wedding-day name-change isn't the only flash of neo-conservatism giving me a migraine. Before the Big Day there will once again be, as there was in Palaeolithic times surely, a Stag Party for him and a Hen Party for her. At least one of them is likely to involve strippers.

To be honest, I like a bit of retro — nana cardy, asparagus rolls, the kiss curl — but I felt like I'd been slapped in the face by a Neanderthal paw when, five years ago, the otherwise delightful, intelligent, charming men in my close circle of friends held a stag party for our groom-to-be involving cricket, poker, pizza … and strippers.

You could call the stripper-at-the-stag-do 'a tradition'. Or take the new view that you can watch strippers 'in an ironic way'. Or maybe you think it's just 'a bit lame'. Whichever chorus my friends joined — mostly the irony argument — I was the voice growling 'sexist and offensive'. I had thought that the smart people had worked out in the 1970s that paying women to take their clothes off objectified them, reducing them to less than the sum of their private parts. I'm pretty sure I still have the memo lying about somewhere.

I knew that strippers still existed, of course, and that in some circles it had never got old. But now my *friends* were doing this? I felt like an African-American discovering that all my white friends were off to see a black-and-white-minstrel show. Or a pacifist finding out my buddies spent Friday night knitting jumpers at a hanging.

ISABELLE ALLENDE SAYS, 'EROTICA IS USING A FEATHER, PORNOGRAPHY IS USING THE WHOLE CHICKEN.' LUNCHTIME IN A STRIP CLUB FELT LIKE BEING THUMPED WITH A FROZEN CHOOK.

My view of strip clubs is a bit like my attitude towards haggis: heard it described, thought it sounded awful and not for me, tried to be opened-minded and gave it a shot, and discovered I was right. Years ago, an actor friend was researching her role as a stripper, and I trotted along to a lunchtime show to give her support in what was, to both of us, an alien and potentially uncomfortable environment. I hated it, if for nothing else than the low production values — bad décor, ghastly music, furtive behaviour, and the absolute absence of fun or joy in any of it. Isabelle Allende says, 'Erotica is using a feather, pornography is using the whole chicken.' Lunchtime in a strip club felt like being thumped with a frozen chook.

Don't get me wrong: I like a feather. I've been known to read erotica, and I like a tickle of burlesque — spoil me with great skill, saucy costumes and a bit of narrative and I will admire and applaud. If Holly had told me she wanted to take up burlesque, I'd have learned how to sew on sequins and gone shopping for tasselled pasties. If she told me she wanted to be a stripper, I'd have wanted to lock her in a cupboard until she was 35, and only let her out to talk it over with a counsellor to establish what I'd done wrong.

I worried for the strippers, because I know that the only time I've ever considered taking my clothes off for money, in even an abstract way, I've been desperate. I've never met a little girl who dreams of growing up to be a stripper. Plus, I couldn't help in this scenario identifying with their mothers at home, not with the boys watching them. That's one of the things that happens when you become a mother: it becomes a lens through which you view the world. And I even worried that your ironically booked stripper at a stag do isn't even being objectified any more with old-fashioned, straightforward leering. There's a cruel joke happening, which she, the woman working, is not part of. Surely that's like a Society of Skeptics hiring a psychic for their Christmas function, just so they can laugh behind their hands and feel smug, and later say the psychic should have seen it coming. I thought we were better than that. Still do.

Once, after an awful corporate gig that felt like death, I found out that I'd been hired by someone specifically because she knew her audience would hate my comedy. She was leaving the firm and wanted me to be her parting shot. 'Here you go — here's something you will hate.' I never knew how to describe how dreadful that night felt. And then I did. I felt like an ironic stripper at a post-modern stag do.

Sexism is still sexism even when it's ironic, or benevolent, or accidental. And on this, there will be no flippity-flop from me.

CHAPTER 17

HEARTBREAK

Cheer up, though. Let's talk about divorce and relationship breakups in general. I've been poised and waiting to coach Holly through a heartbreak for years, but she has been the heartbreaker rather than heartbreakee in romantic endeavours, so the opportunity hasn't properly presented itself, and now I hope it never will. This is not to say her life has been without sadness and loss, just not in the way of a boy sending her a text to say he didn't want to see her any more, lol. 4SRS? SMH. FML.

I'm never sure if this is a good thing or not, this lack of experience in romantic heartbreak. There is something deliciously melancholic about being on the receiving end of a good dumping — tragedy and sorrow without the burden of guilt for being the one who chose it. Also, I've met people to whom bad things have never happened (Holly is not one of them) and they are pretty dire. Suffering through your own tragedies is the thing that makes you able to empathise with other people's tragedies, and offer up less judgement and more kindness. These are wonderful human qualities.

So that's the first thing: welcome some practice heartbreaks, I say. Think of them as useful rehearsals for bigger ones in your more grown-up life. A kind of vaccination where a little shot of flu prepares you to be stronger to fight the super-flu if it turns up later and makes your eyes stream and your nose run.

The second thing is: cake. Cake is remarkably effective as a salve for your spirit when it is hurting. As is going for a walk and listening to birds sing. Taken together, they balance each other out nicely. A slice of cake, a walk, and another slice of cake when you get back. Think of it as 'an exercise sandwich' — a walk slapped between two bits of cake. I'm not a nutritionist, but I'm pretty sure this works.

A SLICE OF CAKE, A WALK, AND ANOTHER SLICE OF CAKE WHEN YOU GET BACK. THINK OF IT AS 'AN EXERCISE SANDWICH'.

Third thing? Friends. Girls are social creatures. We do things in groups. And we talk. A lot. I heard a psychologist explain once that when men need to deal with emotional issues, they do that 'shoulder to shoulder' rather than 'face to face'. They sort through their stuff while playing golf or fishing or watching sport or standing side-by-side at a bar leaner. Or possibly think stuff through while they're alone and tinkering in the shed. Women sit across from each other. We don't knit in a shed, we knit in a circle. Alice Walker said, when I last saw her speak, that if you get a circle of women together and let us talk without an agenda, we will cover every topic we needed to discuss on the agenda we didn't write down.

One of the things I have always admired about Holly and her circle of friends — aside from their apparently innate ability to apply false eyelashes — is their loyalty to each other as friends. One of the biggest sins in my daughter's circle? Ditching your girlfriends' plans in favour of your boyfriend. Despicable. Similarly evil is sleeping with your girlfriend's boy. They move through the world in friend-based circles. They'll visit Family Planning for smear tests and contraceptive advice in groups and make a party of it. They might make a fuss on Facebook about their romantic relationships, but they understand the value of friendship. Nothing — but nothing — makes a girl drop everything faster to race around to her friend's place than a status update that says she is sad. I've seen Holly stop mid-application of false eyelash on a Saturday night with plans, to rush around to her girlfriend's house after she'd posted nothing more than 'No longer in a relationship'. By the time Holly got there, half a dozen other friends had also gathered and popcorn was popping in the kitchen.

That is sisterhood, or what my dear friend Kathryn Irvine described back in our university days as being 'female-identified'. Kathryn was big on this; that there were two kinds of women — those who in any given work or social situation would be looking to support and bond with the other women present, and those who were focused on impressing and engaging the men. It was (and still is) an interesting way of reading a room. Will a woman stop interacting with you when a man arrives? Or will she actively seek out the women who, like her, talk face-to-face. This isn't about not talking to men (heaven forefend!), but about the conversation being *social* rather than sexual. Try it: have a crack at working out which of your girlfriends is 'female-identified' — I bet they're your favourite ones. And have a little think about how you operate when you are being your best self, too. I think it is one of the reasons why girls do so well in all-girls schools: the conversation is about what the conversation is about, rather than being about winning the attention of men.

Kathryn gave me another piece of advice way back then — one of those bits of advice that is incredibly wise and which you wish you'd remembered *before* it became relevant, rather than in hindsight. So let me chuck it out there and see if you can do something better with it than I often did. In looking for a partner, the world likes to give you rules — the kind of rules that aren't written down but which we are all aware of, mostly because of the way the world looks on TV, at the movies and in magazines. Traditionally, a woman's partner is supposed to be four things: older, taller, richer, smarter. Additional requirements are usually that couples should be of matching race, religion and social background.

We know these things are generally required because we make a fuss when couples draw outside the lines in that picture of what a 'normal' relationship looks like. He's shorter than her: how embarrassingly unmanly he looks, and how masculine is she? He's younger than her: he's a toy boy and she's a cougar. She's smarter and earns more money than him: he's a failure and she's a ball-breaker. Look at them! Imagine them atop a wedding cake. Ew! The status is all wrong!

Kathryn would brook none of this traditionalist nonsense about choosing your relationships based on how things looked from the outside. Her advice on partnering up had nothing to do with height, age or any other kind of status. She simply said this: 'Look for someone who has fewer personal issues than you do.'

It is a useful idea to hold in your head. As much as women (and men) want to play Florence Nightingale (or rescue the damsel) and be so extraordinarily clever, kind and powerful that your love will be like a magic wand that heals and restores a broken thing, you are actually, in your romantic life, looking for *an equal*. Or as close to equal in neuroses and tricky-stuff-to-deal-with as you can find. As a very clever marriage guidance counsellor once said to me as I lay on her couch, writhing in agony with guilt and a sense of failure about being unable to save someone from himself: 'You're his wife, not his nurse.' Which is not to say that we shouldn't love and protect our One In Particular. But importantly this: that in that very beginning of a relationship when we get to choose who we will couple with, go for an equal rather than someone less well, and less together than you. Aiming for someone who actually has even *fewer* personal problems than you do is a good goal.

'LOOK FOR SOMEONE WHO HAS FEWER PERSONAL ISSUES THAN YOU DO.'

Kathryn also told me that once you lose respect for a partner, it is nigh on impossible to get it back. That sounds like a tough thing to say but, the older I get, the more I think she was right. One of the worst days you will have is the day you look at your partner and realise they are a douchebag. That's a really awkward moment. 'Oh no. He's a fuckwit. I didn't know.' You can't unrealise that shit.

Breakups, then, and cake and long walks and friends. That's another bit of Kathryn-wisdom. 'You can live without a lover, Michèle, but you can't ever live without friends.' Bloody good point. One of the worst punishments one human being can wreak on another is solitary confinement. We need to talk and touch and have company. But being single is totally okay — essential, even, as a moment to reset, find yourself again, and work out who you are and how you want to live. And always remember: if relationships didn't end, there would be no love songs or poetry, and all our movies would be one long stupid car chase.

Indulge in the delicious melancholy of heartbreak when you get the chance. I take a homeopathic approach and 'treat like with like' — a feast of heart-rending movies and achingly sad music. Tom Waits, Joni Mitchell, Leonard Cohen and Lucinda Williams provide excellent soundtracks to a breakup. When Holly was little and her parents were divorcing, while her friends were listening to the Wiggles in the car, she and I would be singing along to Alanis Morissette and Jewel on the kindy run. Less 'Dorothy the Dinosaur', more 'Jagged Little Pill'. Holly turned out just fine. By the time she was 13 we'd be shrieking along in two-part harmony to P!nk's 'Dear Mr

President' on the way home from her evening dance classes. Good times.

In the event of heartbreak emergency, note that you don't have to run with end-of-romance movies — anything miserable will do. For upliftingly tragic, I go for *Rent*, the 2005 movie based on the Broadway show about a bunch of friends dealing with love, life and death during the AIDS crisis. It stars a young Idina Menzel as Maureen — you will recognise her face from *Glee* where she played Lea Michele's biological mother, and her voice from playing Elsa in *Frozen*. Though my number-one pick for a weep-fest on a bad day is *Rabbit-Proof Fence*. I have to pause that one occasionally to let the sobbing die down. Sometimes it's nice to let the tears flow for someone else's tragedy rather than your own.

Weeping is awesome. I do it all the time. I have a theory that the world requires a certain volume of tears to keep the planet turning. Some people can't or won't cry, so people like me who sob at anything — our own pain, or our friends' pain, or the empathised pain of complete strangers — are doing it for them. Taking up the tear-slack out of a sense of social responsibility. You're all welcome. Pass us the tissues.

Yes to melancholy, then, but keep an eye on anger. Anger is useful fuel for spurring you forwards, but it requires a lot of fuel to feed itself and will eat up everything if you don't watch it. Being angry at someone who is no longer there is exhausting. It's like a blowfly banging around in a bottle — ugly and irritating, and no one ever wants to climb inside the bottle and hug it out with the blowfly, right? In the wise and immortal words of *Frozen*'s Queen Elsa: let it go.

ONE OF THE WORST DAYS
YOU WILL HAVE IS THE DAY
YOU LOOK AT YOUR PARTNER
AND REALISE THEY ARE
A DOUCHEBAG. THAT'S A
REALLY AWKWARD MOMENT.

Letting go is hard. But think of it this way: if someone has hurt you, you wouldn't give that person room in your house, right? So don't give them room in your head. They don't belong there, they're not welcome, they're not paying rent or helping out with the things that need to be done, so chuck them out. Put the idea of them in a pink bubble, release it, and watch it fly away until you can't see it any more. Sure, they'll keep popping back into your head but just don't invite them to stay.

IF SOMEONE HAS HURT YOU, YOU WOULDN'T GIVE THAT PERSON ROOM IN YOUR HOUSE, RIGHT? SO DON'T GIVE THEM ROOM IN YOUR HEAD.

Breakups are a whole different bottle of blowflies when there are children involved. Your life will forever be entwined with someone who is also your child's parent, so you can't quite so easily put them in a pink bubble and watch them float away. You will probably have to see them at Christmas. All I can say is that, sooner rather than later, it has got to stop being about the broken adult relationship and start being about each parent's relationship with the kid.

Outside of my close circle, I've never spoken about the specifics of the breakup with Holly's father. General stuff, sure, the stuff everyone feels and thinks about divorce which, in the context of a comedy club, makes for a good gag. Creative people are a bit lucky — songwriters, poets, comedians, painters, dancers and writers can channel anger and pain into our work. 'Anyone else been through a divorce?' I'd ask an audience, and there'd always be several hands in the air. (One-to-two, people, one-to-two.) 'Divorce is okay. Though obviously, it's better if they die. But you can't have everything the way you want it, right? Sometimes, people, you've got to make lemonade.' So yeah, I did some of that. But I don't talk about the specifics, because it is not really my story — it belongs to Holly's father as well, so the story is not mine to tell.

But I will say these things. In an ideal world, it is wonderful to have both parents living in the same house as the children. I've looked admiringly at those family constructs across the fence. And I've also looked wistfully at the divorced parents I know who share the parenting and find ways to have amicable, grown-up friendships with their ex-person. I reckon that could possibly be a yardstick by which you measure whether you should have kids with someone: can you imagine them, even if they no longer loved you, being responsible and polite anyway? Hard to guess (everyone is perfect when we first love them), but worth maybe asking yourself that question before you commit to a baby's crib.

Raising kids on your own is really hard — the hardest kind of parenting there is, and that's already a big job. But celebrating the solo mother isn't something we do that much. If we handed out a packet of crayons and some butcher's paper to the nation and asked people to draw a picture of a solo mum, we'd probably get several variations on a promiscuous trollop in track-pants, filthy with her own lack of ambition, smoking a fag and watching *Oprah* while her kids scoff instant noodles and run with scissors.

That's certainly the image our politicians rely on when beneficiary bashing is in season and there's a crackdown on entitlements that warns 'the dream is over' for anyone who thinks she can kick back and make babies instead of, you know, *doing something*. I've never met anyone whose dream was to *not* make a living or *not* find a life-partner, although I assume they must exist if only to justify the coining of the phrase 'lifestyle beneficiaries'. But I have met many good women who have had to make the hard choice — or had the choice made for them — to be the sole adult in their household.

So a little word of praise from me, who had childcare backup and emotional support from my own parents and, later, more support from a new partner: solo mothers do an amazing job. They make every decision alone — about what the rules are, when something is appropriate, what is acceptable behaviour, which school they go to, when is bedtime, whether broccoli matters — without either a sounding board or backup. When you're exhausted, you can't tag-team; there's no 'You sleep in on Saturday morning and I'll grab a nap in the afternoon.' The buck stops with you for energy, ideas, money, transport, discipline and for attending to scraped knees, middle-of-night sick-ups, bad dreams and sad hearts.

On Mother's Day, it is highly unlikely that your children's father will turn up with some fabulous gift for the kids to give you. You will take your kids to school on Monday and overhear reports about the great day 'the kids and their dad' put on for other mothers — a coffee machine or a necklace or a café brunch — and you'll have a crack at talking up the card your kid's teacher got them to make which is now in pride of place on your fridge.

I reckon the best gift we could give a solo mother is that, next time we need someone to vilify for being lazy and immoral, we skip the solo mums and instead get all pointy-fingered at the 65,000 non-custodial parents in New Zealand who either pay child support late or not at all. Currently, they owe $1.7 billion (yes, that's a 'b') to some of the 277,000 Kiwi kids whose absent fathers are supposed to contribute to their welfare. Imagine what a fine Mother's Day gift those kids could buy with just a tiny bit of whatever's left over from winter shoes and hot food.

Of course, men matter, too. And finding male role models to wave man-energy around the place is important. Holly always had a father for high-days and holidays, and a grandfather and stepfather for everyday use.

When my parents and I first moved into our combined houses when Holly was two years old, I remember looking out of my upstairs bedroom window on the day we shifted in, and seeing my father in the garden, pushing my daughter on the swing hanging from the puriri tree. The garden swing plus the jasmine growing by the front door were the two things that made me want to buy this house. Two thoughts tumbled into my head in that instant. The first was that I couldn't recall my father ever pushing me on a swing. The second was how wonderful it was that he could do that now with his granddaughter.

Born in the first year of the Great Depression, my father is of the generation that understood being a good father was about being a good provider, and he really was. He worked every hour God sent — at his business, around the home and in the community — and my brother and I, as the saying goes, wanted for nothing. He instilled in both of us an extraordinary work ethic, which means we both survive as freelancers and have never watched daytime TV.

Fatherhood is more complex now, less easily defined by traditional roles. We're all making it up as we go along and it's complicated — not only for the dads. But however you organise a household, I believe there are three things that make a home: jasmine, a swing and a lemon tree. My dad planted our lemon tree the first year we were here. During our first summer, my brother took a photo of Holly and me together on the swing. Framed, it has hung on the wall ever since.

I BELIEVE THERE ARE THREE THINGS THAT MAKE A HOME: JASMINE, A SWING AND A LEMON TREE.

Many years later, I caught a plane and gave the swing to my brother to hang in his garden for his own children. Stored for a time in the cupboard under our stairs, Dad had wrapped it carefully in polythene and labelled it *Holly's Swing From Puriri Tree*. Handing it to my brother with appropriate reverence, I suggested that if he wanted to maintain its value he should keep it in the original packaging. Always the wittier of us two, he declared he'd be taking it straight to Te Papa. Later, he sent a photo of his little girl on our swing. Whatever fatherhood means now, it is nicely traced in the arc of that image.

Anyone who tells you that it's easy to be a family and celebrate its ordinary milestones after a divorce is telling you big fat lies. There has been all that fragmenting — which feels more like tearing — as parents scatter, then the blending as they re-couple. Christmas, birthdays and funerals are scenes rife with subtext and minor plotlines involving the kind of complex dynamics you've never seen in any episode of *The Brady Bunch*. Family dramas not suitable for family viewing. Like I say, we're all making it up as we go along.

But I can tell you at least one joyful story from our lives about a wider family finding a way to come back together. It happened for Holly and me at her twenty-first birthday, which took place while I was writing this book. And it was all down to the women.

The years before and after the divorce from Holly's father were pretty dark times for all of us, which left a lot of wounds which were never resolved. You'd try to let the blowfly out of the bottle, but then someone would deliver a new bottle with a new fly. It is not always this fraught for everyone, but it's rarely, for anyone, a jolly sitcom.

Holly, always brilliant at organising a party, took charge of most of the arrangements and invitations for her twenty-first — her A'Court family, her paternal whanau, her stepfather's parents, her partner's whanau, and lots of friends. We hired a downtown bar. We knew the day before that her father wasn't coming because of a mix-up with dates and other commitments. To be entirely honest, there was relief in some quarters. But not in hers and mine. Over the years, I really have been able to stop thinking of him as my ex-husband, and place him in the world simply as her dad. And a girl needs her dad.

So, at the beginning of the party that night we had a room full of much-loved friends and family, with a piece missing. And then they arrived. Two of her aunties and six cousins with gifts and giggles, sent under orders from her paternal grandmother to represent the whanau from down the line in Te Puna. 'You have to be there,' Nanny Kitty had said that morning to some of the women. And so they came.

We used to party once, all of us. Share each other's homes. Sing and tell stories. Then the divorce happened, and no one really knew if anyone wanted to see each other. Except that I'd had an amazing visit with Holly to Kitty's place a couple of years before this, which had fixed a lot of things for me — for both of us, I think. But suddenly, in that moment when all those women walked through the door at Holly's twenty-first, things went from complicated to simple again. We partied so hard that all the photos of that night are slightly blurred.

Not just the aunties and cousins came, but her dad's new family — my daughter's stepmother and stepsister made the journey, too. We made speeches. I acknowledged where my daughter comes from — my family, her dad's family (and cried a bit), and the life she is making now with her partner's family (and I cried a bit more). We had waiata and haka. The haka was spine-tingling, the aunties' waiata was heart-warming. Our friends were all funny and kind.

And then there was this crazy moment when, on behalf of the Te Puna whanau, my ex-husband's partner, Sarah, presented me with a carving to give to my daughter. A special piece of art passed from woman to woman to woman. And right then, something was healed.

WE PARTIED SO HARD THAT ALL THE PHOTOS OF THAT NIGHT ARE SLIGHTLY BLURRED.

So celebrating family after divorce isn't easy. But it is possible. Even if it takes years; until someone turns twenty-one.

Just a few weeks later, Holly's paternal grandmother, Nanny Kitty — Kiritapu Wilson, née Borell — passed away. We were all there. All 11 of Kitty's children were in the room with her when she died. Holly and I were amongst the last to see her before she left us. Holly's father made sure of that — inviting us down to Te Puna, finding a place for us to stay, and being very kind. When I left the tangi, I thanked him for all the good things he'd done over those days. I told him I couldn't think of anything to be angry with him about any more. He assured me he would probably screw up again at some point. I told him I had no doubt of it. His partner, Sarah, was laughing so hard she had to turn away.

I've felt lighter ever since. Like I said, being angry is exhausting. And now I am humming that song from *Frozen* again.

CHAPTER 18

WORK — MOUNTAINS AND ELEPHANTS

When Holly was a great big kindy girl, she also started going to music classes with the Kids Music Company (KMC). This wasn't piano lessons with a scary lady and her knuckle-whacking ruler, but a delightfully holistic approach to music and movement where the kids learned to feel rhythm in their bodies, run around, sing songs and bash a glockenspiel. KMC's style of learning is, of course, a whole lot more sophisticated than that, but, importantly, the kids experience it as 'fun' and 'play' and then eventually discover they've accidentally learned to read music and play a whole range of instruments.

Holly kept going to KMC for years, singing in the choir at public performances, being part of summer holiday productions, and recording two studio CDs, until eventually she was a teenager and too old to go any more. Over all those years, I waited for the day when I would have to cajole her into attending the after-school classes but that day never came. On a morning when she didn't want to go to school, I'd tell her that if she didn't, she couldn't go to KMC in the afternoon. As a bribe it almost always worked, and when it didn't I knew she must genuinely be at death's door and it was probably time to rush her to A&E and have her put on some kind of drip. She loved her music classes with a passion.

Classes for the younger ones always ended with a rhythmic little ditty sung in a circle that went: 'It's time to say goodbye (boom boom); it's time to say goodbye (boom boom); we've had a lovely time and it's time to say goodbye.' Holly misheard it the first time and from then on always sang, 'fluffy' instead of 'lovely'. 'Fluffy' was as delightful a concept to her as 'lovely' is to most other people. We still sing 'we've had a fluffy time' at the end of a good day.

THIS WAS HER TRUE, EXACT SELF — HAPPY, INVOLVED, ENTIRELY PRESENT.

Quite often I'd stay and watch for the whole class. I remember in the very early days seeing her sitting at a big wooden xylophone, listening intently as the group played a piece of music, feeling the rhythm, knowing exactly what to play and when to play it, totally absorbed in the moment. She looked, I recall thinking, exactly like *her*. This was her true, exact self — happy, involved, entirely present. Her face was arranged in its own perfect way. This is who she is, I thought, and this is what she looks like. And then the song finished and she looked over at me as though she was waking up, and beamed.

There was Holly, being her exact self. I recognised the look because I had seen it on her before when she was less than a year old — old enough to sit up independently but not yet walking. A bit of Deep Forest's world music was on the stereo (I think I've mentioned mama is a bohemian, right?) and she was grooving along happily, absorbed in the moment. There she is, I thought, that's Holly. That's the person this baby is going to be all her life.

So I've always known when she was doing the right thing for herself. You can see it on her face when she's dancing on stage, or just hanging with her friends, or intent on any kind of project that makes her happy. This is the face you don't see when you ask her to empty the dishwasher.

You can recognise that in your kid because you know what it feels like yourself. When people ask me why I do what I do for a job, the best way I can answer is this. When I am standing on stage, making people laugh and also making them think, that's when I feel the most like *myself*. That's when I feel like I am properly being me. So on stage, then, and also when I am sitting in my office in my pyjamas, writing. Arranging words in a new and interesting order that captures and gives shape to the jumble of ideas in my head. These are my two favourite places, because that's where I am *me*.

I reckon if you are lucky enough to find a place or two that feel like that for you, you should try to arrange your life as much as possible so that you can be there as often as you can. And if you can make a living out of being in that place, you are one of the luckiest people on Earth. Which will all sound a bit heady and esoteric, perhaps. But I've seen it on the faces of piano tuners and plumbers, and I can imagine it happening to an accountant pouring over a quality spreadsheet or a road worker pouring a first-rate bit of bitumen. We spend at least one-third of our adult lives working, so it might as well be fun and absorbing and satisfying and match who we are — or at least not make us want to scream and punch things, and run very fast in the other direction.

This is not to say there has been any grand plan to how I make a living and pay the bills. I've shied away from any invitations to give 'motivational' talks to anyone, partly because most motivational speakers I've heard sound like wankers, and I find it hard to relate to people who were born without any actual arms and legs but manage to climb actual mountains. It's not the disability I can't relate to, it's the climbing. I'm never sure how to translate all that scroggin and high-altitude training into something that would work for me. If you ask me what motivates me to get out of bed in the morning and get my shit done, I will tell you it is mostly hunger and fear. If I don't work, I don't eat (I'm a freelancer), and I'm scared of being homeless and/or starving to death. Ergo, I bounce out of bed most mornings and Get The Fuck On With It.

To be honest, I'm not even much of a goal-setter. Mostly, I'd describe my professional life as 'organic', a series of small choices which lead to other choices which occasionally end up in a perfect moment where you think, 'Okay, yes, this is exactly where I wanted to be.'

It would be unwise to share what I am about to say with any prospective or actual employer or co-workers. Let's keep this as a secret just between us. Here's the thing: at work, many of us are faking it. By this I don't mean that we're not doing any work. Though sometimes, that too. We all have days at the office that are the equivalent of leaning on a shovel. Back when I had a job–job in the 1980s, I perfected my skills at 'doing nothing' for a day here and there. I found that if you wander the building looking purposeful while carrying a file and a pen, people will automatically assume you are either on your way to a meeting, or on the way back from a meeting. This won't fly forever if you have the kind of job that requires things to be completed at some point, but it can cover the odd day now and then when you're feeling a bit off because of the flu or tequila.

What I mean when I say we are faking it is that pretty often we are all pretending that we know what we are doing, when, in reality, we have no idea. There are a lot of people gainfully employed who may look like gliding swans but who are frantically paddling with their little webbed feet just beneath the surface, desperately trying to maintain the illusion of forward momentum. Understand? Just nod confidently. There. You're catching on.

THERE ARE A LOT OF PEOPLE GAINFULLY EMPLOYED WHO MAY LOOK LIKE GLIDING SWANS BUT WHO ARE FRANTICALLY PADDLING WITH THEIR LITTLE WEBBED FEET JUST BENEATH THE SURFACE.

Let me tell you about my work philosophy. In my first year of college I read my way through the entire New Zealand Fiction section of my high school library. That's right, both books. Well done, me. One of those two books was Barry Crump's *A Good Keen Man*, the classic coming-of-age tale by the consummate Kiwi philosopher. In it, the lead character is given this sage advice: 'Never tell anyone that you don't know how to do something. By the time they've worked out you didn't know how to do it, you will have worked out how to do it.' I wrote it down and learned it off by heart, that's how much it resonated with me. I have since based my whole career on this.

I read an interview years ago with Estelle Getty, who played Sophia, the octogenarian mother in the 1980s sitcom *Golden Girls*. In reality, Getty was only 62 years old, and just one year older than Bea Arthur who played her daughter when she was cast in the TV show — but, what the hey, this was Getty's big break. It had arrived after 40 years of struggling to find work as a theatre actor and comedian. An Emmy, a Golden Globe and years of stardom followed in the wake of the popular sitcom's success. Yet in this interview, Getty admitted her great fear was that one day someone would walk up to her on set and whisper, 'Excuse me, Miss Getty. I'm so sorry — we thought you were talented, but we've just realised we made a terrible mistake. You have to go.'

You see my point? No one else knows what they are doing either. Everybody carry on.

I have what I like to refer to as 'a portfolio career', which, if you flick through it, features a whole lot of bits and pieces that add up to something that covers the mortgage and buys plane tickets and shoes. I will cheerfully admit to being a comedian, writer, social commentator, voice artist, corporate entertainer, an occasional theatre and TV actor, and a frequent teller of jokes while holding a microphone in pubs.

Sometimes when someone asks 'What do you do?', the potential correct answers are so various that my synapses fuse and I dribble a bit out of the side of my mouth. But I worked out a catch-all term for it a couple of years ago. Jeremy and I spent some time in the mountains of Papua New Guinea with people who hadn't seen white folk for many years. We travelled there as ambassadors for Fairtrade NZ to find out how coffee was grown and get first-hand experience of the good things an organisation like Fairtrade can do to ensure growers get a fair share of the price we pay for latte. In each village we'd be introduced to the locals by our guide and translator, Michael Toliman, one of their few English-speakers. Pressed by him for a way of describing what I did for a job, I suddenly hit on 'storyteller'. It still delights me that I've found one word that pretty much covers all the disparate ways I spend my day.

Still, when I look through that list of 'stuff I do most days' it is fair to say that I didn't know how to do any of these jobs until I started doing them. I've had no specific training to do anything except write a hard-news story, which is the one thing I don't ever do. But in lieu of any formal preparation, I reckon along the way I've worked out some useful tools for getting by that might be useful to share.

10 tools for getting by

1. Ask for help.
This is different from admitting you don't know how to do something. It is admitting that someone else might know different and better ways of doing something. People love it when you ask for help. It acknowledges that they have skills and expertise and, since you put it like that, they're happy to share.

2. Put a value on yourself.
Work out what other people get paid for doing the kind of thing you do, and make sure you get at least that much, too. Not just for your own sake, but also so you are not undercutting them and their work. If someone else is getting $25 an hour for babysitting, for example, and you turn up and ask for $15, sure, you'll get the work because you're cheap, but suddenly babysitting isn't as valuable any more. And if you can get *more* than $25 per hour, go for it. Your friends will be cool if you single-handedly increase everyone's hourly babysitting rate by being confident about what taking care of someone else's little darlings is worth.

3. Know what you are good at.
When Holly was babysitting, she was awesome at amusing kids, making them feel safe and special, reading stories with gusto, and soothing them to sleep. If that's what people were after, she was their guy. If they wanted cordon bleu meals prepared and ovens cleaned, maybe they should call Sharon.

4. (related point) Know what you are not good at.

Lower everyone's expectations on how well you will do those things. 'Sure, I can babysit on Friday. Will you be ordering the pizza, or shall I do that when I get there?' And in the wider world, when you know what you're *not* good at, you can surround yourself with other people who are. I can't set up a sound-system, for example, so I make sure I work with comedians who can. I can write a show, but I can't for the life of me design a poster because I'm not a 'visual' person. But I know a dude who is. So I give him some money and he does that bit. Also see Chapter 3 on 'How to Store Ginger' and my cunning plan of living with a man who finds cooking 'relaxing'.

5. Eat elephants a teaspoon at a time.

No matter how much you love what you do, sometimes work feels insurmountable and exhausting. A particularly big project will seem like a metaphorical mountain that you need to metaphorically climb, and you will end up wishing I'd listened harder to that dude who packed scroggin and I was therefore in a position to pass on his advice. But rather than a mountain, I like to visualise work as an elephant. An elephant that I have to eat. No, really, this is a useful image. There's this massive elephant so big you can't really see where it begins and ends, and it is your job to consume the whole thing. And you know how to eat an elephant? One teaspoonful at a time. That's how I picture the big jobs. I pick up my teaspoon and start eating. It is pretty slow-going at first, but before you know it the trunk's gone and you're passed the ears and then you're running out of elephant and you have to look around for another one because you're nearly hungry again. Honest.

6. In the beginning, say yes to everything.
I can't tell you how many hideous gigs I did in my early years at public bars in industrial areas where I was totally the wrong comedian in completely the wrong room. But it paid for that week's groceries, and toughened me up no end. It's where I learned to swear really well, an admirable skill which I have been trying to unlearn ever since, with limited success. You learn at least as much from your failures as your successes, and the best person you can surprise with a previously unknown skill is yourself. Also, one of the truly great things about being young or new is that sometimes you succeed because you don't yet know how easy it is to fail. That's a really special time in your life — do great things with it.

7. When you let someone down — particularly an employer — limit how much you tell them about the reasons for your failure.
Long stories about cats or funerals or upset tummies or flat tyres aren't entirely helpful, except to give a general sense that you know it was important to do the thing, and you feel bad that you didn't do it. Your boss doesn't really want to know about your personal life. They mostly want to know when you'll get the thing done, and whether they can trust you to do the next thing. Encourage them to picture you as a generally competent person whose life is usually under control except for in this instance. It is better if they don't start thinking of you as living a life that makes *Breaking Bad* look uneventful and chilled out.

8. Always remember what drives you to do what you do.

And be pleased that you get to do it. It's easy to get blasé about work, to approach it with cool hipster reluctance, or to genuinely wish you were somewhere else. Years ago, I noticed I'd be standing side-of-stage, waiting to go on, and I'd be wishing I could just go home and do the ironing. I was appalled at myself for thinking that — this is what I'd wanted! This is what I'd grown up wanting to be allowed to do! So best I put my game-face on and have a bloody good time. I know now that the best gigs, the ones that really fly, are the ones when I cannot *wait* to have my turn at the microphone. So I look for that thrill when it comes bubbling up and embrace it. I've talked about this with midwives and nurses, and teachers and engineers and lawyers and architects. Everyone who chose their job chose it for some really good reasons. Now and then, we need to remind ourselves what those reasons were and let ourselves *feel* them again.

9. You have to really want it, whatever it is.

At the Laugh Factory, the comedy club in Las Vegas, they have a fabulous Green Room — the place where comics hang out before they hit the stage. The walls are covered with framed photographs of the great and good who have played there; there are fridges full of booze, a big TV, a monitor that shows what's happening on stage inside the club, and bags and bowls of sugary and salty snacks. There are squishy couches and armchairs, and you can bring a friend and lounge around, swap war stories, and generally feel good about the business you're in. It's comfortable, quiet, safe and welcoming.

I LIKE TO VISUALISE WORK AS AN ELEPHANT. AN ELEPHANT THAT I HAVE TO EAT. AND YOU KNOW HOW TO EAT AN ELEPHANT? ONE TEASPOONFUL AT A TIME.

Then when you're ready, before it's your time to walk out on stage, you go down the hall to another room. This room is small, with nothing in it but a bench and an empty beer fridge. There isn't even a chair. The walls are hard yellow and as empty as the fridge, except for a mirror along one side and a poster featuring all the species of sharks on the other. You wait there until it's your turn to push through the curtain at the back of this room and walk straight out onto the stage.

THERE IS ONE THING SCARIER ON THIS PLANET THAN WALKING OUT IN FRONT OF A ROOM FULL OF STRANGERS TO TRY TO MAKE THEM LAUGH. AND THAT'S A SHARK.

You are in this room alone. It is too close to the stage to allow any kind of conversation so it's just a holding space for the next comic on. The week I played there, two shows a night, I was MC so I spent a lot of time in that room — pre-show, and then while each of the other two acts were on as I waited to hear them end. I spent a long time looking at that poster of the sharks. There was nothing else to look at except my own face in the mirror, or the empty fridge. I thought a lot about why someone might put a poster of sharks on that wall. On my third night it dawned on me. That poster was there to remind every comic that there is one thing scarier on this planet than walking out in front of a room full of strangers to try to make them laugh. And that's a shark.

I might be wrong. I didn't ever ask Harry, the manager, if that's why it was there. But it certainly seemed that way to me. A way of reminding you that, to walk through that curtain and on to the stage, you really have to want it.

Which brings us to Lesson Number ...

10. Be fearless.

Don't play it safe or find excuses to not take the risk. Understand that scary things are good for you. In my experience, each scary thing you do makes every slightly less scary thing much, much easier. After a week in Las Vegas, a gig in Hamilton or Brisbane feels like a piece of piss. Embrace those big, scary opportunities and don't ever find a reason to go home and do the ironing. There is a comic I don't like very much, but he said a good and useful thing to me years ago. He said to imagine the kind of comedian you want to be one day. And then decide to be that comic right now, on this night, at this show. That works for other kinds of jobs, too. One day you want to be a great and inspiring teacher? Be her today. Don't wait for later.

And thinking about him reminds me of a Bonus Lesson:

11. Be kind.

There are people I admire because they are good comics, and there are people I admire because they are wonderful to be with. Not everyone is both those things. There are some terrific comedians out there who are arseholes. And there are some gorgeous people who are a bit hit-and-miss on stage. I've learnt over the years that if we have to choose — or get to choose — who we will work with, we would all rather work with a good and kind person than a great talent who is a dick and messes with your head in the Green Room. I reckon that translates to other workplaces, too. Knowing your craft is important, but being a nice person to be around matters, too.

So those are some things for you to bring to your workplace. Your place of work has some responsibilities to you, too. There's an old saying I like that goes something like: 'If you want someone to do a good job, give them a good job to do.' What makes a good job isn't always about the task. We're social creatures and we want to feel welcomed and included, with access to all the people, and access to all the knowledge.

KNOWING YOUR CRAFT IS IMPORTANT, BUT BEING A NICE PERSON TO BE AROUND MATTERS, TOO.

Every corporate gig I do — turning up to MC someone's awards evening or conference, or be their after-dinner entertainer — is pretty much like turning up for the first day of school. They all know each other; I'm the new kid. The very best gigs are always the ones where someone — *anyone* — seems pleased to see me. It's not always like that, which seems weird. They've picked you from a line-up and booked you for some reason, but they can still make you feel like a very small, unimportant cog in their mysterious machine. Plus, people say dicky things that can throw you off your game. I keep a list of dicky things people have said to me in the back of my comedy notebook under the heading: *Things Not To Say To Me When I Arrive To Do Your Gig.* Writing them down makes me feel better about it at the time – it's my way of owning that kind of shit. Here's a sample.

From the guy who picks you up at the airport: 'They said you're some kind of celebrity. I've never heard of you.'

Alternatively: 'You're shorter than I expected. And more ordinary-looking.'

On the drive to the venue from the airport: 'It's all ruined round here, mate. Too many Maoris.'

At the venue: 'We really wanted [insert name of dude who plays rugby], but he was too expensive.'

During dinner: 'I hate to say it, but women have wrecked our industry.'

Just before you go on stage: 'The guy we had last year was awesome. It'll be impossible to beat that.'

All of which motivates you to prove yourself and do a great job. But also makes it a little harder to do a great job. Like I say, my best and favourite gigs always turn out to be the ones where someone — *anyone* — says, 'Yay, we're really excited to have you here!'

My mother said something wonderful to me many years ago when I was all frocked up to head off for a corporate gig and feeling incredibly anxious about how it might go. 'Just remember,' she said, 'they're very lucky to have you.' It was a very 'mum' thing to say, but I still let it play in my head each time and try to believe that it's true. Because the better I feel about what I'm about to do, the better it goes, and the better time everyone has. I'm thinking that goes for everyone in every business. 'The kids are so excited that you're coming to babysit,' augurs for a good night. While 'Sharon couldn't make it — she's so popular! The kids are a bit disappointed,' isn't anything like the same.

So find the place that makes you feel like you, the very best version of you. Then pick your elephant, grab your teaspoon, give the sharks a rueful nod, and chow down. Risk failure, and celebrate every success.

Want to know what success is? And this is true whether you are 15 or 50. Success is exceeding your parents' expectations. Do that and you will be fine. And here's a little secret: it's not really that hard, because, right at the heart of it, what your parents want is for you to be happy. Be that.

CHAPTER 19

MONEY

Money is awesome. Make sure you have some.

I heard someone explain once why people buy books. They said when people buy a book, they are not just buying *that book*, they are also visualising that they are *buying the time to read it*. So when you hold that thing in your hand you are not only anticipating the story between the covers, you are picturing the kind of life that allows space for you to lie about and read. Those unread volumes on your shelves represent a glorious future moment when you will spend time with them.

Money is a lot like a book, then. It represents choice and opportunity, the chance to make a good life better, or escape from a life that has become a bit shit. Having some money stashed away in a savings account that you can't easily access with your eftpos card is tremendously good for your mental health. It's your Plan B, your 'running home to Mum' option if everything turns to custard. Occasionally in my life when I've thought I was anxious or depressed, I've thought that through and realised I was just broke. Hiding some money from myself in a savings account is tremendously calming. It's not my only tool for dealing with anxiety, but it's the first shovel I look for in the shed when I need to reassure myself that I could dig my way out of a dark hole if I needed to.

THAT'S WHAT SAVINGS DO. THEY SAVE YOU.

Picture yourself in this scenario. Let's say it's a Wednesday. Wednesday is often a miserable day — as far away as you can get from weekend memories on the one hand, and from weekend anticipation on the other. On top of this, your boss regrets to inform you that her company is restructuring and gives you a month's notice; your best friend tells you she is heading off to backpack around Europe for a year; your boyfriend shaves off his hipster beard and you see for the first time that he doesn't have a chin; your car fails its warrant of fitness; your dad phones to say your mum is not well; and your landlord wants his flat back so he can give it to his daughter and her friends. That's a shitty day, right? Jobless, homeless, friendless, romantically frustrated, and feeling a long way from home. Now imagine that you have $3000 stashed away in a savings account. That's still a shitty day, but you have options, right? A ticket home, or a ticket to Europe, a new car, or the breathing space to find a new flat and a job while your boyfriend grows his beard back. Did you feel your anxiety levels decrease? Maybe even a little excitement grow as you consider new choices? That's what savings do. They save you.

So I squirrel money away as often as I can and pretend it doesn't exist, and never count it as something I can spend on pretty, sparkly things that catch my eye. Because as well as being a pretty good 'rainy day' saver — learned the hard way from weathering the odd financial storm — I am also a passionate shopper. I love buying stuff from shops. Or even just looking at stuff in shops. Shopping is, for me, equal parts thrilling and soothing. It's a distraction from a tough day, or the celebration of a good day; a way to feel grown-up and in control, or indulge myself like I'm my own small child being treated for being good.

I am oddly fascinated by spreadsheets in particular, and economic theory in general. As someone who spends a great deal of her life walking into a room full of strangers and guessing what they will find amusing, I find columns of figures with correct answers at the bottom which match other numbers along the side tremendously comforting. Every two months I prepare spreadsheets of my income and expenditure for my accountant. The glory of taking a number (*a*), then adding 15% GST to it (to calculate *b*), then multiplying *b* by 23 and dividing it by 3 (*c*), and then subtracting that amount (*c*) from the second number (*b*) to miraculously reveal the number I first started with (*a*) never fails to entertain me. Maths is magic.

Stand-up comedy and writing might be the things I do to earn a living, but economics is my passion. Some of you may already know this — it is public knowledge and not a secret — but I won the Economics Prize in the Sixth Form (Year 12 in new-speak) in 19-mumble. Given my expertise in the field, then, let me explain my own version of economic theory. Let's do that anecdotally, with a little anecdote about shoes.

Let's pretend that today I went out shopping and saw a pair of shoes that I liked very much. We'll say they were pink and red. Now, I know what you're thinking. You're thinking: 'Pink and red? Sounds hideous.' But trust me, they were adorable. It worked in these particular shoes. And they had that perfect heel, the one that is high enough to make your calves look good but is not yet so high that at the end of the night it feels like the ball of your foot is on fire, and not so high that you are likely to fall off them after a couple of margaritas. These pink and red shoes were $360. Again, I know what you're thinking. You're thinking: 'Three hundred and sixty dollars? Bargain!' Agreed. Also, can I make it really clear: we're talking $360 for the pair, that's not per shoe. I don't know how they make them at that price. Hard to imagine. The margins involved must be tiny.

'HANG ON, LET'S DO THAT "COOLING OFF" THING I OFTEN DO WHEN BUYING EXTRAVAGANT THINGS.' THAT IS, LEAVE THE SHOP, GO FOR A LITTLE WALK, AND SEE IF I STILL REALLY WANT THEM. PEOPLE SHOULD USE THIS SAME TECHNIQUE ON DATES.

Anyhoo, let's say I was about to buy these fabulous pink and red shoes and then I thought, 'Hang on, let's just wait a minute. Let's do that "cooling off" thing I often do when buying extravagant things.' That is, leave the shop, go for a little walk, maybe grab a coffee, and then see if I still really want them. It's a great technique to take you out of the moment and assess your genuine passion for wanting to take something home. People should use this same technique on dates. So I wandered down the street, and suddenly found myself in a different shop. A much cheaper shoe shop — I won't bore you with what it was called, but it rhymed with 'Number One Shoe Warehouse' — where I bought two pairs of shoes for $30 each. One pair of pink, one pair of red. For some reason, that felt right.

So let's recap. I *didn't* buy the expensive pink and red shoes for $360, but I *did* spend $60. So I saved $300 just like that. Cash money, in my pocket. The beauty of this is that tomorrow, I can go back to the expensive shoe shop and buy the pink and red shoes for $360 but they will only really cost me $60 because I saved $300 this morning. Who's coming with me? Meet you at 10am for a coffee.

Shoppers like me can do this all day. I know a woman who grabs a cheap flight now and then to Sydney and does the end-of-season sales. By the time she has calculated how much she has saved on her airfare, and on her discounted purchases, she reckons the whole trip is fiscally neutral. And I've been known to receive a Goody Bag (we all love free stuff) at an event, filled with things I didn't want and don't need, calculate its retail value, and then go out and spend that amount on the kind of things I actually do want and need, and trick myself into believing I got it all for free because I didn't have to pay for the other stuff. That's how to run an economy, people.

Or possibly not. *Actual* economists (who may or may not have won their Sixth Form Economics Prize — they very rarely say) espouse much more rational theories. Often they emphasise the priority of paying off debt even before you start squirrelling away savings, because the interest you have to pay on debt is always more than the interest you'll be given on your savings. I've taken that on board in recent years and now make a habit of paying off my credit card every month before the bank gets a chance to charge me any interest at all. Which makes it free money, right? I'm pretty sure that's a fair way to view it. In which case … Shoes.

'Debt' used to be a dirty word. My grandparents didn't borrow money at all. My parents only borrowed money to buy a house. My generation only borrowed money to buy a house and a car. Okay, and maybe a fridge. But since Holly's stepfather went to university, we've arranged our economy so that our best and brightest begin their working lives already thousands of dollars behind the eight-ball with student debt. Which has made being in debt — spending money you don't yet have — acceptable and normal. Ergo, flat-screen TVs, smartphones on tick, instant gratification rather than delaying the moment of purchase until you have, you know, the money. I'm very sorry about that. I think we screwed up on your behalf by not keeping your education free through continuing to ask each generation to pay for the one coming after it through their taxes. Our bad.

You see, back in my day (cue wistful music under sepia-toned reminiscence) we assumed that our best and brightest young minds went off to university to learn. These days, the new ideology is that you go to university to get a job. These aren't mutually exclusive goals — a higher education may well lead to better job prospects. But also, it may not. A profound appreciation of the Lake Poets or Cubism might give you a rich interior life, but have little impact on your post-graduate employment. And I seriously, deeply, passionately don't believe that matters. I simply want to know that I live in a society where someone knows something about literature and art history, even if they don't use it nine-to-five, and even if it's not me.

More and more, the funding of universities is based not on how many students want to study, or on their academic outcomes, but on how many of the previous year's students found work as a result of their qualification. I hate that idea. There's something Sir Ed Hillary said in a television interview not long before he died: 'We must take time to read and dream.' This gets harder to do when you have a job and kids. As grown-ups, we grab our Big Thinking Moments when we can — while we're waiting for the traffic lights to change, or to fall asleep at night, or while lying on the osteopath's table getting our shoulders unknotted, God help us.

But when you are a student — no longer 'the child' and not yet 'the adult with complex responsibilities' — that's pretty much what your life is all about. Reading, dreaming, engaging with your community and the world, and finding your place in it, breaking hearts and having your heart broken, taking on the impossible while you still think it is possible, risking failure, failing, and learning to celebrate every success. None of which is covered in any course outline or earns a grade or ticks a box on a job application, sadly. Since the advent of student loans, we have already condemned two generations of students to believing that living in debt is acceptable. It would be pretty sad if we condemned the next generations to not climbing mountains either.

To cheer myself up about all this indebtedness, I quite like to read my credit-card bill as though I was in an English Lit class rather than in Economics. Ignore the numbers for a moment and look at the individual items as though they were journal entries: 'Oh, I remember that dinner — the fish was superb!' or 'The silk blouse — I must give it another wear!' or 'That much for a bottle of wine! I am tickled that I once thought I could afford that!' Also, I am often comforted by the wise words of American comedian Maria Bamford, whom I once worked with at the Adelaide Festival and who stars these days in Louis CK's almost-eponymous sitcom *Louie*. (Yeah, I'm not sure either. Best guess is it is Louis's way of saying that *Louie* is a comedy-based-in-reality, but not a documentary.) Maria has some brilliant gags, and one of my favourites is this one: 'I'm rich. By which I mean I own a lot of stuff I don't need.' Most of us have a bunch of junk around the house that, according to Ms Bamford, defines us as supremely well-to-do.

I understand being broke — paralysingly poor and hungry with no immediate change, loose or otherwise, in sight. As a brief moment in your larger history, this can be good for you: anyone who has ever been really poor puts things in place to keep that ugly wolf from ever approaching the door again. As well as my squirrelled and largely inaccessible rainy-day account, I make it a rule to always have the pantry stocked with sufficient baked beans for a week. And one tin of smoked oysters, for my soul.

When you are feeling a bit miserable, on the back of the envelope your credit-card bill came in you can write down your responses to this 'Are you loaded?' litmus test. You are rich if you own books you haven't even read yet, and some you might read again if there's ever time. If, in your music collection, you have stuff that takes you back to a special time in your life, another album you are still getting to know, and a song that always makes you cry. You are rich if you have enough clothes that make you feel good to wear for a week without doing the laundry. And more wine than you and your favourite people could drink in one high-spirited night. And you are rich if you know that, worst-case scenario, you have friends who would rally around; and that — boot on the other foot — you could afford to take in a friend and cheerfully give them houseroom if they needed it.

Everyone should own one good coat and one really good pair of shoes. That's clearly the kind of advice that might have been given at any point in the past few hundred years — it's probably what a young Blue Stocking was told by her mama — and it still holds true. A good coat because being cold is awful, plus as a first impression it does wonders, covering up as it does whatever else you threw on that day. A properly good coat is as close to an 'investment' as you can get without being able to stick it on your expenditure spreadsheet and claim it off your tax. It will 'see you out' as my grandmother used to say of things that might last longer than she would. Indeed, I lived for many winters inside the coats my grandmother and Great-aunt Ruth saved up for, and two of them still hang in the spare-bedroom wardrobe. They kept me warm through my university years, and occasionally doubled as extra duvets whenever I lived in particularly damp, sunless, manky student flats. So we have a fine tradition in our family of buying 'a good coat' and passing

I QUITE LIKE TO READ MY CREDIT CARD BILL AS THOUGH I WAS IN AN ENGLISH LIT CLASS RATHER THAN IN ECONOMICS. 'THAT MUCH FOR A BOTTLE OF WINE! I AM TICKLED THAT I ONCE THOUGHT I COULD AFFORD THAT!'

it down the line. A few years ago I realised I had been so reliant on Other People's Coats that I had never bought one of my own, so, in my forties and not broke, I bought a fancy lambskin thing that cost about as much as my first car. It's as warm as wearing a car with the AC on, too. It has travelled with me to icy mountains in Queenstown and snow-covered cities in Europe, and experienced a white Christmas in Canada. One day I will dry-clean it and pass it on to Holly if she fancies it. The important thing is that I can.

And when I say 'good shoes' I don't mean the pink and red ones. I mean you should own the best quality pair of shoes you can afford, for everyday use, the kind you can stomp around in all day. Spend as little as possible on the party shoes if you have to, but as much as you can on the everyday. I don't know if you've seen bunions. Or felt corns. Google them. And then save up for something well-made that breathes and won't be mean to your feet.

I FIND IT ALMOST IMPOSSIBLE TO BE SAD WHILE WEARING RED SHOES.

Although you should also have one pair of red shoes. I find it almost impossible to be sad while wearing red shoes. They also cheer other people up when they see you wearing them. Think of it as your social responsibility to spread a little joy. They don't have to sparkle like Dorothy's, and you can't expect them to take you home to Kansas, but they'll do wonderful things for the spirit. I had a flatmate years ago, Barbara, whose theory was that people can't be angry with you when you wear red. This was back in that Wellington flat when I was doing a lot of hand-washing. Barbara made it a thing to always wear red clothes when she had her period — not for any ease-of-laundering reasons, but because she always felt a bit fragile when she had the painters in, so wearing a red dress was her way of shielding herself from other people's negativity. She described it as being 'in sympathy' with herself when it was arts and crafts week at panty-camp. My other flatmate, Fee, and I adopted the same practice ourselves, until we noticed, as inevitably happens when women live together, that our cycles were in synch. Every 28 days we looked like we were playing for the same team.

I'm never entirely sure it was a great idea for Mother Nature to design women to bleed collectively. I see her point: in ancient times, apparently, it was an opportunity for women to gather together in the Red Tent to chat and giggle and feed each other dates and generally have some well-earned time out from cooking for the tribe's hunters and otherwise tending to their needs. It was full-on lady-time. We don't get to do that any more, sadly. And a houseful of women with PMS can be a dangerous place, as edgy as a restaurant kitchen full of burning flames, blistering steam and viciously sharp knives wielded by a team of temperamental potty-mouthed chefs on crack. But eventually, we'd all get up one morning and put on our red frocks and meet in the kitchen for a cup of raspberry-leaf tea (excellent for cramps) and look at each other and go, 'Oh God, sorry — that's why we were all bitches. We were so pre-menstrual, we forgot we were pre-menstrual! Love you. See you tonight for Banoffee pie.'

Whatever you decide to spend your money on, don't save anything 'for best'. Use it, wear it out, break it, lose it — those things happen — but also *enjoy* it. That gorgeous frock you're saving 'for best' will either be out of fashion or too tight by the time 'best' turns up. And what's the point of having 'good' plates or 'nice silver' if they live in a drawer? They may as well not exist. I have friends who lost every wine glass and dish in the Christchurch earthquakes, which was just one of the tragedies during those events. It would have been even worse if those lovely things had never been used.

> WHATEVER YOU DECIDE TO SPEND YOUR MONEY ON, DON'T SAVE ANYTHING 'FOR BEST'. USE IT, WEAR IT OUT, BREAK IT, LOSE IT — THOSE THINGS HAPPEN — BUT ALSO ENJOY IT.

Holly taught me a fantastic lesson about this when she was little. Her approach to fashion was to wear everything. All at once. When she was 10 years old I took her to the Royal New Zealand Ballet's production of *Peter Pan* and we sat down the front where we could lean over the railings and watch the orchestra play. She was wearing everything she loved — her best frock and a tutu, a purple feather boa, every necklace from her dress-up box, and, I seem to recall, a tiara. Coco Chanel insisted that 'Before leaving the house, a lady should stop, look in the mirror, and remove one piece of jewellery.' Even so, Holly would have still looked like a glorious Christmas Tree.

We've all loved something so much that we've put it away and saved it for some special occasion, and then gone to dig it out only to discover it's not quite as sparkly and fabulous as we remembered it being. Use it, wear it and enjoy it while you still think it is sparkly. The only thing you should save for later, dear squirrels, is money.

CHAPTER 20

FAME

Everyone, apparently, wants to be famous. Which is entirely do-able now, thanks to social media. Your face, your thoughts and whatever you've been up to this afternoon can be communicated to the whole world in a way that used to be available only to movie stars and entertainers, élite sportspeople and world leaders. I can follow your life on Facebook, see what you're wearing and who you're hanging out with on Instagram, and find out what you think on Twitter. Back in the Olden Days, 20 years ago, I could know that much about someone I hadn't met only if they were a world-class actor or singer, or a world-champion athlete, or were in charge of a war.

Now anyone can be famous. And that's good, right? Because being famous is fun. It's like being popular. Sometimes now, when you ask kids what they want to be when they grow up, they'll say 'famous'. Not 'a famous *something*', like an actor or dancer or writer or sportsperson. Just famous.

Probably the most famous people in the world right now are

the Kardashians. And I don't even know what they're famous for. Now that they are famous, they do things like design clothes and make TV shows. But they didn't become famous because they designed great clothes or starred in a terrific TV show — they started doing those things *after* they became famous. This is new. You used to have to do something first. I'm not fond of the Kardashians. You can probably already tell. I'm middle-aged, so it's kind of in my job description to disapprove of them. About the only thing I am pleased about is that they don't suggest you have to be skinny to be a confident woman. They're proud of their curves. Which I would applaud properly with both hands, instead of just one with my finger sticking up, if those curves weren't so artificially constructed and therefore the result of a seriously discomforting level of self-obsession. Hey ho.

THE KARDASHIANS ARE PROUD OF THEIR CURVES. WHICH I WOULD APPLAUD WITH BOTH HANDS, INSTEAD OF JUST ONE WITH MY FINGER STICKING UP, IF THOSE CURVES WEREN'T SO ARTIFICIALLY CONSTRUCTED.

We have, in a very short space of time, redefined celebrity and re-routed the cause of fame. Fame used to be about recognition for doing something super-well. You wanted to be really good at doing something you loved — like rowing or playing the guitar — and be so damn good at it that people would notice. They'd go: 'Look, that's Tina. She can really *play*.' Celebrities were the people we literally 'celebrated' for their talent and the hard work they put into entertaining us. Now, celebrities are just as likely to be people we enjoy denigrating as celebrating. Celebrity magazines don't celebrate them, they criticise them for getting too fat or too thin, for having too much plastic surgery or letting themselves go, adopting and then abandoning a monkey, punching a photographer, crashing a car or violating themselves with an inflatable banana. Mostly, when we talk about them, we talk about *their lives*, not their work. And not in a nice way. We can't get enough of that shit.

And yet we all still want to be famous. Maybe we like to think we could handle the fame better than they do. Or maybe we just want the money and the incredibly cool stuff we imagine goes with all that fame and scrutiny. But before any of you go putting 'famous' in the box marked 'job title' on that form your careers counsellor wants you to fill out, let me tell you a very small story.

I had a wee taste of fame a couple of decades ago when I appeared weekly on *What Now*, which played on one of the two available TV channels. Back then, pretty much everyone knew who I was. I knew that was likely to happen when I got the job, and I was pretty excited about that. I wanted people to like what I did, and I thought it would be fun to go places and for people to be nice to me. That sounded like a cool way to live. My first celebrity moment occurred at a supermarket one Saturday. A family of shoppers, excited to see someone from that morning's small screen in this afternoon's freezer section, stopped me for a chat. Overcome with it all, they also rifled through my trolley to establish 'what you TV people eat'. They were deeply disappointed and oddly disapproving that I wasn't a vegetarian. 'Chops, Brian! She eats chops! I wasn't expecting that!' We all fell silent when they dug deeper under my loaf of bread and my bananas and uncovered my preferred choice for personal feminine hygiene. It was really awkward. I distracted the kids by asking them about their favourite cartoons from that morning's show, and then we all moved off quite swiftly. I hid in the pet food aisle (I didn't have a cat) until I knew they'd been through the checkout and were gone.

My second celebrity moment made me cry. At that point in our lives, my brother had developed a penchant for running half-marathons, and was one weekend competing in a half-marathon near where my parents were living at the time. I was living far away from all of them, so decided I'd catch a plane and be there with the rest of the family to cheer for Stephen when he crossed the finish line. It was all going well until a family — not the disapproving vegetarians, another one — again recognised me from that morning's TV and asked for autographs. Which was, you know, something you might think you wanted. Except that by the time we'd all found pen and paper and dealt with how to spell their names, Stephen had finished his run and I'd missed it. I burst into tears. I really wasn't sure this fame thing was what I had hoped for.

These days, I mostly get 'Don't I know you from somewhere?', or they think I'm Jackie Clarke, because somewhere in our New Zealand psyche there is only one amusing lady-person about my age who does stuff. Jackie gets the same in reverse. We both live in fear that she will be asked to do a 40-minute comedy set, or that I will be asked to sing. Though I suspect she'd be better at the comedy than I would be at the show tunes. Occasionally I'm tempted to give it a whirl just so the word would get out that we're actually two separate people, and one of us isn't going to thrill you with a sensual rendition of 'Fever'.

It is good to know you are less famous than your manager tells people you are — it stops you throwing your weight around and acting like a dick. Very recently I was on my way to MC a glitzy event at a big venue. I had already been mistaken for Jackie that morning during rehearsal, as it happens. Still, I was feeling pretty special as I sashayed my way into the cab, all frocked up in my fancy evening dress, glittering stilettos, face full of makeup and best glossy hair. The driver looked me up and down and said, 'So what's on at the Arena tonight? Bob Dylan?'

IT IS GOOD TO KNOW YOU ARE LESS FAMOUS THAN YOUR MANAGER TELLS PEOPLE YOU ARE — IT STOPS YOU THROWING YOUR WEIGHT AROUND AND ACTING LIKE A DICK.

'Yes,' I agreed, 'I threw this on for the mosh pit. Like to look my best for Bob.'

A week after I didn't see Bob Dylan, my mother and I called emergency services at 4am to take my father to hospital. Dad was really ill and couldn't walk. While they were carrying him out to the ambulance, one of the paramedics glanced at the wall where my mother keeps my university degree framed next to my brother's. 'Michèle A'Court?' the medic said, reading it. 'The celebrity?'

My father, bless him, whispered, 'Yes, she's my daughter.'

At which point the medic stared at me. I was looking the way I always look at 4am when my dad is being rushed to hospital. Clearest description: not like I am going to a Bob Dylan concert. 'Is that her?' the medic asked in a tone of disbelief.

'No,' I assured him as I pulled my nana cardy around my tatty pyjamas and smoothed my bird's nest hair, 'I'm Jackie Clarke, the singer.'

I emailed Jackie to let her know what I'd done. She wrote back immediately: 'Jesus — I have a cardy on and a bird's nest hair-do as we speak!!! xxx.' She's a bloody good sort, that Jackie.

Holly is pretty chilled about the fame thing. She has grown up thinking it is normal for everyone you know — your mum, your stepdad, their friends — to be on TV. And she's seen what it is like out the back end of the glitz and palaver — the angst and sweat — so fame doesn't look as shiny to her as it might to other people. She knows first-hand what it takes to be a dancer on stage, plus she sang on her first CD with Kids Music Company when she was seven, and worked out then that being in a recording studio mostly involved a lot of waiting and eating sandwiches. She also knows what it's like to watch your mother on stage making jokes about her daughter while you're actually in the room. I've always checked with her that she's okay with the stories I tell. Mostly, she has been. Once, at a gig in the Auckland Concert Chamber, she waited for the end of one of my mother-daughter jokes and stood up and took a bow.

Another night, during that difficult sixteenth year, she asked me before the gig not to tell any jokes involving her. I didn't. Afterwards, I asked if she'd enjoyed the show. She said, yeah, kind of, but she was a little disappointed that I hadn't mentioned her. I understood. Fame can be a bitch. But she's fun at parties.

I was upset about a review not long ago in which the reviewer, who generally didn't find me amusing, also wrote 'she obviously doesn't like her daughter very much'. Given that the jokes about my life with Holly always come from a place of love (and given also that I adore her) that freaked me out, so I rang my daughter from the road, read her the review, and asked what she thought. 'Dick,' she said. 'Can't he tell the difference between comedy and documentary?' Smart girl. Beautifully raised.

IT IS BETTER TO BE RECOGNISED FOR DOING SOMETHING. THEN AT LEAST YOU'VE GOT SOMETHING TO TALK ABOUT WITH THE PERSON WHO RECOGNISES YOU.

There is an upside to not being rich and famous. Sometimes, when I can't sleep, I think about Michael Jackson. Michael suffered from insomnia, too. When he couldn't sleep he'd call up his personal physician, who would make a house-call and give him sedatives. And we all know how that turned out. Ordinary people, when we can't sleep, count sheep and drink warm milk. Or we get up and watch re-runs of local dramas

FAME CAN BE A BITCH.
BUT SHE'S FUN AT PARTIES.

we didn't catch in prime-time and are pleasantly surprised. Occasionally, when I can't sleep, I've been known to clean out the kitchen cupboards. That's not an option if you've got a personal assistant, a housekeeper, a valet and a chef. No wonder Michael couldn't cope with insomnia — he probably didn't know where his kitchen actually was.

I like it that around these parts, no one let's you get too up-yourself about being famous. But really, these cautionary tales gleaned from my very small experience of a tiny bit of fame are about something else. What I'm suggesting is that, if you are going to be recognised, it is better to be recognised for *doing something*. Then at least you've got something to talk about with the person who recognises you. Otherwise you're just left staring at chops and tampons in the bottom of a shopping trolley with nowhere to go, conversationally. And that really isn't an experience I'd recommend.

CHAPTER 21

SAYING STUFF OUT LOUD

As well as popping baby Holly behind the bar in her car seat while I told jokes in pubs for grocery money, I also took her as a little girl on political protests. There are people who disapprove of that sort of carry-on, viewing it as some kind of exploitation of minors, akin to sending them up chimneys or making them stitch sneakers. My skin crawls, too, when I see a kid carrying a banner or wearing a T-shirt with a slogan, but taking Holly with me on protests against sporting contact with Zimbabwe or to support imprisoned Algerian refugee Ahmed Zaoui was something I did for both pragmatic and ideological reasons. Pragmatic because, generally speaking, many parents who want to spend their Saturdays walking uphill in the rain (why do marches always have to go *uphill*?) don't have a nanny to leave the kid with while they do it. And ideologically, I wanted Holly to know that you should care about lives other than your own, and when you care about things you should say so, out loud. And it can be fun to gather together and say so out loud in groups.

I come from a long line of seekers of social justice of various political persuasions. My maternal great-grandfather, John Rogers, was a passionate socialist, with a fondness for raising a fist and saying, 'See this hand? I'd rather cut it off than vote Tory.' I wish I'd been born soon enough to see that. All along my mother's side of the family were staunch Salvation Army soldiers, driven as much by the desire to care for the vulnerable as by their faith in God. John and his wife, my Great-grandma Edith, held regular prayer meetings at their home: convivial fellowship, and also a chance to check that their neighbours had enough to eat. Before the family sailed to New Zealand in 1914, one of my great-great-aunts, Sarah Holmes, was renowned in England — and later New Zealand — as a stunningly fierce fire-and-brimstone preacher. I like to think there's a genetic link, some quirk in the family DNA, that travels down to me, three generations later, getting all shouty in a comedy club about something I passionately believe.

WHEN YOU CARE ABOUT THINGS YOU SHOULD SAY SO, OUT LOUD. AND IT CAN BE FUN TO GATHER TOGETHER AND SAY SO OUT LOUD IN GROUPS.

My parents leant somewhat more to the economically conservative than my socialist great-grandfather — Mum baked cakes to fundraise for the National Party for years — but it was still all about social justice and community support. Dad was a dedicated member of the Lions' service club, raising funds and organising activities for families in need. As a kid, I drove with my mother to deliver meals-on-wheels, and went door-to-door collecting money with her for Save the Children, IHC and Red Cross at weekends. This was when I first observed that fairly often the people who looked as though they had the least to come and go on were the most generous and kind.

This roll-your-sleeves-up mucking-in didn't make our family unusual; it made us normal. New Zealand and Australia are two countries built largely by working-bees, I reckon. That same pioneering spirit that made our predecessors up-sticks and travel halfway around the world — Maori by waka, Europeans by ship — to have a crack at building a new and better life, also got us out there at weekends to knock up a playground or paint someone's fence. When Anzacs want something done, we've slapped a public notice in the local newspaper, got Marge to activate the phone tree, and everyone's come over with hammers and paint.

I probably need to explain some of those terms.

Glossary of terms

The phone tree

The 'phone tree' was an early form of Twitter where someone would 'phone' you and give you some information. 'Phoning' is like Tweeting except you actually talk to the person. It is done on a landline, which is like a mobile, but it's not mobile. In the Olden Days, it would be a telephone attached to the wall by a cord so you'd have to have all your conversations wherever it was installed, like in the hall (freezing in winter) or in the family room. Quietly, so everyone else could still hear the TV. Someone would phone you (you had to be at home when they called — there were no voice messages), and you would 'write the information down' with a pen or pencil on a pad kept by the phone for this express purpose. You would then 'phone your friends' to pass the information on, which is like re-Tweeting to your followers. Then they'd phone their friends (more re-Tweeting) until everybody knew about the working-bee.

The working-bee
Oh, okay, yes, a 'working-bee' is essentially a Flashmob with tools. Very little dancing. Maybe afterwards.

One more thing:

Public notices in the local newspaper
A 'public notice in the local newspaper' was a bit like posting an event on Facebook. You'd write the information down (maybe on the pad by the phone, maybe a bigger piece) and drop it into your local newspaper office (this was when we knew where that was), and a few days later it would appear in the back section of the newspaper that arrived in your letterbox.

Oh, okay, one other thing:

Newspapers
A 'newspaper' is like an iPad or smartphone but made out of paper, as the name suggests. After you finished reading it, you

could use it for other things, like wrapping up fish'n'chips. That was awesome. You'd poke a hole in the top of the package, and take out chips and bits of fish while the rest stayed hot. Newspapers were brilliant. They should bring those back.

Hennyhoo. I was raised to think we have two civic responsibilities: to take care of each other, and to speak up for those who can't speak for themselves or who need our voice to make theirs louder. Like feminism, this was one of those things I assumed was self-evident and/or would be absorbed by Holly through osmosis during the marches against the invasion of Iraq or in support of Palestine, or at all those cheery fundraisers in dismal bars and dreary church halls I dragged her along to. So an organic understanding of civic duty — although we also had actual conversations about individual issues. Hence the singing along in the car as harmonious hoydens to P!nk's 'Dear Mr President' (see Chapter 17: Heartbreak) with the kind of gusto you could only whip up if you were properly cognisant of George W. Bush's ludicrous views on war, gay rights, women's rights, homelessness and poverty. 'Let me tell you 'bout hard work!' Ah, good times, again I say.

Our kids tend toward 'clicktivism' rather than activism, showing their support online by 'liking' a page, engaging in discussion threads, chucking buckets of ice over their heads, or taking makeup-less selfies rather than by trudging uphill of a Saturday afternoon in June. All of which might involve more fun and less sacrifice than an afternoon drinking terrible community-hall tea, but it is still awareness, and it's still making their voices heard. And although Holly has less interest in geopolitics than I did at her age ('I can't find Palestine on the map, Mummy.' Exactly, darling. 'What, Mummy?'), she and her friends do see themselves as citizens, which is a tremendously good thing.

The year Holly cast her first vote in a national election — 2011 — I was as proud as other mothers might be witnessing their daughters take their first communion. I genuinely adore democracy so much that I have a little cry every three years in the polling booth. Voting actually *moves* me. Putting a tick in a box is a tiny thing for an individual to do, but I can't help being aware that when we all do that tiny thing it adds up to something huge. Having a tendency towards the melodramatic, I also take a moment to remember that people die to be able to do this. We can be casual about it around here, but not in other places. I've seen what that looks like.

I GENUINELY ADORE DEMOCRACY SO MUCH THAT I HAVE A LITTLE CRY EVERY THREE YEARS IN THE POLLING BOOTH.

Back in 2001, Jeremy and I travelled to East Timor to entertain New Zealand's peacekeeping troops. During our time there, we visited the site of the Suai massacre. Eighteen months earlier, the East Timorese people had overwhelmingly chosen independence from Indonesia in a 1999 United Nations referendum. They wanted the right to vote and to choose their own government. The Indonesians were not happy at the prospect of losing control of East Timor with its valuable land and seas full of oil, and punished the East Timorese immediately after the referendum with a string of atrocities. In one of them, Suai villagers fled to their local church, hoping for sanctuary. The militia simply walked into the church and opened fire at point-blank range. Those who escaped the first bullets ran out past the school and tried to hide in a half-built cathedral nearby. The stairs inside this cathedral-in-progress led to an exposed mezzanine floor that offered no cover, and the militia who followed picked them off one-by-one as though they were ducks in shooting gallery. The bodies — some say 100, others say more — were dragged back to the courtyard in front of the chapel, piled high, and set alight.

Because there can be no graves for these people, survivors placed little stone plaques over the blackened, oily earth, and there was a handwritten list standing at the centre with names of some of the dead. As we were reading it, speechless, the church choir started singing in a neighbouring building and, at the same moment, 50 schoolchildren came outside to watch us and smile.

The still-unfinished cathedral was being used then as an extra classroom. The kids' lessons were written in chalk on the walls, long-division worked out among unmistakable bullet holes. There were two things I couldn't comprehend at the time: which part of humanity allows you to open fire on unarmed women and children in a church; and which part of humanity survives that experience to keep going to school, keep building new homes, having babies, welcoming strangers, and believing that things are going to get better. All these years later, I

'I CAN'T FIND PALESTINE
ON THE MAP, MUMMY.'
EXACTLY, DARLING.

understand that second part a little more; but I still cannot for the life of me understand the first.

I think about that every three years in the polling booth, and about the suffragettes and suffragists, too, who fought incredibly hard so that I could take an orange feltpen and put my tick in a box. It always makes me wish polling booths were more elegant. If this is our moment to be alone with our personal vision of democracy, I'd prefer something fancier than just a Corflute box.

Our family tries to give it some flair. Without discussing it, voting day has become an outing for grandparents, parent and child (even before she was old enough to vote), all of us travelling together to the local polling station, ice creams on the way home. Given the differing political persuasions amongst the adults, our votes probably cancel each other out, but no one would ever suggest it might be more efficient if we just stayed home. Around here, we like giving our democratic rights a bit of exercise. And, of course, I'm only guessing that we're voting different ways. There may be robust dinner-table discussion about policies and politicians on any given evening, but again, without discussing it, we respectfully keep our actual votes private.

I didn't nag Holly about many things — not bed-making nor dishes nor getting her laundry done at weekends — but I harped on sufficiently about democracy to ensure she'd registered online in time to vote that first time. Out for coffee in the lead-up to the election, she asked me for advice on who she should vote for. I said I didn't mind who she voted for, so long as she voted, and admitted that on the odd occasion I have cast an 'informal vote' because I didn't love any of the options but still wanted to be part of the democratic process. Then together we made a list of the things she cares most about (money for the arts and youth rates, for starters) and talked about various parties' policies on those issues. The fun bit was when we made lists of MPs we each thought were either evil or stupid, or smart and kind, and continued to apply those labels as we watched the news and party political broadcasts during the campaign. It might not have been high-level political analysis, but we were engaged. And I've read worse commentary.

WE PARENTS PICTURE OURSELVES AS BOOKS FULL OF WISDOM, AND ASSUME THAT THE KIDS WILL ASK US TO OPEN OURSELVES UP TO REVEAL THE STORIES INSIDE. MAYBE WE SHOULD DO LESS OF THE WAITING TO BE ASKED.

Parents can be nervous about expressing our political views in case the 'expressing' comes across as 'imposing' instead. Lord knows why we think that — it's not as though they let us tell them what to think about anything else, right? Robust discussion, people, and sharing some wisdom and experience. Because we've got some, generally. Without ever articulating it, I suspect we parents picture ourselves as books full of wisdom on a shelf, and assume that at some point the kids will ask us to lift ourselves down and open ourselves up to reveal the stories inside. Maybe we should do less of the waiting to be asked.

Sometimes I also think we need to call a village meeting to remind ourselves — and explain to our children — what a democracy is all about. Every time I hear someone say 'It's not my job to feed someone else's kid,' for example, I feel obliged to politely tap them on the shoulder and say 'Um, yes, actually, it is.' That's our deal. We all chip in for roads and schools and healthcare — the stuff that our community uses even if we, individually, don't — and we agreed a long time ago that we'd keep a special eye out for the vulnerable ones. No one would stay sick or go hungry or live in fear or without hope, not on our watch. I believe that was the plan.

Turns out, according to the teachers at the coalface, that a significant number of our kids — kids who might not live at our house, but who live nearby — are hungry. So I reckon we should feed them. We should also find out why they are hungry. Not enough money? Bad handling of money? Lack of parental interest? We'd all like to know. I find it hard to believe that there are many parents who deliberately fail to feed their children. You would have to fight quite hard against the very strong instinct to do your best by your child. We are hardwired to nurture and protect. If something has gone wrong with that wiring of late, we'd better get it sorted. But in the meantime I'm really happy to chip in with my taxes and feed the kids.

Being poor is horrible. When Holly was small, I got a taste of the crushing, panicked, chronic state of grinding fear — it's like metal in your mouth — that we wouldn't make it week by week. Choosing between bills and food, choosing between bread and milk, sometimes knowing only one of us would eat that day and making sure she didn't notice. Which is why we've built safety nets for families like her and me — benefits like the DPB, established in 1973 to support women and children who received no support from the father when he had wandered away, as men sometimes do. And also to make it possible for women and children to leave violent and dangerous relationships, and still make rent and buy Weetbix. In the end, Holly and I survived without any safety nets. But I am more than happy to join hands and stretch out those nets for other people like us.

In 2013 there was a dramatic news story about a 12-year-old Napier boy, Josh McQuoid, who almost drowned on the Napier seafront — a notoriously dangerous beach that looks inviting but can pack a serious tidal punch. Josh was dragged 150 metres along the beach and fought for air for eight minutes. A German tourist and a police officer both tried separately to save him, but neither of them could hold onto him by themselves in the heavy swell. So the cop organised all the onlookers into a human chain, then grabbed Josh, who was then passed up the beach through each pair of arms to safety. That's how I sometimes picture democracy: a remarkable thing, like the human chain. We should all probably get together to practise that move at our next village meeting.

So taking care of each other, and also speaking up for what we believe in. Down here at the bottom of the world, I reckon we're in a unique position to be a bit lippy about things. Quite often, because New Zealand is small and Australia is an individual continent and both countries are reliant on trading with bigger markets, Australasians are encouraged to be socially and economically conservative. Too small to make a difference, people suggest, so don't try any mad ideas about saving the planet or taking risks with the way we make our living in the global market. We're discouraged from being critical of those who are bigger and more powerful, especially the ones who buy our lamb chops.

Somewhere along the way, as a small person working in a tiny industry in this little country, I formed precisely the opposite attitude. I figured if it didn't matter what I did on a global scale, I might as well do what I want, in the way I want to do it. So I cheerfully chuck mad ideas out there — on stage or on the page — in the hope they will find agreement or inspire debate. Clearly, the idea that small people and small countries should be loud and opinionated is one of these mad ideas. And I know exactly where it came from. I can trace it back specifically to 1973 when my government sent two navy frigates with a Cabinet minister on board to Mururoa to protest French nuclear testing in our part of the Pacific. It's hard to picture that happening now: a prime minister drawing a name out of hat (Norman Kirk literally did that) to send one of his team (Fraser Colman) off on a protest, and using our military to make a political point.

As a schoolkid, I thought that's what governments did. I got used to the idea that New Zealand did things before other countries, like granting every woman the right to vote and adopting an eight-hour working day. And we've been at the spearhead of groups of countries that have taken a stand against apartheid or declared that gay men and prostitutes aren't criminals, and allowing anyone, regardless of gender or sexual orientation, to make a family. I still want my government to be that kind of world leader. Because, really, that's what small countries should do.

One of the tremendously useful things about being a political activist is that if you can't quite remember what you did in the 1980s, you can apply under the Official Information Act to read your own Security Intelligence Service (SIS) file. I did that. After writing for the Victoria University student newspaper, *Salient*, for a few years and being active in the anti-Springbok Tour movement in 1981, I wanted to know what our spies 'had on me' as it were. Curiosity, more than anything. Maybe they could fill in the gaps in my memory of those heady, turbulent times? Could they maybe remember where I moved after leaving that great flat on Willis Street? And could they help me find that really nice jersey I lost in the shift?

The SIS felt I wasn't subversive enough to warrant having my *own* file, but my name turned up in a lot of other people's files. This felt both creepy and a tiny bit exciting. Most of the material containing my name was withheld, but they did send me a few pages, most of it redacted. I had, unbeknownst to me, been interviewed by SIS agents and they had tracked where I worked for a few years. In 1984, one agent reported that 'as a former *Salient* worker who might be a member of the WCL [Worker's Communist League] MA'C impresses as knowledgeable about WCL policies'. I was touched — I never really thought I got a proper handle on dialectical and historical materialism. I, of course, had no idea at the time that I was being interviewed; I thought some dude was just chatting me up in a pub. If I'd known he was a spy and they'd been watching me, I would have asked him if he knew anything about that jumper.

The final page in the file sent to me by the SIS was a photocopy of a 1987 clipping from Wellington newspaper *The Evening Post*. It's a publicity picture of me with Frank Flash and Danny Watson, being introduced as *What Now*'s new presenter. That seems to be the last time the SIS showed any interest in my doings. I guess they assumed that, once I started working as a children's entertainer, I was no longer a danger to anyone. Fair enough. Although I'm guessing that way of thinking has changed now after the revelations about Jimmy Savile and Rolf Harris.

YOU LOOK AROUND AND REALISE THAT THE NUMPTIES ARE GETTING ALL OF THE AIR-PLAY AND COLUMN INCHES, SO YOU'D BETTER MAKE A NOISE.

Obviously, no one needs to spy on me any longer to know what I think or what I'm up to. (Although anyone is welcome to buy me a drink and ask.) I have taken to chucking it all out there and seeing who salutes. There was a brief time — maybe a few years — when I was busy paying the mortgage and parenting and I lost my voice a little, stopped saying what I thought about political and social issues, and didn't challenge people whose attitudes and assumptions offended me. I would second-guess myself about what right I had to speak out and bother anyone with my ideas. It was what Leonard Cohen had said (see Chapter 4: Middle Age) about the world conspiring to silence us. But then you look around and realise that the numpties are getting all of the air-play and column inches, so you'd better make a noise or no one will know that you — and people like you — are there. You find your voice again and, on a good day, discover you are not alone, that you're not the only one who thinks the way you do. I love it when we're *all* like that: openly saying what we think, arguing for what we believe in and listening to each other's point of view. This doesn't mean that all our ideas are right, or that we need to have an opinion on everything, but when we have a view we have a right to express it, and a responsibility to share. And then to turn up at the next working-bee and get stuff done.

CHAPTER 22

FINDING YOUR TRIBE

Every now and then, I remember that it would be wise to take my own advice. When I'm a guest speaker for various industry groups, I hear myself waxing lyrically about the importance of knowing where you come from, knowing who you are, and 'finding your tribe'. And then I realise it might have been weeks — months, even — since I hung out with my people. So I round up the girls and we go out for dinner.

When I say 'your tribe' I mean the people who don't make you feel 'other'. There can be all kinds of things that make you hum the *Sesame Street* 'One of these things is not like the other' tune quietly inside your head. You'll be in a work or social or family environment and feel acutely aware that you are from another culture, differently-abled, less financially empowered, not as married, oddly childless, too smart, too soft, the wrong gender, or suddenly very young or dreadfully old. You are, in that group, defined by being in some way *different*.

So your 'tribe' is the group of people who best match the important things about you — the things you most like about yourself. If you are proud of your creative bent, your tribe is likely to be found somewhere amongst a bunch of other creatives. Although other factors will come into play, too — world view, life experience, your moral and ethical values. You will know you are in the company of your tribe because you will be less aware of your differences, and more aware of your sameness. Sometimes, you'll just feel yourself suddenly relax, breathe out and feel a bit more comfortable about being you. Not that there is anything wrong with visiting alien places and engaging with metaphorical foreigners. But now and then it is nice to be at home with your own kind.

Depending on how many things are important in defining who you are, you might have more than one tribal group to belong to. Ethnicity, gender, social status (the stuff you were born with) plus all the stuff you have experienced since birth, and all the stuff you want in your future, play a part in developing your tribal identities. Sometimes, you'll be dying to hang out with your geek friends, or your yoga friends, or your old friends. Once you've left school where they put you in classrooms and teams, you have to consciously organise this for yourself. You're going to need a bunch of people you think of as your team or your gang, your crew or your posse. One of my tribal groups is called 'Every Comedian You Ever Meet Anywhere In The World', and you will find it holding a meeting and getting down to business in Green Rooms and bars 24/7 around the globe. My other tribal group is the one I like to think of as 'The Coven'.

When I say 'Coven', I don't mean that me and the ladies

gather around a cauldron to boil newts' eyes and cast spells — although if one of us suggested it, I'm sure we'd give it a go. A meeting of The Coven is 'networking' in business-speak, just an informal group of like-minded women, giving and receiving support and affirmation, backing each other up over a pot of tea or a glass of wine. Most of us, whose primary personal and professional relationships are with men, will hanker after a night out with the girls. I totally understand why other women take up scrapbooking or get a group together for Chippendales — it's not actually about the handcrafts or theatrical eye-candy; it's about hanging out with people who talk the same language. And talking is what the ladies do best.

Meetings of The Coven, I've learnt, have to be scheduled. We're busy. According to sociological research, the most common complaint amongst working women in general, and working mothers in particular, is lack of 'me-time'. Apparently we're lucky to get 40 minutes a day to ourselves as we juggle work and home life.

But with a bit of planning, I can knock a week's worth of me-time into one night of lady-time by grabbing half a dozen hoydens to meet up for a few Happy Hour wines and half-price-Tuesday pizzas. The thirst and hunger is mostly for each other's company, but a girl's gotta eat. One memorable evening I threw together a giggle of women I knew who didn't know each other but should. The pool I drew from included several writers (magazines, film, plays and books), a TV editor, a sculptor, a singer, a sometime-model, a politician, a hairdresser and two comedians. I don't think I've ever managed to have them all in the same room at the same time since, because, you know, we're busy. Though when push comes to shove, the sculptor and TV editor and I can usually manage a meeting of The Coven Hardcore at the drop of a desperate-for-your-company hat.

On the night in question, we managed to gather most of the writers, the TV editor, the model and a comedian. For a relatively highbrow bunch, we got down to the nitty-gritty pretty fast: modern heart-throb Ryan Gosling versus the classic charms of Alan Rickman (classicism won); and revelations about more than one of us being thrown out of the Girl Guides. It didn't really matter what we talked about; we were just happy to be out, and laughing, and being shocking and kind to each other. Somewhere in there, we also swapped useful information about work contacts and project ideas. Which made the entire evening tax-deductible for those of us who are self-employed (which is almost all of us).

We always vow to do it more often. We've even considered giving our loose group a name and making it a monthly rendezvous — hence the possible title, 'Club 28'. Or just 'Ladies Who Drink'. We don't, of course, manage to do it as frequently or as casually as we'd like. Some of us need childcare, another needs handy disabled parking, some of us work nights, several of us travel, and all of us could make good use of a sober driver. We're working on all that. And I'd be surprised if our combined organisational skills can't make that happen again sometime this side of Christmas.

This thing of spending time with our tribe doesn't just matter in terms of our own personal mental health. It is also the most effective tool for social change. I don't know for sure, but I suspect Margaret Thatcher didn't have a Coven for Tuesday-night half-price pizzas. I've seen no evidence that she

I SUSPECT MARGARET THATCHER DIDN'T HAVE A COVEN FOR TUESDAY-NIGHT HALF-PRICE PIZZAS.

identified tribally with women — in fact, there's evidence that she specifically did not. No sisterhood, no making a lady-shaped space at the table, no mentoring of other women to follow in her footsteps. And when Second Wave Feminists suggested that if women ruled the world, the world would be a better place, I am pretty sure they meant that you needed more than one woman sitting at the table with the men. One woman isn't enough. For women to make a difference, we need multiple women bringing our gender perspective, our culture, our collaborative approach to the Parliament and the boardroom and the shop floor. We are making a mistake if we think sending one individual woman into a leadership role is going to make things better for everyone — or make it possible for even one other woman to follow later.

FOR WOMEN TO MAKE A DIFFERENCE, WE NEED MULTIPLE WOMEN BRINGING OUR GENDER PERSPECTIVE, OUR CULTURE, OUR COLLABORATIVE APPROACH TO THE PARLIAMENT AND THE BOARDROOM AND THE SHOP FLOOR.

We do our knitting in a circle, not a shed, remember? We get things done in groups. And so we need to meet each other, know each other, introduce each other to the rest of our tribe. It's good for business, and good for our souls. So find your version of The Coven. It is how magic happens.

CHAPTER 23

HOW TO TELL YOU ARE A GROWN-UP

Young people are disarmingly enthusiastic about becoming grown-ups. From a distance, adulthood looks like Freedom and Independence. It tends not to feel like that close-up, but we don't tell them that or they'll all turn into Peter Pan and never go flatting.

I am already a grown-up. I know this because in my handbag I carry painkillers, tissues, a functioning credit card, a comb, tweezers, several pens and something to write on. If pressed, I could also come up with two hairclips, some cotton buds and a safety pin. You could be sick, dirty, unkempt, torn, bewildered, hungry, limping from a splinter and miles from home, and I would have the means to fix any and all of it.

Being a grown-up is not just about having a large handbag. There are other indicators that indicate you have travelled a fair way along the journey on the highway of life. You will, for example, as a grown-up know a good shoe-mender. This is because grown-ups understand some things aren't disposable and get more comfortable with age. Mending shoes is about respecting the ageing process. I have a Danish guy, Gerd, whom I've been taking my shoes to for new soles and re-heeling for years. He treats them with reverence, like I'm dropping loved ones off at the doctor. We chat a bit.

Probably you will also have made friends with the lady at the dry-cleaner, and will know a dressmaker who alters your clothes because you've reached a point where you've stopped blaming your body for not fitting the stuff on the rack, and started adjusting the clothes instead. You will have a good mechanic and call him by his first name. You've accepted that you can't be an expert at everything, but you take responsibility for finding someone who is. And you're smart enough to know he is more likely to source good re-treads if you say nice things about his hobby car tucked around the side of his workshop. 'Wow, Kevin, that's come a long way since I last came in for my WoF. Can you do me a deal on radials?' It's just good manners.

You can tell you're a grown-up because in your diary (you still keep a paper diary, because you once dropped your phone in the loo and that thing with the bag of rice doesn't really work) on some page it will say 'Gynaecologist' and 'Mammogram', and in your head it feels like the same thing as taking the car to the mechanic. Just checking it runs right and that there isn't a crack in the big-end you hadn't noticed. A mammogram, for the uninitiated, is like slamming your tits in the fridge door, and then lying down on the floor and slamming them sideways in the freezer door straight after. But there is a magical moment when they don't find anything and you skip like a kindy kid out to the car, feeling that for another year you've evaded some disaster that was both inevitable and unexpected.

There's a great grown-up day when you finally find a dentist who listens when you tell her you don't want a lecture every six months about flossing. You hate flossing. She might give you a sample of those little brush things you can push between your teeth instead which, she readily admits, aren't as effective as floss, but they're still better than the not-flossing you've been doing. And then she'll whack a bit of anaesthetic in before she scales and polishes around the sensitive bits down the back of your gums because you're a regular client and she likes you.

YOU WILL HAVE LEARNT THE HARD WAY NOT TO OPEN TUBES OF ANYTHING – CONCEALER, HAND CREAM, TOOTHPASTE – WHILE ON A PLANE.

You will have learnt the hard way not to open tubes of anything — concealer, hand cream, toothpaste — while on a plane, because the cabin pressure causes it to gush out as soon as the cap is off and before you've even started squeezing the effing thing, and it won't stop until the tube is empty. It's something to do with physics that you can't explain, and, even if you could, the guy sitting next to you in the business suit would be unimpressed because he's got a meeting when he lands and is wondering how he's going to explain the white mark on his thigh that smells vaguely of lavender. You, however, will be fine because you have a pretty scarf stuffed in the corner of your laptop bag for just this kind of emergency, and will drape it casually over your chest-front, where most of your moisturiser ended up in the first instance before you threw the tube in the air in a panic and it landed on his pants.

You will have a hammer of your very own (not borrowed) and two screwdrivers — one flathead, one Phillips — and you can tell the difference between the two. It is possible you might never use them for anything other than banging in a picture hook or prising open tin lids, but you like to think you could knock up an ark someday if it didn't stop raining. You know where the fuse box is and can point to it with confidence. Pliers, tin snips and secateurs are also signs of maturity and independence. It is important to know where to find the right tradespeople, but there is something empowering about having a crack yourself first. I have a theory they charge less per hour if they can see your spanner lying in plain sight — you will appear less easily bamboozled.

And you know you're a grown-up when you can introduce an old friend to a new one by saying, 'This is Judy, we've been friends for … gosh … 35 years!' and then you both giggle like schoolkids, exactly the way you did when you first met.

You will have at least three scars — one accidental, one surgical and one emotional — and a bloody good story to go with each one. And you'll have at least one secret that you've never told anybody, and probably never will. There will be one person of your acquaintance whom you would literally cross the street to avoid, and another you could phone at 3am for a restorative chat if you really need to. You have stopped being nervous when you walk into a room, because you've worked out by now that, actually, no one is looking at you. At least, not in a judgy way. And there will be at least one person you would willingly die for, and you can name them.

And you know you are a grown-up when being a grown-up stops being your ambition: what you are looking forward to now is being a curmudgeonly old grump. You start fantasising about being a very old lady who might elicit shock and awe by saying something as simple as 'Get fucked' to someone who doesn't expect that from a very old lady. I'm not saying you'd do it, necessarily, just that it is a fun arrow to keep in your quiver should the need arise.

> ## YOU KNOW YOU ARE A GROWN-UP WHEN BEING A GROWN-UP STOPS BEING YOUR AMBITION: WHAT YOU ARE LOOKING FORWARD TO NOW IS BEING A CURMUDGEONLY OLD GRUMP.

I'm not a curmudgeon yet, but I like having a little go at it in the same way small children play dress-ups — just to try it on and see how it feels. I find I am making a good start by being easily annoyed by meaningless pleasantries from young male shop assistants. It seems someone has trained them to ask 'Doing anything special this weekend?', which I find overly inquisitive

YOU WILL HAVE
AT LEAST THREE
SCARS – ONE
ACCIDENTAL, ONE
SURGICAL AND
ONE EMOTIONAL
– AND A BLOODY
GOOD STORY
TO GO WITH
EACH ONE.

from a total stranger. Do they want to know when I'll be out so they can come around and nick my stuff? Are they in the employ of the GCSB? Do they need me to explain dialectical and historical materialism again? Can't I just buy this shirt for my dad without an inquisition? I am working up the courage to respond with something equally over-familiar like 'Trimming my minge' or 'Worming the cat.' Or I might just freak them out by smiling coyly and replying: 'Free as a bird, as it happens. Where would you like to meet up?'

CHAPTER 24

DEATH AND TATTOOS

Before I left home and moved to Wellington, my brother would tell me about this amazing woman called Kathryn Irvine who worked as the typesetter for Victoria University's student newspaper, *Salient*. She was, he said, passionately intelligent and worldly wise, very funny (important) and beautifully spoken. She said 'fark' rather than 'fuck', Stephen told me. I couldn't wait to meet her.

In 1979 I enrolled at Wellington Polytech in the one-year journalism course, but lived at a university hostel on the other side of the city, just down the hill from Victoria's campus and the *Salient* office. I did some writing for *Salient* that year (and for several more years once I became an actual university student) and hung out a bit in the office, mostly to be with my brother and in the vicinity of the wondrous Kathryn Irvine.

Kathryn was different from the rest of us — more sophisticated and self-assured. She and I were thrilled that we almost shared a birthday — she was six years and two days older than me. Kathryn had done a wildly sensible thing in completing a secretarial course after finishing high school, which meant she was now supplementing her university studies with her very grown-up and professional typing skills. It was one of the many things we bonded over, this typing expertise. I explained to Kathryn that back at high school I had swum against the tide by choosing Typing as a subject. This was in an era when students were streamed into either 'professional' or 'trade' subjects depending on academic ability. Kids in my 'professional' stream were supposed to take History and Geography as opposed to Typing and Home Economics. I had insisted on crossing the stream to take History and Typing instead, figuring that, if I was going to be some kind of writer, being able to use a writer's tool properly was going to be handy. It caused a bit of fuss at my school at the time, but I had stood my ground. Kathryn was impressed with my chutzpah.

The *Salient* offices in the student union building comprised four rooms. There was the editor's office, which Stephen occupied for a couple of years, a windowless hidey-hole mostly used for overnight kips when deadlines rendered the trek home impossible; the main workroom filled with typewriters, cigarette smoke, layout tables littered with scalpels and glue, a million half-drunk cups of instant coffee, and a bunch of spotty, long-haired, pea-jacket-wearing youths who dreamed of being Woodward and/or Bernstein; a photography darkroom; and the typesetting room. The typesetting room housed the machine we used in the Olden Days to turn badly typed copy and handwritten scrawl into long, column-shaped strips which we then cut up and laid out to look just like a real newspaper.

The machine was almost as big as the room which housed it, and it hummed and chugged, and smelled of the photographic chemicals used to print galleys of wet copy which were hung up to dry from twine with clothes pegs. Yet this room was an oasis of calm, because this was where Kathryn lived. Two days a week, sometimes more, you could find Kathryn here with her pot plants (alive!) and a Thermos of real coffee, fingers flying over the keyboard as she turned our rants and raves into something that seemed almost like journalism because it suddenly looked so much like the real thing. She was possibly the fastest touch-typist in the world, never looking at the places her fingers went on the keyboard, sometimes even chatting while she typed, correcting spelling and grammar as she went, and amusing herself by racing the machine — she could type faster than the typesetting machine could absorb her input, so from time to time she would stop, stand up and stretch, untie her long hair, pour herself a cup of her own fine coffee, and wait for the machine to catch up with her.

Every 18-year-old girl should have a Kathryn. Older, wiser and just enough removed from your circle of peers to be able to say 'Of course you must!' or 'Don't be ridiculous!' without it sounding like a crushing admonition or an order. I could say anything to her, try out any of my half-formed ideas about life, politics, love and sex, and get a considered, respectful, illuminating response. She gave me books, introduced me to Nina Simone's music, told me stories of her visits to Italy (Florence was her happiest place on Earth), and brought wisdom to this new grown-up life I was trying out. For almost a decade she was my touchstone for everything — Was I right to think this? To feel this? Was I making the right choice? — and I can't think of any big decision I made that Kathryn wasn't consulted on. I didn't always take her advice, but, with the benefit of hindsight, I can say I always should have. Sometimes when her partner, Brent, was away I'd stay over at her place to keep her company, eat pasta, drink red wine, listen to Nina and talk all night. We even, from time to time, hennaed each other's hair — a remarkably intimate thing that sounds like such a girly cliché, but it was a genuine, natural part of our friendship. The only other person I've ever done that with is Holly. It felt very much the same.

After university, when we were both working, we'd meet for lunches and dinners. For a few years, Kathryn and my brother worked together in the Continuing Education Unit at Radio New Zealand, and I would find any excuse to drop by their office to talk to them — so often I got into terrible trouble from their boss for distracting them from their work and had to stop. When I left Wellington in 1987 to move to Christchurch and work on *What Now*, Kathryn and I wrote each other letters. I still have them, as well as the postcards from Florence sent on her regular visits to her cultural home.

Kathryn was diagnosed with cancer — lymphoma — in 1987. We wrote more letters, and I visited her in Wellington as often as I could.

Always tremendously outspoken and firm in her principals, Kathryn refused to play docile cancer patient. When her waist-length hair fell out and the government provided a hideous synthetic wig, she wouldn't wear it. I can't remember now if she actually *did* attach it to a dog leash and drag it round the

Oncology Ward, barking, or if she just threatened to. I like to think that she did. And when people gave her those 'cure your own cancer with something unscientific' or 'understanding God's plan' books of which she disapproved, she'd cheerfully tell them to 'fark off'.

We talked about dying, which is a tremendously hard thing to do once you know someone is actually about to do it. But because we'd always been so honest with each other, you couldn't skirt around it. You'd get to that part of the conversation with a sick person where usually you would say 'But you'll be better soon,' and realise those words weren't going to fly. Certainly not with Kathryn. She'd never been one for platitudes, and she had even less time for them at this point in her life.

WHEN PEOPLE SEND YOU LOVE AND KIND THOUGHTS AND LET YOU KNOW THAT THEY ARE THINKING OF YOU, 'IT'S LIKE HAVING A PIECE OF YOURSELF STUCK BACK ON'.

Which is not to say she wasn't open to kindness and love. One of the many things Kathryn said that has stayed with me is that, when people send you love and kind thoughts and let you know that they are thinking of you, 'it's like having a piece of yourself stuck back on'. The surgeries, chemo, radiation, sickness and fear were like having pieces of you stripped off and taken away, but every kindness and connection was like having a bit of you returned. Like Post-it notes, she said, stuck back onto you, and she'd pat herself with her hand to show what it felt like.

It became clear that no amount of chemo was going to make a difference. Our shared friend Victoria, a film editor at TVNZ, came up with a brilliant plan to shoot a short film with me at Kathryn's place. This gave us all an excuse to fill up her house one weekend with activity and drama. *The Assignment* was inspired by a strip from French feminist cartoonist Claire Bretécher. I played a writer on a deadline who spent most of the film making coffee and hanging out the washing, which is what writers do. As well as a chance to demonstrate my skills as a touch-typist (quite shit compared to Kathryn's), it was our way of keeping her involved in the world by bringing a little piece of it to her. We wore her out and she loved it. It was a delightful weekend, and almost our last time together.

Kathryn died in August 1988. She was 33 years old. Victoria and I were pallbearers. Our death notice said our friend had died 'with dignity and courage'.

Sometimes when people die, the space they held in your life eventually gets filled in or closes over — time, new people, busyness, changing lives. But there is always a Kathryn-shaped gap in my life. I think of her every day and still have things I want to ask her and tell her. As much as I can, I imagine her voice, her response, her warmth, her laugh. I feel tremendously lucky to have known her, and to still feel both her presence and her absence. Like I say, every 18-year-old girl should have a Kathryn.

If it had ever come up, Kathryn would probably have tried to talk an 18-year-old-me out of getting a tattoo. I tried to channel the arguments she would have used when Holly first expressed an interest in getting one. When you're 18, sweetheart, you don't yet know what your fully-grown self might want, so don't go imposing something permanent on her that she will have to live with forever. And, darling, why don't you save some things for later so you have some stuff to look forward to? You don't have to have *every* life experience now. Plus, honey, you don't want to present people with too many opportunities to make assumptions about you before you've had a chance to speak. You know how I dislike titles like 'Miss' and 'Mrs' because they're flagging your relationship status before anyone has even got as far as 'Hello'? A tattoo is not a million miles from doing the same. Maybe it's wise, darling, to limit the visual clues that might be a barrier to you and them *getting on*.

It's not that I'm against tattoos *per se*. Secretly, and despite what I've just said, I have always wanted to be the kind of person who had at some point had the courage and confidence to have a vine of flowers inked artfully onto my forearm, or a tui on my shoulder, or a word of wisdom on my wrist. I am entranced by other people's stunning vintage-inspired artwork or culturally significant designs that suggest right upfront that the owner is confident and sassy, and doesn't spend a lot of time worrying about what other people think. On visits to New Orleans I gaze wistfully at all the tattooed women who fill the French Quarter with their bohemian style and attitude. And I mean *all* the women. Jeremy and I once played a drinking game where we'd take a drink whenever we saw a woman there *without* a visible tattoo, but we got very thirsty and had to give it up. We didn't dare try the game in reverse or we'd have been hammered by morning tea.

So I've always liked body art in theory, just not for me. Nor for my teenage daughter — am I right, every-mother-in-the-world? It's our job to stop you doing things you can't undo, and few things are as permanent as a tattoo. You can have a hasty and imprudent marriage dissolved comparatively swiftly, but the wrong design in the wrong place is going to require a laser and a lot of pain. But, sigh, we are swimming now against a tide of tattoo ink — body art is ubiquitous in the new millennium.

'SOMETIMES YOU NEED TO LET THINGS GO' IS GREAT ADVICE, BUT SHOULDN'T BE PLACED IN THE TRAMP-STAMP POSITION.

As it happens, the 'divorce tattoo' is hot right now, especially with women. Big, visible statements marking the end of one chapter and the beginning of the next. Not so much old-school butterflies and dolphins, more skin novellas intended to affirm and inspire. Though you'd want to be careful where you put them. 'Sometimes you need to let things go' is great advice, but shouldn't be placed in the tramp-stamp position in case it ends up looking like a warning label for what happens nearby. 'Always a lesson, never a failure' is undeniably a positive spin on emotional turmoil — though again, placement is crucial. You wouldn't want just that last word peeking out at the world from under your T-shirt. 'This too shall pass' is another pearl of wisdom, though not terribly encouraging when etched on your spine to be read by your next partner. Cher's approach, according to legend, is to celebrate each new lover by having their name tattooed on her bum, then covered up with a rose once the relationship has run its course. Delightful.

I am still intrigued by the young lady I walked behind in Costa Mesa who had a story etched on her back that began 'I am selfish and arrogant and ...' — before it slipped below her bra strap. I am hoping it led to a witty and affirming punchline around her hips, but worry that her ex-boyfriend was the tattooist exacting a cruel revenge, knowing as he did that she was crap at reading mirror-writing. Awesome breakup story, dude.

Parents, then, have started striking deals with their kids in the hope of delaying what seems nigh-on inevitable. Michelle and Barack Obama have told daughters Sasha and Malia that if they get tattoos, Mom and Dad will get the same tattoo in the same place and post photos of the matching family body art online. Their plan is that the prospect of this will significantly reduce the 'cool' factor. Good thinking, but pretty high stakes with potentially drastic consequences if either of the girls goes properly off the rails and the Leader of Free World has to turn up to a meeting with Putin sporting a neck tattoo of a spider.

So when Holly started talking about wanting a tattoo, I said all these things to her and made it clear it wasn't something I would support. She was too young, it was too permanent, she should wait until she was older and knew more about the kind of life she wanted, and what she might be willing to wear forever as she lived it.

She was 18 when she came home from a visit to her whanau in Te Puna with an angel's wing tattooed on her right ribs, created by an artist from Holly's Pirirakau hapu to represent her family and Ngati Ranginui iwi. I couldn't find it in myself to be angry or disappointed; it was done, so there seemed no point in railing against it. The conservative part of me was relieved that it was in a place that wasn't always on show. The romantic part of me admired its artistry and meaning, just quietly. Given some of the other things we've been through, it didn't feel like the major drama I had thought it would be. No harm done. We all carried on.

IT MADE AN IMPRESSION ON ME – THIS IDEA THAT SOMETHING THAT YOUR KID DOES WHICH IRKS YOU MIGHT ONE DAY BECOME SOMETHING YOU'RE GRATEFUL FOR.

Somewhere in the back of my head, I had tucked away a story I'd heard in the late 1990s about a young Kiwi killed in a horrific accident overseas. His devastated parents flew over to claim his body and bring him home. They said that, some time before, they'd been cross with him for getting a tattoo — for all the reasons we've talked about here. Not because it was a terrible tattoo, just that it was a permanent thing that might be regretted later. But they said it was their son's tattoo that made it possible for them to know they'd found his body in the wreckage. It made an impression on me — this idea that something that your kid does which irks you might one day become something you're grateful for.

Which doesn't mean everyone should rush out and get a label placed somewhere in case there's a tragedy. Just that there are matters of life and death, and then there are tattoos. They are different things.

In 2005 I had a mole removed. I didn't want to do it — I loved that little heart-shaped mole which had been sitting on my chest since I was a child. However, I'm not actually a doctor, and a couple of people who *were* doctors seemed to think it needed to go. We take our moles seriously in this family, so of course I agreed. The whole experience was vile. The surgeon had the bedside charm of slime mould, and barely spoke a word — certainly not a comforting one — throughout the process. It was done under a local anaesthetic without so much as a whiff of Valium to float me through it. Because the mole was deep, he dug at me with his scalpel for all the world like he was using a jackhammer. I'm not usually overly bothered by the visceral, but the whole hacking, cauterising and stitching process (all of which I could see, what with my chest being quite near my face) left me weak, speechless and weepy.

The mole was, as I'd predicted, entirely benign. Ha. Even if it had been something evil, I still doubt I would have forgiven Dr Jackhammer entirely for taking away something I was so fond of, with so little compassion. I've missed the mole ever since; the scar left behind is shaped like a frown. It's not my only surgical scar — I'd had a hysterectomy not long before this — but it was the one I felt most traumatised by, oddly. Maybe because I'd felt so dismissed during the process, and the scar was so public.

So nine years later — while writing this book and just before my fifty-third birthday — I went to see my friend Richard's tattooist. Just for a chat, really, to see if Stefan thought he could put a heart-shaped mole back on my chest just below the scar. Yes, he said, he could. I'd figured that would be the case — Stefan has over several years created for Richard a complete sleeve of full-colour New Zealand native birds all down his right arm, an impressive work of art, so a very small heart-shaped mole was entirely within his purview.

With serious tattoo artists, there's usually a cooling-off period between consultation, design and actually doing the tattooing. But since I was so clear about what I wanted, and since it was so tiny, would I like to do it now? Yes, I said, I would. And so I have a tattoo — a little piece of me that was taken away and has now been stuck back on. And I pat myself with my hand on the tiny heart quite often, and remember Kathryn, too. I am very pleased to have it back.

THERE ARE MATTERS OF LIFE AND DEATH, AND THEN THERE ARE TATTOOS.

CHAPTER 25

I AM SORRY THAT ...

You will make mistakes. Heaps of them. Big and little. Irrevocable and revocable. (People don't use 'revocable' enough. It's one of those words where the antonym gets all the play. We should balance that out. Same for 'disgruntled' — I want 'gruntled' to catch on when we're contented. But I digress.) The only people who never make mistakes are people who don't do anything, ever. You'd have to live alone in a cave, never speak and never move to avoid screwing up at some point. Which would be the kind of life one could characterise overall as one massive mistake. Booyah with the irony.

Your mission, then, is to get more things right than you get wrong (that's what we would have called a 'pass mark' in the Olden Days — an 'Achieved', right?) and to learn from your screw-ups. I'm pretty sure that's why a lot of people have two kids — one to practise on, one to get things right with. Yeah, that'll never work. (a) We are all entirely capable of making the same mistake several times over. And (b) my observation is that each new child presents you with new and different opportunities for blowing it. Am I right? I think I am.

So don't let fear of screwing up paralyse you, and let yourself learn from mistakes when they happen. Comedians have a fondness for saying that you learn more from your bad gigs than you do from your good ones. Although the good ones are still our favourites. Still, occasionally we even go out there and self-sabotage a gig to see if we can win an audience back after we've lost them. It's a dangerous sport, but in the right hands displays a considerable level of craft. In the back of my comedy notebook, where I keep almost everything important, I make a note of things I've done wrong — 'Don't assume she's not a hooker', 'Don't call the guy in the sunglasses a wanker; he may be blind' — that kind of thing, so I remember not to do it again. As if.

TRAGEDY + TIME = COMEDY.
MISTAKES + ESPRIT DE L'ESCALIER = COMEDY GOLD.

As well as offering teaching moments, screw-ups also provide excellent fodder for great stories or — in professional parlance — 'new material', once you've applied the comedian's best friend, *esprit de l'escalier*, to that moment of crushing failure. Literally 'spirit of the stairs', it is the brilliant and witty thing you think of to say *after* you've left the room and the moment has gone. Pretty much any time you hear a comedian come back with a searing

THE ONLY PEOPLE WHO
NEVER MAKE MISTAKES
ARE PEOPLE WHO DON'T
DO ANYTHING, EVER.
WHICH WOULD BE THE
KIND OF LIFE ONE COULD
CHARACTERISE OVERALL AS
ONE MASSIVE MISTAKE.
BOOYAH WITH THE IRONY.

retort to a heckle, it is because someone has thrown that heckle *before*, and on the drive home the comic thought of what they wished they'd said. In our line of business, a second chance often presents itself. And if it doesn't, we'll fake it. 'I said that another night and this guy shouted ...' You get the picture. Tragedy + time = comedy. Mistakes + *esprit de l'escalier* = comedy gold.

My Grandmother Edith was fond of saying that it isn't the falling down that matters, but the way you get back up again. The inference was that you should do it quickly, and with dignity. As a little girl, I always imagined someone falling down and managing to get back up again without her knickers showing. Grandma had some hard things to deal with during her life, but she always 'clogged on' with great style and aplomb. When she was in her twilight years she literally did fall down a bit, and I can always see her in my mind's eye, carefully getting back on her feet, straightening her skirt, and picking up her handbag, which invariably matched her shoes. She also in later years had issues with wind. She could be walking to the kitchen and, involuntarily, audibly break wind. Grandma would simply pause for a moment, look behind at the floor, and say, 'Someone should see to that squeaky floorboard.' She's still my role model for moving on from mistakes with dignity and courage.

IT ISN'T THE FALLING DOWN THAT MATTERS, BUT THE WAY YOU GET BACK UP AGAIN.

You can take your time with finding the lesson in the mistake and getting back on your feet if you need to, but there is something you need to do immediately. Apologise to anyone your mistake has hurt. The important part of the apology is not the word 'sorry', it is the ones that come after it. 'I'm sorry if you …' isn't worth a tin of beans to anyone. You've just qualified your sorry-ness by putting a question into the sentence and throwing the onus for offence caused back on the victim. Think about it for a minute. 'I'm sorry if you were offended by what I said,' suggests (a) they might not have been offended (hence the use of 'if'); and (b) 'you were offended' implies the taking of offence was their choice.

THE IMPORTANT PART OF THE APOLOGY IS NOT THE WORD 'SORRY', IT IS THE ONES THAT COME AFTER IT. 'I'M SORRY IF YOU …' ISN'T WORTH A TIN OF BEANS TO ANYONE.

Now try this: 'I'm sorry that I offended you.' Better. That's you admitting you were the one who gave offence, and there's no question about it. Or this: 'I'm sorry that I offended you by behaving like a dickhead.' Best. Now you've really owned it by including a description of your mistake. It's about what you did, not about how they reacted to it. Being sorry for how someone reacted to you isn't really apologising; it's just observing their reaction and commenting on how you feel about it.

'I am sorry if …' is of course a fabulously passive-aggressive way of getting out of saying sorry — it smells like an apology, but in fact contains no admission of guilt. It lives right next to

'I am sorry that you feel that way', which is a superb way of saying you're not sorry about anything you have done at all. Save those constructions up for people you don't want to be friends with — and keep an ear out for them when people in the public eye have to apologise for stuff under instruction from their public relations consultant. But for anyone who matters, keep practising 'I am sorry that I ...' It can be hard to remember to do it right when you're all hot and bothered with humiliation. I am quite crap at it. But if you cock it up, say you're sorry and try again. Also, crying helps. And gifts.

And I must apologise. There isn't really such a word as 'gruntled'. There was once, but it is no longer in use. Only its antonym remains in common parlance. You will look like a dick if you say 'gruntled'. I am very sorry that I lied to you.

See? Easy.

CHAPTER 26

YOUR LIFE AS A BOOK

Think of your life as a book. A book with lots of different chapters which might have a link from one chapter to the next but they will be separate, too. Different phases in your life, the focus shifting from one event to another, various other characters who come and go, and the potential for a change in direction or location from time to time. It is nice to think of life in terms of 'Okay, this bit of my life is about this — but it will be about something else later. Phew.'

And make it a really interesting book. At regular intervals, find the time to take a step back and look at your story so far and imagine, if it was a book you were reading, what you would want the next chapter to be about to keep it enthralling. Imagine the next possible adventure that would make your life a good story.

Cast yourself as the lead character in the story of your life. This narrative of yours needs a star, and it has to be you — you're the only one who can carry your story. Sure, you have to be aware that everyone else is the lead character in their own book, and in their story you are playing a supporting role or the love interest or a recurring character or whatever. Play those roles for them with commitment and enthusiasm and truth — as Stanislavski said, 'There are no small roles, only small actors.' But in your own life, think of yourself as the hero. Heroes drive the action, make decisions, behave with courage, solve problems and embrace adventure.

I talked to Holly about this 'think-of-your-life-as-a-book' thing. She said she liked movies more than books. So yeah, think of your life as a movie and, every now and then, work out what could happen in the next scene that would make your movie a blockbuster. Not too many car chases, though. Think light and shade. Mostly, just keep it *fascinating*.

IN YOUR OWN LIFE, THINK OF YOURSELF AS THE HERO. HEROES DRIVE THE ACTION, MAKE DECISIONS, BEHAVE WITH COURAGE, SOLVE PROBLEMS AND EMBRACE ADVENTURE.

Also, make sure that if your life was a movie, it would pass the Bechdel Test. Alison Bechdel is an American cartoonist and author who, in 1985, drew a cartoon that features two women discussing a film. One of the women says she will only go to movies that (a) feature at least two women who (b) talk to each other about (c) something other than a man. And the punchline was that she hadn't seen a film since *Alien*.

I love this test. It is a revelation to discover how few films earn a pass, and therefore how many movies don't present female characters who are real enough to have, like, *a friend* or something to care about other than *boys*. Films that fail the Bechdel Test aren't necessarily terrible, and not all films that pass the test are great, but it is interesting to keep an eye on how women get presented on screen. I like keeping it in the back of my mind when I watch TV and read books, too, and I think about it when I'm putting a comedy set together. Bits of my comedy (less and less these days) are about men. Some of my comedy is about women, and being one. And some of my comedy is about 'stuff'. I try to get the balance right.

Applying the Bechdel Test to your personal life isn't a crazy idea either, right? Think of all those times when you and the girls get together and the only thing you talk about is boys. What's that you say? That never happens? Right on, sister. It has genuinely never occurred in my life, either ... in a conversation that's lasted more than two minutes. That's one of those lady-myths that kicked off when they started segregating our bathrooms and we decided we'd always go together — for the company, and because you can never be entirely sure when you might need to borrow a tampon. If men knew how often we didn't talk about them, they'd weep and cling to each other in the urinals. Even so, make sure this movie you are making (or the book you are writing) is filled with interesting characters who care about a whole range of things, and each other. And keep looking for your next adventure.

STUFF MY DAUGHTER TAUGHT ME

We all have dreams for our children. There's the big overarching dream about them being happy and fulfilled. And there's a more particular dream about them living a *better* life than we do, with more choices, more experiences, more comfort, more thrills. Right back at the beginning of their lives, all we wanted (remember?) was for them to be born healthy with all their fingers and toes. As they grow, we keep adding to the list of things we want them to have and be. So we teach them the stuff they need to know: to eat and sleep, to talk and walk, use a bathroom, say please and thank you, to read, be kind, be curious, to have manners. Before we know it, the things we want for them get even more specific — throw a ball, learn algebra, achieve Level 2 NCEA, get a job, fall in love, make us proud.

At some event I was hosting years ago, I got into an intense conversation with a lovely woman I'd never met before or since — it happens more often than you'd think — this time about raising children. She said something that wasn't radical or revolutionary, but she made it resonate for me that evening. Children, she reckoned, were like plants in a garden. You prepare the soil, make a place for them in it, water and feed them and clear the weeds away so they have space, and protect them from the harshest elements. But at some point, she said, you've got to stand back and just let them grow the way they are designed to. And trust that you've done everything you needed to do to allow them to flourish.

Of course, what we really want to do is nothing like as poetic as nurturing a flower. If we could, what we'd like to do is lay our kid's head on a table, shove a funnel in their ear, and stuff all our ideas and plans and dreams quite hard into it. Jam all our hard-won knowledge in there, then stand them up, point them in the right direction, and give them a shove to send them on their way. But apparently, you can't do that. At some point, you really do have to let go, stand back, and see what they choose to do with all the stuff you've told them.

It is a strange phase of parenting, this bit where the children start independently making their way in the world. My friend Lesley and I talk about it a lot whenever I am with her in Vancouver, and we catch up on what her son Jason (my godson) and Holly are each doing. Although not just *what* they're doing, but *how* they're doing. Lesley says she has noticed a tendency amongst the parents of adult children — the kids Jason grew up with — to talk about them by simply listing their activities and achievements. A register of graduations and qualifications; a catalogue of careers; an inventory of countries they've visited.

If you ask how Peter is, you might just get the name of his employer. 'Sometimes I want to ask them — because they haven't said — if their child is *happy*,' Lesley says. 'They don't mention that. Just what they *do*.' Like those interminably boring Christmas newsletters (kill me now) that record a year's worth of exams passed and awards won, but tell you nothing about what kind of people are doing these things.

Holly spent her first year out of school studying at Unitech for a Performing Arts degree. She wasn't happy there. Dance was — and is — her first passion, but student life didn't suit her generally, and there wasn't quite enough hip-hop involved specifically. So she made a call and left, and found a job in clothing retail and a flat with friends. She is awesome at retail — the hours are brutal and her feet hurt, but she's fantastic with people and great with sales. Dance went back to being an extra-curricular activity with regular public shows. They made her fizz with excitement and joy.

Without being aware of it, I had quite a specific dream for Holly. I'd never articulated it (not even to myself), but I was harbouring a pretty detailed ambition about wanting my daughter to join the Mark Morris Dance Troupe in New York and live in a studio apartment in Brooklyn where I would go and stay several times a year. I'd buy her groceries and quirky furniture, take her shopping, and we'd go together to Broadway and off-Broadway shows and to jazz clubs in the Village. Maybe we'd share a White Christmas one year and go ice-skating in Central Park. She would live this bohemian but very cosmopolitan life, and I'd get to visit it. I mean, *her*. Yes, I know. When you boil it down, that dream was pretty much all about me, right?

WHAT WE'D LIKE TO DO IS LAY OUR KID'S HEAD ON A TABLE, SHOVE A FUNNEL IN THEIR EAR, AND STUFF ALL OUR IDEAS AND PLANS AND DREAMS QUITE HARD INTO IT.

Holly had a very specific dream of her own. She wanted more than anything else in the world to become a mother. Which is exactly what she did. Shortly before I debuted my comedy show *Stuff I Forgot To Tell My Daughter*, in April 2013, Holly told me she was pregnant. I was — and she won't mind me telling you this — shocked. It was during that period of shock and surprise that I realised I'd been harbouring the Mark Morris Dance Troupe dream. And then quickly realised that that dream more accurately belonged to me. Not that I wanted to be a *dancer*, I wanted to be *the mother of a New York dancer*. I am, of course, not the first mother in the world to be surprised and dismayed by the choices her daughter makes. It's just that when it happens, you feel like you are.

TURNS OUT I RAISED A DETERMINED YOUNG WOMAN WITH HER OWN VERY CLEAR IDEAS ABOUT HOW TO LIVE HER LIFE. WHO SAW THAT COMING? I BLAME THE MOTHER.

We talked about it a lot. We all cried and got a bit shouty, and I believe a door may have been slammed at some point. But it became clear that this was exactly what she wanted to do, and if I would just trust her, she said, she would make it work. Turns out I raised a determined young woman with her own very clear ideas about how to live her life. Who saw that coming? I blame the mother.

When Holly was six months pregnant, she and her partner,

Harley, decided to move to Australia to live with his ex-pat Kiwi family — his mum, his gran, their cousins — where he could go back to the job he was doing before Holly became pregnant. His family were all incredibly welcoming and supportive, and couldn't have been kinder to my girl. Safe hands, strong love. So one Friday morning we all went out to the airport — Jeremy, me, Harley's New Zealand family, Holly's friends — and waved them off. I came home and cried for six hours, then slept for 12.

I've always known that the thing you to do with your children is love them and keep loving them, no matter what. That's your job. I talked a bit with Jeremy's Aunt Kim, who lives in Toronto. Kim is a wonderful person. We're about the same age, and she also knows what it is like to have a daughter who has a baby relatively young, when it can be a surprise. More significantly in terms of wisdom and perspective, Kim's much-adored first grandchild arrived into the world exactly one year before her much-adored son, Luke, left it. A private in the Canadian military, Luke died accidentally in July 2010 when he was in training for possible deployment to Afghanistan. The grief of death throws a special kind of light on the joy of birth. Embrace it, Kim told me. And of course, that was what I was always going to do. Wrap my arms around my daughter and her baby, and hug them tight.

Holly and Harley's baby was due in late November, but, because of one or two medical factors, her midwife planned to induce the birth on 15 November. I booked a flight over on 13 November so I could be there in time. They live in a tiny town in New South Wales, so two flights really — one to Sydney, then on to the nearest hospital in Wagga Wagga.

Timing is everything. Holly's waters broke at 6am on 13 November at the exact moment I was checking in for my flight across the Tasman to be with her. By the time I reached Sydney she was five centimetres dilated. When my domestic flight landed near her new home town, she was almost ready for the final push. I was admirably calm in the car that came to pick me up, right up until the moment I stepped inside the hospital lift, pushed the button for the fifth floor, and the lift broke down.

I spent the next 15 minutes phoning the delivery suite upstairs to talk to her through contractions; and also briefly let her get on with it without me and phoned Jeremy back in New Zealand for comfort. I alternated between laughing at the absurdity of it all, crying with frustration, and over-sharing with the nice hospital clerk trapped in the lift with me. Once emergency services had us out, I ran the five flights to Holly's room (something I couldn't do under any other circumstances) and held my daughter's hand through those last gruelling minutes of labour and those slippery, shining moments of birth.

When we left the hospital two days later, me with the honour of carrying my granddaughter in my arms, my finger marks were still clearly visible in the lift where I had tried to prise the doors open.

Grandparenthood is different from parenthood. The clue is in the name. It is majestic, splendid and grand. It is motherhood without the anxiety but all of the joy. It is a story in which you are no longer a lead character, and the revelation of this is liberating. It is understood that, in this story, you are a guest star, making cameo appearances to move the narrative along, deliver wisdom where you can, and offer comic relief. Your own role models shift. Suddenly you have in mind the recent work of Robert De Niro and Diane Keaton. You find Ellen Burstyn and Candice Bergen incredibly hot. You start thinking about buying fewer but more expensive clothes, and doing something chic and possibly classical with your hair. You begin to understand that you might have been a fierce mama at times when danger approached, but you will constantly be a ferociously protective grandmother.

GRANDPARENTHOOD IS DIFFERENT FROM PARENTHOOD. THE CLUE IS IN THE NAME. IT IS MAJESTIC, SPLENDID AND GRAND.

For the first five days of my granddaughter's life, I was on burp, change and laundry duty while her paternal grandmother cooked and directed visitor traffic. We called each other 'Nana G' and 'Nana Michy', trying out our new names and liking how they sounded. I struggled to remember how to swaddle a baby, until, in the middle of the night, my hands remembered the correct origami fold that keeps a baby womb-like safe. I taught my daughter how to do the things I once did for her, and then stood back to watch how she will choose to do these things.

On the second day, baby got a name — Ariana-Rose. Day Three, we took Ariana out for coffee. Day Four, we took her shopping. Day Five, I had to leave. A delayed flight was a gift of extra time, and Holly and I wept at final boarding call. Against airport protocol, I ran back from security for one more kiss with my two girls. As I squeezed her, my granddaughter produced a magnificent burp, audible across the terminal. It was the most hilarious thing, ever. Timing is everything.

Ariana has a passport and uses it frequently to come and visit us, bless her, and I use mine to go and see her, too. She was here with us when her mother turned 21 and the aunties came; and at the party we had when my mother, Donna, her maternal great-grandmother, turned 80; and she was back here again when her great-grandmother, Nanny Kitty, died.

In between all the comings and goings there are almost-daily photographs and videos, and when we Skype she waves at me and kisses the screen. She is the most beautiful, gifted and advanced grandchild ever in the history of grandchildren — she was walking at 11 months. And I know all nanas say that, but in this case it is true. When she took her first steps — viewed on video — Great-Granddad John, my dad, joked that she walks even better than he does these days. Ariana's favourite song right now is Nathaniel's 'Live Louder', and when she hears it she stops whatever else she is doing to dance, lost in the music and the moment. Just like her mama did.

And Holly is a wonderful mother — relaxed, at ease, taking everything as it comes, entirely in her element. You can see it in her face when she's feeding and bathing and playing with her little girl. I've seen that face before. This is when Holly looks the most like herself, when she looks like who she really is.

She is happy. I was — and I don't mind telling you this — wrong about some things. I wasn't sure it was going to work out this well. Like we agreed before, success is exceeding your parents' expectations.

Holly and I have had the chance now to talk about all the things in this book — the stuff I forgot to tell her while she was growing up, when we were busy with all the big and small things. And now? Now I have a granddaughter to tell all this stuff to. Maybe I'll save some of it until she is a little older. In the meantime, I thought you might like to know all this stuff, too.

One more small story. Remember the day I got my heart-shaped mole back? On the way out of the tattoo studio — literally as I was walking down the stairs — I got a text. It was from Holly with a photograph of the new tattoo she'd just had done on her wrist. A pink rose, in honour of Ariana-Rose. What's a mama to say? It was beautiful. So I said that. And sent her a photo of mine. Holly was shocked. She'll get over it.

AFTERWORD

Back at the beginning (see 'Prologue') I said I hadn't experienced the 'empty-nest syndrome' angst I've heard other mothers suffer when their last — or only — child leaves home. And that was true ... back then. Three years later, though, I'm getting an insight. It's not that I don't have enough to do, or that I'm no longer sure what my role is in life. Just a general sense of nostalgia for those 18 years. I catch myself lingering in the snack aisle of the supermarket, gazing wistfully at lunchbox treats I used to buy — straps of dried fruit, tiny packets of cheese and crackers mostly made of plastic (including the cheese), biscuits in the shape of small bears. My eyes go misty. On rare Saturdays at home, the day feels limp and unstructured without a dance rehearsal to drive to or a carload of squealing pre-teens to drop at the mall. I drive past Holly's old primary school and automatically search the playing field for her little dark head. I'll be sitting on the deck and suddenly see in my mind's eye the big-girl's bicycle her godmothers, Sue and Jo, delivered one

Christmas, wrapped entirely in pink paper and festooned with tinsel so you couldn't see a single bit of bike, but you could still tell what it was. I miss the smell of wet paint on kindy art paper. I've started to find the permanent tidiness of Holly's room creepy. I have begun to understand why another kind of person might have turned it into a sewing room or a gym.

I miss being a mama — or, to put it properly, I look back at those years of being a 24/7 mother with huge fondness and a touch of grief that this part of my life is over. We remain mothers forever, of course. Some of us experience the boomerang-ness of today's kids. They'll come back to the nest, dragging impossible amounts of ex-flat furniture behind them and cluttering up our briefly well-kept kitchen benches with overly complicated hipster espresso machines. Invariably, they also bring with them an attitude that suggests they'd like you to think of them more as a flatmate now — though they also wouldn't mind if you put through a load of washing for them while they are out being adults, and maybe had something available for them to heat up whenever they get back, can't say what time that'll be, they're not a kid any more. There will be a noticeable spike in your supermarket bill — not necessarily because they eat a lot, but because you find you need to drink more.

Many of us experience the special heartstring-tug of our kids living overseas. I still get a jolt when I realise I can't just get in the car and go visit Holly. After knowing where they are every minute of the day for 18 years, you can feel somewhat adrift when you suddenly lose sight of them. Though — hoorah, social media and technology! — we can text and Skype, write and talk every day. I like to think the quality of communication is elevated from our previous day-to-day chatter. Holly and I talk about plans and feelings and the wider world. It is possible I know her better now than when I was asking her to empty the dishwasher and tidy her room. I already have more photos of my one-year-old granddaughter than have been taken of me in a lifetime. On a daily basis I know what Ariana is wearing, what she had for dinner, and what her voice sounds like. Long-distance grandparenting is bittersweet: I can play the videos of special moments over and over, but I can't smell her head.

Unlike parenting, grandparenting hasn't been sexed-up by popular culture. Yet. Give it time, and there might be a next-generational equivalent of Yummy Mummies and MILFs. Hot Nanas? Grannies I'd Like to Grind? Maybe once Angelina Jolie, mother-of-six, gets to that life-stage we'll think of something that works. The image of 'grandma' is so clear and fixed in our heads that it has become a handy descriptor newspapers like to chuck into headlines just for the thrill of juxtaposition. Given that grandparents aren't supposed to do anything more notable than quilting and playing lawn bowls, there is an extra frisson if you can add 'Nana' (even when it is contextually irrelevant) to something the kids would do. 'Granny charged with drug-running' will inevitably turn out to be about a 61-year-old career criminal rather than the 85-year-old sweetie you were encouraged to imagine, tottering through Customs with cocaine packed tightly inside the bars of a Zimmer frame. We're having our kids later, so if mums are older we automatically assume a grandma will be properly aged. Retired. Settled. Resting. Like roast beef or a cake, out of the oven, done, and put to one side.

Being a grandparent is delicious, but it does elicit the occasional public double-take. 'You're too young to be a grandma!' people say, as I bore them with pictures of Ariana, 259 of which I have on my phone. Doubtless, it's my stilettos and the margarita that I'm waving in the other hand that throws them. 'You're too young!' is meant as a compliment, I think. Though sometimes it also comes with a look of mild dismay that my daughter has taken this path so soon. Wrong order, surely career first, then family? Isn't that how we do things now, finding that sweet spot in our thirties somewhere after youth and before infertility? I am, though, the same age my grandmother was when she became a grandmother. I remember the postcards she sent from her trips around the world, and the presents she brought home for us — gifts of gold and silver stuffed into her bra to avoid Customs duty, and an asthma attack faked to ensure swift processing at the border. 'Gran charged with jewellery smuggling' the headline might have said if they'd ever caught her. In large part, I learnt to be adventurous from her.

And then I think about the feminist dream (Chapter 15: Why Mummy Thinks You Should be a Feminist, Too) of a future for our daughters that was rich in choice and possibility; with satisfying work, motherhood (if and when she was ready), and a relationship based on equality and shared tasks. And they could, we said, do those things in any order, always choosing independence and dignity; and every child would be a wanted child, and they would be raised to be the best that they could be. Then I look at those 259 photos of Holly and Ariana-Rose, play the videos for the thousandth time and smile. 'Nana Michy,' I think to myself, 'we've nailed it.'

And as much as we will think, post-parenthood, about all the stuff we forgot to tell our daughters, we should also take a moment to feel good about all the stuff we *did* remember to tell them. And then pour ourselves a cocktail, and dance like the girls we still are on the inside.

ACKNOWLEDGEMENTS

It takes a village to raise a book. When you get to the bit here at the end where you tip your cap to friends, family and all the other villagers, it is usual to save thanking your partner — your 'One In Particular' — until last, but I'd like to start there. Jeremy has been enthusiastically supportive and stoically patient throughout. I think we both imagined this business of Writing A Book would be a calm, dignified, steady affair. I visualised a lot of green tea being drunk, invigorating walks in the local bush reserve, languid days luxuriating in being creative. Yeah, not so much. There were long days when I was incommunicative and unavailable, and when I *did* reappear I could be a bit whiny. Jeremy consoled, cajoled, made coffee and tea, read bits of what I'd done, and soothed. At one point I recall him saying 'I love my Wife. I can't wait to see her again,' as he gently placed a cup of tea by my computer and slipped away. I love my Husband. He is a good person.

I owe huge thanks to my good friend and manager, Richard Carrington, who heard me describe the comedy show I wanted to write about the stuff I forgot to tell my daughter and said, 'I want to produce that show.' Richard is the best person in the comedy business to work with. I told him that once. He said, 'Don't ever speak to me like that again.' So I won't. I'll just write it here.

And for supporting the show that gave birth to this book, thanks also Lauren Porteous for the music, Ziggy Ziya for the room, Jodi Wright for the tent; and the NZ International Comedy Festival and the Christchurch World Buskers Festival for the opportunity.

The book is all Finlay Macdonald's fault. 'Have you ever thought about turning your show into a book?' he asked. 'Yes, yes I have,' I said, because that had been my vague plan all along. And then I realised Finlay was offering to publish it. I don't really understand the skills required of a publisher, but I can tell you Finlay is the sort of person you can imagine calming a hissing, spitting, cornered feral cat with a well-placed bowl of milk and an encouraging word. Superb. As is Kate Stone, my editor. Kate knows everything about how to use words properly but still allowed me my own linguistic quirks. She has admirable views on cake.

I am deeply grateful to the people who let me weave parts of their own stories into mine: Donna, John and Stephen A'Court; Lesley Donaldson; Victoria Quade; Kim O'Donnell; and Tommy Wilson.

Warm thanks to the Ladies of The Coven who kept saying 'Of course you can do it!' and 'When can we read it?' and 'Have you put that bit in?' and 'Let's get another bottle!': Ali Jones, Debbie Harwood, Barbara Ward, Romola Lang, Linda Joy,

Ruth and Kristen Spencer, Kathryn Burnett, Tina Plunkett, Anne McMahon, Linda McKay, and Margaret O'Hanlon.

For general enthusiasm: David Slack and Karren Beanland, whose daughter, Mary-Margaret, gave me someone to think of when I wanted to imagine a reader.

A grateful acknowledgement to the newspapers and magazines where some of my ideas took their first steps before this book gave them a chance to run: *The Press*; *Sunday Star Times*; *Next magazine*; *Metro*; and *Political Review*.

Most of all, my endless thanks and love to Holly Ruth A'Court, who has throughout her life let me tell stories to her, and about her. That is no small thing. She is beautiful, brave and clever. I love her to the moon and back.